The Methodists

The Methodists

A History of Methodism in New South Wales

Don Wright and Eric G. Clancy

ALLEN & UNWIN

While every effort has been made to trace the copyright for illustrative
material used in this book, further information would be welcomed by
the authors and publisher.

© Don Wright and Eric G. Clancy 1993

First published in 1993

Allen & Unwin Pty Ltd
9 Atchison Street, St Leonards, NSW 2065 Australia

National Library of Australia
Cataloguing-in-Publication entry:

Wright, D. I. (Donald Ian), 1934–
    The Methodists: a history of Methodism in New South Wales.

    Bibliography.
    Includes index.
    ISBN 1 86373 428 7.

    1. Methodist Church—New South Wales—History. 2. New South
    Wales—Church history. I. Clancy, Eric G. (Eric Gerald), 1909– .
    II. Title.

287.1944

Set in 11/12½ Bembo
by DOCUPRO, Sydney
Printed by Chong Moh Offset Printing, Singapore

10 9 8 7 6 5 4 3 2 1

Contents

Abbreviations

ACW	*Australian Christian World*
ADB	*Australian Dictionary of Biography*
AMHS	Australian Methodist Historical Society
Aust. Conf. Mins	Wesleyan Methodist Church of Australasia, Conference Minutes
BT	Bonwick Transcripts
CA&WR	*Christian Advocate and Weekly Record*
CC	Crusade for Christ
CMB	Committee Minute Book (of WMMS)
CSES	Wesleyan Methodist Church Sustentation and Extension Society
DCC	Methodist Department of Christian Citizenship
District Minutes	Wesleyan Methodist Church District Minutes, Aust. and NZ
DL	Dixson Library
HMD	Methodist Home Mission Department
JRH	*Journal of Religious History*
LMM	Leaders' Meeting Minutes
MCP	Methodist Church Papers
ML	Mitchell Library
MMSA	Methodist Missionary Society of Australasia
MN	Mission to the Nation
MWF	Methodist Women's Federation

NCMM	Newcastle Central Methodist Mission
NL	*Northern Light*
NMH	*Newcastle Morning Herald*
NSW Conf. Mins	Methodist Church of Australasia, NSW Conf. Minutes
PM Messenger	*NSW Primitive Methodist Messenger*
PM Magazine	*Primitive Methodist Magazine*
QMM	Quarterly Meeting Minutes
RAHSJ	Royal Australian Historical Society *Journal*
SMH	*Sydney Morning Herald*
SQC	Social Questions Committee (of NSW Conference)
UCA	Uniting Church Archives
UMFC	United Methodist Free Churches
VDL	Van Diemen's Land
WA	*Weekly Advocate*
WAOM	Women's Auxiliary to Overseas Missions
WHML	Women's Home Mission League
WMMS	Wesleyan Methodist Missionary Society
YPD	Young People's Department (NSW Conference)

Acknowledgements

This book has taken a number of years to write and many debts of gratitude have been incurred. Each author received considerable assistance from various librarians and archivists at the Mitchell and State Libraries and at the Auchmuty Library of the University of Newcastle. Eric Clancy is himself archivist for the Uniting church and this has been of great benefit. The University of Newcastle also made life easier for one author by providing funds to microfilm *The Methodist* and its associated papers. Many other people have helped either by providing individual references or by allowing access to their often excellent histories of their own local churches. We owe a deep debt of gratitude to those people who collected the various Methodist archives over the years—though we have often wished that the archives of the minor Methodist bodies had been as diligently collected as those of the Wesleyans. Anyone who attempts to write Methodist history in New South Wales inevitably owes a great debt to Rev. James Colwell—our own will be obvious and we acknowledge it with gratitude. Don Wright's thanks go to Debbie Malcolm, Marian Mason and Sue Owen who carried out various research tasks for him. Pauline James transferred substantial amounts of typed material to disk. We are also grateful to Mark Tredinnick and Annette Barlow of Allen and Unwin (Sydney) for overseeing publication and to Rev. Norman McDonald, Secretary of the New South Wales Synod of the Uniting Church, who has ensured the church's support for the project. We owe an enormous debt to Janice Wright for reading proofs and compiling the index.

While each author has written individual sections of this book,

ix

the whole has been read and worked over by both. Responsibility for the creativity, interpretation and any errors which may have crept in is joint.

Don Wright
Eric G. Clancy
October 1991

Introduction

The Methodist church was born in eighteenth century England as a result of the religious experience and activity of the Wesley brothers, John and Charles, sons of the Rev. Samuel Wesley, Rector of Epworth, and his wife, Susannah. Both brothers graduated from Oxford University and became ordained clergymen of the Church of England. In 1735, both men travelled to Georgia, North America, with General Oglethorpe—John to be pastor to the English community in Savannah and Charles as Oglethorpe's personal secretary. Two years later, both men returned to England, each convinced that he had failed in his work there.[1]

On their journey to America the Wesleys had encountered some Moravian missionaries who had convinced them of their need to acknowledge Jesus Christ as their personal Saviour and, on their return to London, each man, feeling dissatisfied with his spiritual condition, received further help from London-based Moravians. Their conversion experiences brought joy, peace and power beyond anything each had previously known. John's conversion became archetypal for future generations of Methodists, and occurred on 24 May 1738:

> In the evening I went very unwillingly to a society in Aldersgate Street, where one was reading Luther's preface to the Epistle to the Romans. About a quarter before nine, while he was describing the change which God works in the heart through faith in Christ, I felt my heart strangely warmed. I felt I did trust in Christ, Christ alone for salvation, and an assurance was given

me that He had taken away *my* sins, even *mine*, and saved *me* from the law of sin and death.[2]

Henceforth he invited the masses of the British Isles to enter into a like experience and, with his brother's assistance, embarked on a programme of evangelistic and philanthropic outreach which, in John's case, continued for more than half a century. The Wesleys proclaimed the love of God as 'the medicine of life, the never-failing remedy for all the evils of a disordered world, for all the miseries and vices of men'. Phenomenal crowds listened to their message and thousands responded to the invitation to accept Christ as their Saviour.

The Wesley brothers travelled constantly throughout England and Wales and made frequent visits to Scotland and Ireland. With but few exceptions the buildings of the Church of England were closed to them. Because of this, and despite his personal abhorrence of the practice, John Wesley, at the urging of George Whitefield, began to preach in the open air at Bristol in 1739. This 'field-preaching' became the principal means by which he and his helpers proclaimed the Gospel to the unchurched masses, many of whom received his message gladly. At the instigation of squire and parson, mob violence often ensued and preachers were frequently physically assaulted. The Wesleys also regularly visited gaols to offer prisoners the gift of new life in Christ.

The decades before and after the conversion of the Wesleys saw an enormous surge in the population of England and Wales from five-and-a-half million in 1700 to six-and-a-half million in 1750 and nine million by the end of the century. No less important was the shift in the location of that population, brought about by the Industrial Revolution, from the southern counties to the midlands and north, and from the country to the towns where many lived in squalid conditions. Neither the established church nor the Dissenters were geared organisationally or spiritually to meet the challenge of this demographic revolution.

It was left largely to John Wesley, whose heart 'was exceedingly warmed to them', and his followers to take up the spiritual challenge of the masses who appeared to him as 'sheep without a shepherd'. He maintained his evangelistic work energetically until his death in 1791 at eighty-eight years of age. In addition to constant preaching, usually three times a day regardless of place and weather, he was responsible for a prolific output of over four hundred publications. He also maintained an extensive correspondence and proved to be an effective 'postal pastor'. As well, he kept a tight rein on the affairs of the ever-expanding Methodist community.[3]

Wesley was reluctant to use laymen as preachers until his mother persuaded him that, Thomas Maxfield was 'just as truly called of God to preach the Gospel as ever you were'. Thereafter, he appointed lay preachers locally. The foremost task of his ever-increasing band of preachers was 'to provoke the regular clergy to jealousy, and to supply their lack of service towards those who are perishing for want of knowledge, and above all to reform the nation by spreading scriptural holiness over the land'. Acknowledging that 'God owns women in the conversion of sinners', Wesley also used them as preachers, class leaders, prayer leaders, sick visitors and teachers.[4]

From among these local preachers he appointed some as 'travelling' preachers to large geographical areas which he called 'circuits'. Although they had the authority to preach and superintend work John Wesley resisted pressure to ordain them until after the War of American Independence, when the exigencies of the situation in the New World forced him, in 1784, to ordain men and also to develop a church structure for Methodists in America. Later, he ordained men for work in Scotland and England.

From the outset, Wesley gathered his converts into a weekly fellowship called the 'class meeting' designed to enrich their Christian experience and place them under the direct and immediate supervision of more experienced class leaders. The only qualifications for membership were 'a desire to flee from the wrath to come, and to be saved from their sins' and a willingness to attend weekly, though it was also expected that they would live a life in conformity with their declared faith. Such people were issued with quarterly tickets of membership. Until 1795 the right of admission to, or exclusion from, membership belonged to the Superintendent Minister, thereafter it was vested in the Leaders' Meeting. What was initially membership in a 'society' eventually became recognised as membership in the Methodist church.[5]

A number of classes were organised into a 'society' and it was there that the Wesley's converts met for regular weekly congregational worship services conducted by 'travelling' preachers (who were not called ministers until much later) and by local preachers. It was also through these societies that weekly prayer meetings, periodical love-feasts, quarterly fast days and annual Watchnight and Covenant Services were organised. For the children there were Sunday schools and, in some places, there were meetings both morning and afternoon.

The first Methodist 'United Society', comprising seventy-three people, was formed in London on 23 July 1740. Other societies followed but, until the end of the eighteenth century, Methodists continued to be exhorted to attend the parish church for worship and Holy Communion for Wesley had no wish to break away from the Church of England. However, many of the clergy were unwilling to admit his converts to Communion, and many of the converts, who often had no previous religious affiliation of any kind, were equally disinclined to attend. They therefore agitated for the celebration of Holy Communion in their own chapels and, by 1800, this was becoming more widespread. Inevitably this situation led to the emergence of a new denomination.

Methodism's ecclesiastical structures evolved gradually during John Wesley's long ministry as he used whatever methods best enabled him to fulfil the mission to which he believed God had called him. The various societies, with their chapels, were linked together into a larger unit—the circuit—to which a Superintendent Minister was appointed by the Conference. Circuits were usually very large and, invariably, 'assistants' were needed who functioned under the direction of the Superintendent. The affairs of the circuit were administered by the Quarterly Meeting, comprising ministers and representatives from each congregation.

The supreme policy making body of the church was the annual Conference. As early as 1744 Wesley established a ministerial Conference to which authority was transferred at his death. However, during his lifetime, John exercised an absolute authority and determined the discipline and structures of Methodism which remained basically minister-controlled for many decades. Only after 1800 were joint committees of ministers and laymen established to manage the various funds of the church.[6] This was strange in view of the significant role which the laity played in pastoral, preaching and local administrative activities.

Despite the fact that, at Wesley's death, Methodism had an apparently well-structured system, unresolved issues concerning its relationship with the Church of England and the place of the laity in the Methodist organisation produced tension, conflict and schism before the century closed. The first split occurred within a few years when Alexander Kilham, a minister, contended for the rights of local trustees to determine who could administer the sacraments and for lay participation in Conference. He did not accept the Plan of Pacification drawn up by the Conference and, in 1797, resigned to found the Methodist New Connexion. In the first half of the nineteenth century other offshoots emerged, of which the Primitive Methodists (1811) and the Bible Christians (1815) were the most important. Yet it was not until the second half of that century that laymen were given a seat in Conference, a development which might have prevented at least some of the dissatisfaction within the Wesleyan Methodist body.

A rationalistic and deistic philosophy pervaded the eighteenth century. The upper classes laughed at religion, the masses were ignorant and the criminal classes menaced society. Except for a few parish priests who provided occasional bright spots in a generally gloomy moral and spiritual environment, the Church of England was not equal to the tasks of proclaiming the Gospel in its fullness and of effecting moral regeneration and 'it had ceased to merit the description of a Church Militant'.[7] The Dissenters were hardly in a better position. Nonconformity had gone into spiritual decline and the Presbyterians, for example, were drifting into Unitarianism.

During the course of the century, the preaching of John Wesley and the hymns of his brother enabled the doctrines of Christianity to take on new meaning and become infused with a new vitality for thousands who shared the same life-transforming experience which the brothers had undergone in May 1738. The Methodism of the eighteenth century was a 'revival Church in spirit' and 'represented in [its] origins a revival of theology as well as a revival of life'.[8] Each of the brothers had experienced and understood 'the genuine gospel of present salvation through faith, wrought in the heart by the Holy Ghost, declaring present, free, full justification and expressing every branch of inward and outward holiness' and it was this which they sought to convey to their fellows. The Wesleys proclaimed that God's grace was 'immense, unfathomed, unconfined'. Through Christ's death on the cross God had provided an atonement for the sins of mankind. The Atonement was the 'burning focus of faith' for Wesley. Wesley taught that, normally, the Holy Spirit grants to every child of God an assurance of his forgiveness and acceptance by God—a doctrine unacceptable to eighteenth century theologians and labelled by Bishop Butler as 'a horrid thing, a very horrid thing'.

As a consequence of his justification, a Christian refrains from doing wrong and possesses a new motive for living—the motive of love. Justification leads to sanctification. The life of the Christian, which is the life of holiness, produces the fruit of the Spirit. Wesley particularly stressed the doctrine of Christian Perfection, or Perfect Love, stating that this doctrine was 'the grand depositum which God has lodged with the people called Methodists, and for the sake of propagating this chiefly he appeared to have raised us up'. For Wesley, Christian Perfection meant purity of motive, with love of God and neighbour guiding every thought and action in a person's life. Such a condition was not static, for 'one perfected in love may grow in grace'.[9] Accepting the orthodox doctrines of the Christian faith, Wesley placed particular emphasis on three of them—salvation by grace through faith available to all, assurance and Christian Perfection.

No one held more firmly than Wesley that orthodoxy of doctrine 'was but a slender part of religion' and so, in his *The Character of a Methodist*, he gave a description which went beyond the mere words of doctrine to the very spirit of his teaching:

> The distinguishing marks of a Methodist are not his opinions of any sort . . . A Methodist is one who has 'the love of God shed abroad in his heart by the Holy Ghost', given unto him; one who 'loves the Lord his God with all his heart, with all his soul, with all his mind, and with all his strength' . . . And while he thus always exercises his love to God . . . this commandment is also written in his heart, 'that he who loveth God, love his brother also'.[10]

By 1815 all branches of Methodism were making great progress and even those parts of England which had been untouched at Wesley's death were hearing the message of Primitive Methodist and Bible Christian preachers. The influence of Methodism on life in England was considerable and growing and, because Methodism was not only 'a revival Church in its spirit' but also 'a missionary church in its organisation', it was also well-established in the United States of America and had begun to witness in Canada, the West Indies and South Africa. One man who had contributed greatly to this missionary outreach was Dr Thomas Coke, an ordained Church of England clergyman who had thrown in his lot with Wesley. By the 1816 Conference, one hundred and eleven missionaries were working in twelve countries.

The last of these men to commence duty had been the Rev. Samuel Leigh who had reached the colony of New South Wales on 10 August 1815.[11] Leigh found himself in a difficult situation, striving to bring his message of salvation and scriptural holiness to a raw new colony peopled mainly by convicts and soldiers, or those not long released from such positions. Added to this was the problem of working many thousands of miles, and many months in time, away from a Missionary Committee which believed that it should exercise effective, hands-on control of all but the most routine day-to-day matters. Despite these difficulties, Wesleyan Methodism made progress, albeit painfully slowly, for the first fifteen years. Thereafter it spread more rapidly with the laity playing a particularly vigorous role as they moved out with the expansion of the settlement, established the most basic of religious ordinances themselves, and then called on the Missionary Committee to send clergy to serve their needs.

From the time of Wesleyan independence in 1855, they, and to a lesser extent the smaller Methodist bodies, spread with great rapidity across the face of the colony for the rest of the century. As it grew in extent the mission also broadened in scope and Methodists became involved in social witness as well as in the work of the conversion of sinners and the building up of the faithful. During this time, the machinery of the church had to be adapted to meet the needs of the local situation, though the basic idea of the connexional church, with a delicate balance between the local structures of circuit and society and the central

Conference organisation remained broadly unchanged and of vital importance. The itinerant ministry was the lubricant which kept this mechanism working satisfactorily, just as the uniquely Methodist office of local preacher, and the equally unique pastoral institution of the class meeting, provided a basis for the success of the itinerancy.

The many social changes during the late nineteenth and early twentieth centuries found the church totally unprepared and made its witness increasingly difficult, for example, the social conflict ushered in by the Depression and strikes of the 1890s, the 1914–18 war and the subsequent industrial and social divisions. and the Great Depression of the early 1930s. With the advent of nuclear explosives from the end of World War II, the church had to face a world which, for the first time, had the capacity to destroy itself, and that at a time when it was deeply divided by the Cold War so that the final conflict sometimes seemed perilously close. At the same time, the expansion of education and the growth, through scientific achievement, of an increased capacity to control the physical environment led to the development of a confident secularism which challenged the church in many ways and sometimes made it uncertain of its own role.

There were changes in the church too. The most notable of these was the increasing breakdown of the old balance between centre and periphery as centralisation grew and local initiative seemed to decline. The Church developed new machinery to meet the growing problems of delinquency, poverty and racism and to attempt to find answers to the great overall difficulty of a shrinking world which was nevertheless increasingly divided.

So difficult was the way forward that it seemed axiomatic to many that progress could only be made if there was a broad amalgamation of Christian bodies. Thus Methodism participated willingly in both the world ecumenical movement and in less ambitious discussions to bring about organic union in Australia between the Congregational, Methodist and Presbyterian churches. The partial success of those discussions brought an end to the independent existence of the Methodist church in New South Wales, and indeed Australia, in June 1977.

This, in broad outline, is the ground to be covered in the pages which follow. Yet this book does not set out to be a chronicle of Methodism in New South Wales. Such a task was carried out for the nineteenth century many years ago by Rev. James Colwell and needs no repetition for he did his work well. No one could treat the twentieth century in the same way, even were that desirable—the task is simply too complex and time-consuming. The reader will therefore find that many events which he or she may personally consider to be important are not recorded here. Many (most) circuits are not mentioned and the names of many thousands of earnest and hard-working Methodists do not appear in the index. For this we make no apology, for the task we have set ourselves is quite different.

The basic aim of this book is to interpret the broad sweep of Methodist history in New South Wales and to illuminate the great themes raised by the life of the church in the community: why did Methodism make such a poor start in the colony? Why was it able to spread so rapidly in the second half of the nineteenth century? How well adapted to local circumstances was the peculiar machinery of Methodism? Who were the Methodists? What did it mean to be a Methodist in nineteenth century New South Wales? How did the church respond to the great questions raised by war and depression and by industrial and social conflict? How did the church relate to both individuals and the community at large? Was Methodism able to find an adequate response to the rampant secularism of the twentieth century? How did Methodism cope with the challenge of Christian disunity? The approach to the story is therefore general and local events and details are drawn on to illustrate general trends rather than for their own sake.

Whether or not this book achieves these aims, it is hoped that it will promote interest in the writing of Methodist history for there inevitably remains ample scope for more work on particular aspects which may either confirm or modify the view that we offer and the immense riches of the Uniting Church Archives and the Methodist collection in the Mitchell Library invite such work.

It is also a part of our view that the Uniting church, which has so short a history of its own, needs to be vitally aware of the traditions handed on to its members by the constituent denominations. The history of Congregationalism, of Methodism and of

Presbyterianism is now the prehistory of the Uniting church. Any institution or community which is uninterested in its own past is undeserving of a future. This volume is an attempt both to create and fulfil such an interest.

Part 1
Sowing the seed

1

'Send us a preacher'

Methodism made its first appearance in New South Wales in 1812 when the convict settlement was still less than twenty-five years old. Although colonial society was hardly congenial soil for the faith of 'the warmed heart', both the Wesleyan and Primitive variants of Methodism had been planted there by lay initiative before the mid-century. Wesleyan Methodism was firmly established, the fastest growing denomination in the colony; Primitive Methodism was still in a tentative position, its future uncertain.

The Wesleyans: years of struggle

Thomas Bowden arrived in Sydney on 28 January 1812 to begin duty as a teacher. A Wesleyan class leader in England, he quickly established a class meeting in Sydney and encouraged John Hosking, another Methodist teacher who had arrived three years earlier, to do the same. The first of these was held on 6 March 1812. Another was established separately in Windsor by the converted Irish ex-convict, Edward Eagar, at about the same time. Eagar had become involved in active Christian work at the request of Rev. Richard Cartwright, one of the colonial chaplains, who had asked him to read the Anglican service in some of the neighbouring country places. On his own initiative, Eagar proceeded to hold a class meeting after the services as well as various mid-week meetings. Cartwright accepted this without demur, apparently believing that, in such a society, any presentation of the Gospel was better than none at all. Given the

3

primacy of the class meeting among Methodist institutions at that period, these events must be seen as marking the real beginning of Wesleyan Methodism in the colony.

A month later, on 3 April, the Wesleyans from Windsor and Sydney combined to hold a love-feast, another characteristic Methodist event. As a result of this, two letters were sent to the Wesleyan Methodist Missionary Society in England requesting that one or two Methodist preachers be sent to New South Wales to guide the infant Society now tenuously established by the laity, and to improve a colonial society considered to be almost totally depraved. The laymen foresaw no difficulty with the Anglican chaplains provided the Methodists acted in unison with the church rather than as a distinct body. To this end, the missionary sent should not be 'radically a Dissenter' but one who would work in harmony with the chaplains.[1]

The Wesleyan Methodist Conference of July 1814 responded by sending Rev. Samuel Leigh, a Staffordshire man who was thirty at the time of his arrival in the colony on 10 August 1815. He was very much the kind of man sought by Bowden in his 1812 letter. On the morning following his arrival, Leigh was taken to meet Governor Macquarie, who was opposed to the introduction of sectarianism to the colony and indicated some displeasure at having a Methodist preacher land unexpectedly on his shores. Leigh's assurances of his friendship towards the Church of England won the Governor over and he promised to look kindly upon the missionary's work. The Anglican clergy themselves were entirely friendly.[2]

The situation in Sydney was less promising than the Missionary Committee had been led to believe. Local financial support for the missionary's maintenance was minimal and there was clearly going to be a long period of dependence on the English Church. Of the three class meetings of 1812, only one with six members remained in 1815. Within two weeks of his arrival, Leigh opened another in Sydney and, as opportunity allowed, one each in Parramatta, Windsor and Castlereagh. He was soon able to claim forty-four members. At the same time he established a regular pattern of services in the Sydney area without clashing with the official Anglican services.

Within a few months, Leigh began to travel extensively around a circuit of 240 km (150 miles) which included Parramatta, Liverpool, Windsor, Richmond, Castlereagh and a number of smaller places on the Hawkesbury River. At Castlereagh, he met a remarkable layman, John Lees, who offered him the encouragement and support he so much needed in a strange land and who later built at his own expense, on his own land, the first Methodist chapel in Australia.

Leigh managed affairs by spending ten days in Sydney, then proceeding on his rounds for a further ten or eleven days. It was a gruelling and debilitating programme in a climate to which he was completely unaccustomed. Just how trying the physical conditions of the colony were to the early missionaries may be illustrated by a later note from the diary of Leigh's first colleague, Rev. Walter Lawry:

> March 19, 1819. Set out from Sydney for Parramatta, 16 miles, when I arrived the thermometer was at 91 and every inch of my clothes as wet as if it had been in a bath . . . in this state I went to preach in the government school house . . . here with my roasted skin, steaming sweat and fainting spirits I offered the evening sacrifice.[3]

By March 1816 Sunday schools had been started in the major centres and a benevolent society, the first in New South Wales, had begun operations on Leigh's initiative and with the patronage of Governor Macquarie. Such progress led the lay supporters to the view that a substantial chapel (at a likely cost of £1200) was needed in Sydney, along with smaller ones at Windsor and Castlereagh, if the cause was to advance further. It was proposed that if the Committee could send a small supply of goods which could be sold at a profit, it should be possible to remit the principal in eighteen months or so. More ministerial help was also obviously needed, but no financial support was available locally for a second missionary.

The London Committee, delighted with Leigh's progress, decided to send a further missionary to assist him and to adopt the plan proposed to finance the Sydney chapel. It would regret the latter decision.[4] Leigh ran into a number of problems in 1817. In particular, he felt the need for an older, more experienced man and begged the Committee to 'pray for your stripling that he may not be slain and the sheep scattered'. He conducted services at fourteen places and had invitations to many more, but he could not accept these without neglecting others. His preferred arrangement was to create three circuits based in Sydney, Parramatta and Windsor and to operate them with five preachers. Alone, he could not 'keep alive the spark of grace in the heart of the people'. The scattered nature of the settlement compounded the problem. It was not feasible for members to travel long distances to worship as absence from home often led to the theft of the entire property of a family. A more personal problem was also pressing on Leigh's mind. No more single men should be sent to New South Wales as the sexual temptations were great and it was easy to arouse unjustified suspicion in colonial society. Later, others would raise the same point.

One new development in 1817 which must have cheered him, however, was the formation of an Auxiliary Bible Society in Sydney to overcome the desperate shortage of scriptures in the colony. Leigh was a prime mover in this and was also a member of the committee along with his fellow Wesleyans, Eagar, Hosking and George Howe.[5]

Leigh's first colleague, Rev. Walter Lawry, arrived on 2 May 1818 to alleviate some of the loneliness of his situation. A warm-hearted Cornishman of twenty-five years, Lawry responded eagerly to the task, but as quickly fell into despair from the isolation. He was rescued from this, however, by the love of Mary Hassall, a god-fearing young woman from Parramatta.[6]

Initially, Leigh and Lawry appeared to get on well together, the latter informing his parents that 'Bro. Leigh is just about everything I could wish for a colleague'. But this was short-lived; in fact the two men were ill-suited to working so closely together. Leigh was a humourless, intense, single-minded man, quite prepared to kill himself in the fulfilment of his mission; Lawry was warm, even emotional, found it difficult to remain serious in company for long and, while willing to work hard, placed rather more importance on his home comforts than did Leigh. Lawry could also be difficult, however, and this is shown by a comment about the relationship with Leigh which he (Lawry) made much later in a letter to his parents: 'I discovered in him most glaring deficiencies and inconsistencies—of these I used faithfully and affectionately to apprise him'.

Jealousy also played a part in worsening their relationship, for Leigh had previously courted Mary Hassall unsuccessfully and found it galling to see his younger colleague succeed where he had failed with perhaps the only young woman in the colony suited to becoming the wife of a Wesleyan missionary.

A serious decline in Leigh's health because of overwork also affected their relationship. Early in 1819, Leigh went to New Zealand at the invitation of the Colonial Chaplain, Samuel Marsden, to investigate the possibilities of missionary work there and also to recover his health. However, a year later, there was no alternative for him but to return to England. He must have left with a heavy heart since his departure cast the whole burden of the mission upon Lawry and prevented the proper consolidation of the congregations, especially in Sydney, because of the solitary missionary's frequent absence and the lack of a sufficient and adequate lay leadership.[7]

Yet the mission had made some progress. The colony's first Wesleyan chapel had opened at Castlereagh on 7 October 1817. Its donor, John Lees, had also given an acre of land for the maintenance of the cause. A second had opened in Princes Street, Sydney, on 17 March 1819 (largely the work of John Scott, another devoted layman), and a third at Windsor early in 1819 on land donated by Samuel Marsden. A foundation stone for a chapel in Macquarie Street was laid by Leigh just before his departure, although this chapel would not be opened until the middle of 1821.[8]

When Leigh reached London, he was able to report to the Committee that there had also been spiritual progress in the colony. There were, he claimed, eighty-three members of the Society, while 230–350 persons heard the Word each Sunday in Sydney at two Wesleyan services. There was a Sunday school which attracted from 50–100 children. There was preaching on Monday and Wednesday evenings, prayer meetings on Tuesday and Saturday evenings and Sunday morning and a class meeting on Friday evening. He referred to the assistance of a growing band of laymen: Edward Eagar, J. Forbes and John Scott in Sydney, magistrate Thomas Moore in Liverpool, J. Milard in Windsor, William White in Parramatta and John Lees in Castlereagh. Leigh also commented favourably on the help given to the mission by Governor Macquarie. He recommended that missions be established in New Zealand and the islands of the Pacific and offered himself to lead the former.

There remains some doubt about the accuracy of the number of members reported by Leigh. When the men in Australia saw the report, most of them disputed it. Rev. Ralph Mansfield, a new man with no axe to grind, suggested that sixty was a more realistic number once the 'irregular' had been removed from the rolls.

It was probably while talking with the Committee that Leigh discovered that it had already sent Revs. Benjamin Carvosso and Ralph Mansfield to New South Wales and that Rev. George Erskine had also been ordered to proceed there from Ceylon. At the meeting to which he reported, the Committee further decided to send a missionary (Rev. William Walker) to the Aborigines and another, Rev. William Horton, to replace Lawry who would be sent to Tonga; Leigh would go to New Zealand. One missionary, Carvosso, was to go to Van Diemen's Land, leaving two in New South Wales proper. New South Wales would shortly become a District with Erskine as its Chairman. Leigh himself would arrive in Sydney en route for New Zealand on 16 September 1821.[9]

The mission had been bedevilled by problems from the start and several came to a head about this time. The unusual method of financing the mission (by sending out goods which the missionaries sold, using the proceeds for their work), and especially for financing the chapels, was unhelpful despite eliminating a potentially expensive credit problem for a society which was not at first well-known. The situation was not improved by the missionaries' failure to submit proper accounts on time. As early as March 1819 the mission was £150 in debt and a little later an unauthorised sum of £500 had to be drawn, an action which brought a stern rebuke from the Missionary Committee.[10]

The Macquarie Street chapel involved the mission in an expenditure of about £2000, half of which was covered by a loan from the government and half by a loan from Eagar on the promise that the Committee, which would be able to borrow money more cheaply in England than could be done in the colony, would repay him on demand. The Committee accepted the charge only with the greatest reluctance and after considerable delay. The preachers had acted contrary to rule and the fact that the chapel attracted a larger and more respectable congregation than that in Princes Street was no mitigation of the fault. The loan from the government dragged on and was repaid only in the 1830s, during the superintendency of Rev. Joseph Orton, after an involved negotiation and with the aid of a timely legacy.[11]

A further financial dispute, which arose but was not settled at this time, related to missionary living expenses which were much higher in the colony than in England. The preachers wanted substantial increases but the Committee would never go far enough. A letter detailing the prices of such essential items as bread, butter and cheese had no effect. Leigh, newly returned to Australia and thoroughly out of sorts with his colleagues, ended their chances by accusing them of extravagance.[12]

The other problem which greatly troubled the young Society was that of its relations with the Church of England. This also soured the relationship between the missionaries and the London Committee. The initial letter of request for missionaries had urged the sending of a man capable of working with the chaplains. Leigh, who was such a man, had been instructed to pay proper respect to Marsden and he obeyed that direction sedulously. Impending trouble might have been sensed as early as mid–1819 when Lawry described the chaplains other than Marsden as being 'highly Calvinistic' and as looking upon the Methodists as intruders. This same tendency at Windsor and Richmond troubled Carvosso two years later. Possibly because Leigh, in London, had indicated that Lawry was not honouring the original instructions, the Committee renewed them in January 1821 and forbade all interference and controversy with the Anglican clergy. While Leigh was in England, both he and the Committee wrote a number of letters to the Anglican clergy in New South Wales supporting them against Carvosso, Lawry and Mansfield. This evident disloyalty, coupled with the sense of being unjustly censured, was bound to anger the young and struggling missionaries.[13]

Lawry, who had come into money on the death of his father-in-law, built a chapel at Parramatta to forestall the preaching of Calvinist doctrine there. This chapel opened on 20 June

1821 and a Sunday school was started which operated at the same time as the Anglican school. Marsden professed to see this as a deliberate attempt to alienate the rising generation from the Anglican church, though he claimed that he would not have minded if the Wesleyans had merely gathered children not attending any school. Lawry protested that he had done no more than Marsden wished. About five children had been attracted from the Anglican school by superior teaching (Lawry had a trained teacher, Marsden did not), the remainder of the seventy to eighty who joined in the first month came from the streets where there were many more waiting to be won.[14]

The quarrel entered a new phase in October when the lay leaders of the Wesleyan cause in Sydney wrote to the Committee saying that the Sacrament of the Lord's Supper had been celebrated provisionally in the Sydney chapels in response to the pressing requests of members. They sought confirmation of this act, urging that the foundations of Methodism would be weakened if the privilege were to be removed. The times of services had also been changed so that there was now some overlap with the Anglican services.[15]

Leigh, back in Australia on his way to New Zealand, gave every appearance of at least partially accepting his colleagues' actions. However, he wrote to the London Committee attacking his brother missionaries over preaching in church hours, the unnecessary celebration of the Lord's Supper and Lawry's Parramatta Sunday school, all of which, he said, gave great offence to the Anglican clergy. Worse, Mansfield was lecturing on Wednesday evenings for the sole purpose of contradicting what the clergy had said the previous Sunday. The whole problem had originated with Lawry, who had deliberately set out to disturb and annoy the clergy. Leigh's colleagues remained unaware of his disloyalty and Mansfield informed the Committee confidently that 'our beloved superintendent' [Leigh] had 'fully acquiesced in the propriety' of at least the change in church time.[16]

The London Committee was enraged that the Sydney men should so act on their own initiative. It accepted Leigh's account without question and claimed that he had been 'put on trial' for refusing to disobey the Committee's instructions. Each missionary received a letter of reproof and was told that he would be recalled if he persisted in error. The Committee did not feel able to reverse the decisions on preaching in church hours and on the Sacrament, though it obviously wished to, but urged its missionaries 'to cultivate the spirit of deference to the clergy'. They were virtually told to work in the backblocks, leaving the larger towns to the clergy, and there was a strongly implied accusation that they had largely neglected Leigh's pattern of itinerating out of town. The opportunity was also taken to criticise them sharply on a variety of other matters.[17]

It was not until a year after Leigh had laid his charges that the Sydney brethren had a chance to answer them—a clear illustration of the problem of control from afar. At a District Meeting on 2 October 1822, Carvosso, Mansfield, Walker and Rev. William White expressed surprise that complaints, which they had thought withdrawn by Leigh a year before, had reached the Committee. They had a logical and reasoned answer to every criticism levelled at them, but the true basis of their problem eluded them: they saw their task as building a strong and independent Wesleyan church for people who often had little link with the Anglican establishment; Leigh and the Committee saw the Wesleyan mission as an adjunct of the Church of England.[18] This serious colonial problem was a reflection of the one which had occurred in England in the 1790s and which has been referred to earlier.

There had been some discussion about the possibility of a mission to the Aborigines from the start, but nothing was done until August 1820 when William Walker was appointed to the task mainly, it would seem, because his health was found to be unsuited to Africa, for which continent he had volunteered. The early months of Walker's ministry were a time of non-achievement. The nomadic habits of the Aboriginal people and the multiplicity of their dialects made a regular Wesleyan itinerancy impossible and all that could be done was to establish a small mission settlement at which some native youth might be taught. No worthwhile opportunity came Walker's way until early 1824, when the government dismissed the committee of its own Native Institution at Parramatta and gave him the use of the lands, cottages and schoolhouse for one year. There was also a subsidy of £20 per child and an additional £5 for every one who attended school.

11

Less than a year later, Walker had left the Aboriginal mission to become superintendent of the Government Orphan Institution. His brethren ordered him to quit this task and rejoin their work, but he would not. For Walker, there followed suspension, investigation, recrimination and eventual expulsion from the ministry and, for a time, from the church itself. For the Aboriginal mission there was nothing but failure after further extensive attempts by a locally recruited man, John Harper, to begin something in Wellington Valley and Batemans Bay. The only important result of all of this was further ill-will among the missionaries and with the Committee and bad publicity in the colony for the Wesleyan mission.[19]

Marsden had early urged upon Leigh the need for a Methodist mission in New Zealand and the Friendly Islands, and Leigh's first trip to New Zealand in 1819 had been partly designed to allow him to assess the opportunities there. Lawry was also interested in the concept of a mission to the islands and wrote to the Committee on 15 July 1819 saying 'I do long for a mission in the Friendly Islands and unto none is the opening so fair as unto us'.[20] With some reason, the Committee understood Lawry to be offering to go to the islands himself to inaugurate such a mission, though he had not intended his letter to be read in that way and was surprised when he was ordered to New Zealand with Leigh for a time and thence to Tonga. There were certain practical difficulties with this, but, more importantly, it raised the major problem of how these two men, who had been proven incompatible, could again work closely with each other. Discussion with the brethren in New South Wales led to a general agreement, supported by Leigh, that it would be better if Lawry proceeded directly to Tonga.

This he did in mid-April 1822, but he had disobeyed the Committee's instructions, albeit with the approval of his Sydney brethren, and it should have caused him no surprise that, when the Committee wrote castigating all the preachers for their various misdemeanours, it singled him out as 'the foremost in irregularity and disobedience to our rules'. Soon after this a depressed Lawry returned to Sydney and, ultimately, without the Committee's permission, to England to attempt to clear his name. He arrived there early in 1825 to find that only one member of the

Committee was prepared to speak to him in the first instance and even he regarded Lawry with great coolness. When he appeared before the Committee in a formal way, he must have been very persuasive as he was exonerated from all blame and the Committee admitted to having been misled.[21]

Another initiative taken by the Sydney missionaries, on the prompting of prominent layman and journalist Robert Howe, and rejected by the Committee, was the attempt to begin a missionary press and to publish their own journal, *The Australian Magazine*. With the support of Governor Macquarie, it had made a moderate start before it was abandoned on the Committee's orders. The fear was that such literary activity might distract the man based in Sydney from his real evangelistic and pastoral work.[22]

Despite the many disputes during the period 1819–22, all was not negative. The decision to station Carvosso at Windsor was a good one: it helped bring religion to the settlers of the increasingly important Hawkesbury district, it was in line with the Committee's wish that its missionaries should spend more time in outlying areas, and it provided a further base from which the Wesleyans could counter the Calvinism of the chaplains. Early in 1821 Carvosso's Cornish eloquence was attracting congregations of between 70–100 people on Sunday evening and about 30–50 on Wednesday evening. Mrs Carvosso ran a Sunday school class of thirty and nine attended the Monday evening class meeting—a few women also met with Mrs Carvosso on Friday evenings for prayer and Bible reading. There was a prayer meeting in the chapel on Saturday. Carvosso went to Castlereagh to preach fortnightly on Sundays and Tuesdays, drawing fifty on Sunday and twenty-five on Tuesday to a 'decent little chapel' built by John Lees. There were only four or five class members and a very small Sunday school but this could be accounted for satisfactorily by the scattered nature of the population.

Carvosso preached regularly at Richmond and visited Portland Head, Wilberforce and Pitt Town. As each of these places was several miles from Windsor, Carvosso and his horse spent much time on the road tending the tiny congregations. In a little more than two years he travelled over 6000 miles, preached almost 800 sermons, and conducted some hundreds of class and prayer meetings. Together, he and his wife had converted probably eleven people and ministered to a total of twenty-eight in class. On the surface much effort had been expended for little result, but such were the exigencies of church building in early rural Australia.

Figures given at the District Meeting at the end of 1822, however, indicate that some progress had been made. In New South Wales proper there were 110 full members, 271 children in Sunday schools and six chapels seating 1560 people and bearing a debt of £1500. The scattered nature of the population outside the major centres remained a serious problem, as did the relative lack of lay leaders without whom the Methodist church could never be truly effective in the colonial situation. The missionaries were frequently the only class leaders available and this not only imposed a heavy burden on them but meant that the penetrative power of the church was greatly reduced.[23]

An entry in Carvosso's journal for 7 October 1822 presaged a related problem which was to concern the Wesleyans as the nineteenth century wore on: the class meeting was proving a stumbling block to many, with its insistence on public personal testimony. At least one member, a steward in the Sydney district, left the Society about this time because he was reprimanded for not attending the class meeting. Carvosso noted disapprovingly that were the Methodists disposed to abandon the class meeting as the test of church membership they might soon greatly increase their following.[24]

Affairs were expected to improve with the arrival from Ceylon of the new Superintendent and later Chairman of the District, Rev. George Erskine. In notifying his appointment to the Australian missionaries, the Missionary Society Secretary, Rev. Joseph Taylor, had described him as 'a lively zealous man' who would be 'a great blessing' in the colonial mission. The description was less than apt. Erskine reached Sydney on 4 November 1822 in a state of serious ill-health. Almost immediately he sided against Leigh and with those working to establish a separate, identifiable, Wesleyan church. Erskine had neither the health nor the organisational talent for the job and some also thought that a late marriage to a woman of property diverted his interest from spiritual concerns. In 1825, Ralph Mansfield, the ablest of the missionary group, and himself a useful administrator, hinted broadly that Erskine was not a satisfactory District Chairman and should be replaced by Rev. Joseph Taylor who possessed, to a high degree, all the appropriate qualities. Mansfield need not have troubled himself with this clandestine disloyalty to his Chairman. Erskine was painfully aware of his own shortcomings and, from April 1826, regularly asked the Committee to appoint someone more suitable to the post, promising unswerving loyalty to his successor. In any case, the Committee, which blamed him for weakness as well as for serious financial irregularities, began to seek a successor from November 1826. It was a pity for everyone, especially Erskine, that they took so long to find one.[25]

Meanwhile, relations between the Committee and its New South Wales missionaries worsened. A meeting of the Committee in May 1826 decided to reduce the allowances paid to the missionaries. This decision was reaffirmed a year later and strong censures passed against the men on the spot for excessive and unexpected claims. It is likely that the Committee acted on the basis of out-of-date information about prices given by well-meaning men who had been away from the colony too long. Finally, the Committee asked a Sydney businessman to cash bills for the missionaries at the ruling rate of exchange and to limit them to a specific sum each year.[26]

One other dispute also deserves mention since it appears not to have sprung from the basic financial disagreement which so seriously soured relations between the Committee and the missionaries. In 1822 the Sydney preachers appeared to have been given power to appoint 'assistant missionaries' or 'missionaries on trial' who would later be ordained if they proved suitable. This they did, honestly believing it to be the will of the Committee. However, they again ran into trouble, particularly when they not only allowed one (J. Weiss) to marry but sent him to Tonga before permission had been given by the Committee. All costs associated with this exercise were ordered to be paid by the Australian preachers themselves.[27] Mansfield, who acted as secretary throughout this conflict and who was therefore deeply immersed in the argument, decided to accept a lucrative offer from Robert Howe, editor of the *Sydney Gazette*. He further charged the Committee with robbing him of his character, of breaking its pledge to care for the needs of the missionaries, and of oppressing him with a debt which he could not possibly bear on his meagre stipend. Mansfield, who had resigned his missionary office but retained his ministerial status, later sought full reinstatement, but the Committee would only accept him on the most humiliating of terms and so he was lost to full-time work for ever. He did, however, continue to preach and thus provide valuable aid to the hard-pressed Sydney missionaries. So young a mission could not afford to lose the full-time services of its most able preacher, even if he was partly wasted on congregations of limited education.[28]

Despite some small achievements, the Wesleyan mission in New South Wales could not be considered as a success before 1831. Methodism had exercised a presence in the colony since 1812, and had ministerial presence since 1815, yet the District Meeting of 22 March 1831 indicated that there were only 112 members of the Wesleyan Society in New South Wales. In addition, twenty Sunday school teachers and 137 scholars were reported. Even these figures were inflated and a cleansing of the rolls in 1832 by the new Superintendent, Rev. Joseph Orton, reduced the number of members to seventy-six and the number of Sunday school teachers to twelve. As the outcome of the considerable efforts of the half-generation which had passed since the landing of Leigh, it was very little.[29]

There were many reasons for this relative failure. The convict origins of the bulk of the population made them unlikely recipients of the doctrines of full salvation and entire sanctification. The scattered nature of the settlement prevented the regular contact necessary to bring people to the point of conversion. The lack of a significant lay leadership, especially class leaders and local preachers (two very important groups in the traditional Methodist system) was particularly debilitating. But the most crippling factor of all was the endemic disharmony among the missionaries themselves and the constant niggling warfare between them and the London Committee. Leigh was not a suitable person to be Superintendent of the mission. He was hard working and dedicated, but he did not know how to guard his strength and he lacked judgement, patience and administrative skill. He did not relate well to his colleagues and, when he fell out with them, he was too willing to make false reports to the Committee.

Leigh was a conservative churchman and was prepared to make almost any concession to the colonial clergy to maintain the peace. Lawry, Carvosso and Mansfield were more in the Dissenting tradition and had few inhibitions about acting for the best interests of Methodism regardless of the effects of their actions on the Church of England. They were young and, at times, impetuous, needlessly stirring up trouble which might have been avoided, but Methodism would have made little progress in New South Wales had it persisted in the Leigh tradition.

These conflicts led to extremely difficult relations between the missionaries and the London Committee. That Committee, itself far from blameless for the imbroglio, steadfastly refused to give distant missionaries the necessary discretion in the application of instructions to their local situation. Nor did it ever make the necessary effort to determine whether the missionaries were as extravagant as it supposed. In this regard it is significant that Orton had not been there very long before he was recommending increases for the men. In the case of Erskine, the Committee pursued to the very edge of the grave a man whom it must have realised was not competent to carry out successfully the task to which it had appointed him and whom it should have allowed to retire quietly. In so doing it stirred his supporters to a disaffection which lasted for some time.

By 1830 Lawry and Horton had gone home in disgrace, though the former had been forgiven once his position was explained. Mansfield had taken a secular occupation. Walker had been dismissed from the ministry. Carvosso had returned to minister in England. Leigh, who had spent much of his time in New Zealand, was ill and about to return to England permanently. Erskine was on the verge of a dishonourable retirement. It was to the advantage of the mission that the first generation of missionaries all passed from the scene at this time, but it was perhaps a pity that the London Committee did not share the same fate! In the view of Joseph Orton 'The Society was little better than a wreck'.[30] It would be hard to argue that there had been much gain to either the colony or to Methodism from its presence in New South Wales.

The Wesleyans: better times

The problems of the Wesleyan mission were not immediately cured by the appointment of Rev. Joseph Orton in 1831, though he did bring a wiser and stronger leadership than had previously existed. The two Wesleyan chapels in Sydney, in Princes and Macquarie Streets, were badly placed and well away from the population centres of the growing city. The missionaries wished to sell the Macquarie Street chapel and build another in a better location, but it took several years to overcome the problems associated with the sale of the land which had originally been given as a government grant. A new site then had to be obtained in a suitable position and a new chapel built. It took a further nine years before the York Street chapel, 'the cathedral of Methodism' as it came to be known, was opened early in 1844—well into the McKenny superintendency. Yet, as Orton claimed at his departure in 1836, there had been an enormous increase in the number of full members (i.e. regular participants in, and contributors to, class meetings) during his time with the New South Wales Society.[31]

Other encouraging signs also appeared from time to time, especially later in Orton's period, and these usually related to cases of entire sanctification or to multiple conversions. One example occurred at the love-feast held in Sydney on 15 January 1835 when the two missionaries, Revs William Simpson and William Schofield, experienced entire sanctification while a number of adherents were converted.[32]

The most interesting development in Orton's period was his move to enlarge the scope of the mission to include territory beyond the Blue Mountains, especially the region of Bathurst—the Hunter River region was also mentioned for the first time as a possible area for expansion.

Though the London Committee, which saw Orton's task in New South Wales as one of consolidation and revival rather than expansion, gave him no great encouragement to do so, in each of the three years from 1833–35 Orton undertook the long and difficult journey across the mountains to the Bathurst plain. There he met laymen William Tom, William Lane, George Hawke and John Glasson who had already established a class meeting and who were holding services. It is not clear how long these men had been active in the area but, as Tom seems to have been the driving force, it may have been since his arrival in 1830. Orton's journeys were made in response to requests from the laymen concerned who were acting as Bowden, Hosking and Eagar had done before them—and as many would act subsequently. They wanted ministerial assistance to help them evangelise 'the City of the Plains', and they were prepared to pay for it. In Orton, they found a champion for their cause and his pleading led the Missionary Committee to send a man there. 'Parson' Tom, at least, continued to do his share of the hard travelling and preaching work, going east as far as Kings Plain (Blayney) and west to Molong, though in later times this area too would have its problems with inadequate lay preaching assistance.[33]

None of this would do Orton himself much good. Gradually he noticed that the Committee was simply not corresponding with him as it should and, in due course and without warning, it sent him to Van Diemen's Land and appointed Rev. John McKenny in his place. The Committee later denied that this was in any sense a banishment or that it had lost confidence in Orton. Whatever the London Committee thought, Colwell's judgement remains just, that it was Orton who laid the enduring foundations of Australian Methodism.[34] Nevertheless, it seemed otherwise at the time and Orton felt that he had been supplanted.

A new problem arose in the late 1830s which was part of the much wider community-based problem of the relationship between emancipists and free settlers. Rev. Daniel Draper, at Parramatta, raised it first at the beginning of 1837 and Rev. Frederick Lewis, at Bathurst, took it up again a few months later. This problem related to the employment of ticket-of-leave men in the lay offices of a church that was all too short of good laymen. Draper was prepared to allow the relevant class members and officers to judge whether or not a particular man was worthy to hold office. Lewis, on the other hand, thought that ex-convicts could be employed as Sunday school teachers, class leaders and visitors of the sick, if fully emancipated, but never as local preachers (though he would have allowed those already appointed to that office to continue in it). Two years later a new missionary, Rev. Samuel Wilkinson, put respectability before evangelism

19

when he told the Committee that it was to the credit of the Wesleyan Society that few convicts or emancipists had found a place in it!

It was as well that not everyone thought like him. At Castlereagh, the congregation included almost equal numbers of emancipists and freemen but there was no division between them. The latter never reflected on the former but rather 'glorified God on their behalf'. And well they might. A local revival in 1840–41 was largely instigated by a Mrs Byrnes, a former prostitute who had been transported for stealing from a client. She and other convict converts proved themselves to be invaluable members of the Christian body.[35]

This problem was exacerbated by the gradual spread of Methodism. Draper was expanding out from Parramatta to other smaller centres and Schofield was moving from Windsor down the Lower Hawkesbury and into places like Colo, Mangrove and Lower MacDonald. It was here, on 3 February 1838, that he converted John Joseph Walker who was later known as 'the apostle of St Albans', and who began the greatest family saga in the history of Australian Methodism. This same general area also produced other great local preachers like George Everingham (the first Australian-born local preacher), George Douglass and John Laughton.[36]

Everywhere preachers and chapels were needed but nowhere were they readily available. Many Methodist immigrants were coming to New South Wales but they were quickly scattered over the colony and left without pastoral oversight. Some easing of the situation occurred after mid-1838 when an amendment to the *Church Act* put the Wesleyans on the same footing as the Anglicans, Catholics and Presbyterians with respect to aid—under certain conditions, a grant equal to that raised by the denomination was paid by the government towards the construction of a chapel and a sum was paid towards the maintenance of a preacher proportionate to the number of hearers available to him in the district. This did not solve all problems, but it was of great assistance in chapel construction and in increasing the number of ordained missionaries in the colony. It also led to some competition between the denominations to increase their respective 'shares' of the settlers.[37]

According to the District Minutes of January 1838, there were 241 Wesleyan full members in the colony distributed as follows: Sydney, 139; Parramatta, 37; Bathurst, 35; Windsor, 30. The number continued to rise rapidly throughout McKenny's period as Superintendent and the figures from the Australian District Minutes for 31 July 1845, indicate 1497 full members, with a further 96 on trial. The circuit distribution was now Sydney, 619; Parramatta, 213; Windsor, 260; Bathurst, 189; and Hunter River, 216. This was more than six times the number in 1838 and almost twenty times that in 1832. It was a phenomenal increase and marked a dramatic change from the stagnation of the early years. There were many reasons for this but the increasing stream of free immigrants and the *Church Act* were the most important. Also, the Wesleyan tentacles were stretching out into areas previously unreached and enrolling as members those who, in earlier years, could not have been included. One of the newer preachers, Rev. Benjamin Hurst, also assured the Committee that the increase was substantially due to conversions.[38]

The growing outreach of Wesleyan Methodism at this time was not planned in any systematic way, least of all by the London Committee which was running seriously short of funds. Rather, this growth was the unplanned result of free immigration which brought to New South Wales substantial numbers of Wesleyans who found their way to many parts of the colony and established the ordinances of their religion wherever they went. They then called on the District Committee, and through it the London Committee, to provide ministerial oversight.

In Ashfield, Church and suburb 'grew side by side' with Wesleyan services being conducted in the home of Mr and Mrs John Fyle soon after the municipality was established in 1838. Likewise, cottage services began in Newtown in 1840, though that location did not come onto the Sydney circuit plan as an official place of preaching until 1841 after which it developed rapidly. The situation in Chippendale was similar. These and other developments led to the splitting of the Sydney circuit into North, South and East circuits by the end of the 1840s. At that time, the city and suburbs also saw the strong development of Sunday school work and the establishment of The Wesleyan

Methodist Sunday School Society of Sydney, a development which will be discussed more fully later.[39]

If we neglect the false start made there by Leigh in 1818, the Hunter was the second country district to come under the influence of the Wesleyans. In the early 1830s, William Lightbody, a schoolteacher and local preacher, began to conduct worship in Newcastle for a group of nonconformists who were mostly Wesleyans but who included a number of Primitive Methodists and some others. However, it was in the larger and livelier upstream town of Maitland that Methodism developed more strongly. Jeremiah Ledsam, an Irish coach builder and local preacher who went to West Maitland in 1837, began by establishing preaching services followed by a class and prayer meeting. A chapel was well under construction before the appointment of the first missionary, Rev. Jonathan Innes, in 1840. Innes and his successors were then able to develop the Maitland region and offer support to laymen who had already found their way to such widely separated places as Newcastle, Singleton, Sugarloaf, Wollombi, Raymond Terrace and Dungog.

The great problem of the Hunter River Circuit was that ministers were constantly tempted to over-extend their activities. It was only the presence of lay preachers like Ledsam, Robert Belford, Isaac Rose, William Plummer and, later, Silas Gill at Maitland, and Lightbody and others at Newcastle, that allowed the work to prosper. More than one such preacher walked from his home in West or East Maitland to Mulbring and Brunkerville and home again, a total journey of about 45 km as the crow flies, preaching three times along the way.[40]

By the end of the McKenny period, the most remarkable development in the Hunter region had occurred in its most secluded corner, the Upper Allyn, where there was a thriving cause. In 1845, the District Meeting reported that in an area totally neglected eighteen months earlier there was now a Society of forty persons. This development had occurred because two laymen, T. Doust and W.S. Grenfell, had not only sought a lay preacher—teacher for their district, but had also been prepared to move him there and to ensure that arrangements were made to pay him. The man chosen, T. Paterson, proved ideal for the task. At much the same time, a similar, but less dramatic, development took place in the Upper Hunter through the agency of W. Currey, a hired local preacher.[41]

There was an equally important development to the south from similar causes. In the late 1830s there had been a gathering of unusually talented Methodist laymen in the Cobbity (Camden) area. They included James Noakes, Thomas Baker, Thomas Foster, John Vidler, Joseph Doust, Silas Gill, John Wheatley and Tom Brown. After serving in the area for some time, the group began to move out, Brown, for example, going to the Jerrawa area, near Goulburn, where he tried successfully to convert the cattle thieves for whom the area was well-known. He established a church of seventy members, built a place of worship and became one of Methodism's best loved and most devoted local preachers. At Goulburn itself, Matthew Trenery, John Wheatley, Robert Blatchford and Henry Goldsmith prepared the way for the organisation of the full ministry of the church by Daniel Draper in the mid-1840s and the appointment of William Lightbody, founder of the Newcastle cause, as minister.[42]

Meanwhile, when William Schofield visited the Illawarra in 1839 he found a Society (with sixteen members) already in existence at Dapto, along with a Sunday school. There was also a Society at Wollongong. The great names in the Illawarra were those of John Vidler and John Graham. Vidler arrived in 1838 and began services almost immediately in his own hut. He transferred to Dapto in 1839 and linked up with the Somerville brothers and the Black family who shared his devotion. Graham operated from Marshall Mount. It was several years before this region had its own missionary but it was, to some extent, supplied from Sydney—though this still left it very dependent on those 'plain but good men', the local preachers.[43]

There was a continuing problem between the Wesleyans and the Anglicans which arose largely because the new *Church Act* put other denominations in the colony on an equal footing with the Anglicans. Bishop Broughton had considerable difficulty in accepting the erosion of the special position of his own church as it simply became one among several. The problem was worst in the Windsor–Lower Hawkesbury area where there were deliberate attempts to prevent the Wesleyans from celebrating the sacraments in a jointly used chapel and, indeed, where the validity of the whole Wesleyan ministry was questioned. At Parramatta, the Bishop tried to prevent a member of the MacArthur family from laying the foundation stone for a new chapel for the Wesleyans. He lost badly as MacArthur not only performed the ceremony, but was supported vigorously by both the *Sydney Morning Herald* and the *Colonist*.[44]

The missionaries continued to be worried by the excess of costs over allowances, even if they deprived themselves of the wine and ale they regarded as 'indispensable' in the Australian climate, and by the penetration of some congregations by Ranters (Primitive Methodists) whom they regarded as 'ignorant' and 'uncontrollable'. But these were minor matters. More serious was the declining health of the Superintendent, Rev. John McKenny, who, before he came to New South Wales, had spent nineteen years in India where his health had been impaired. McKenny's problems were first commented on as early as January 1841 when they were attributed to overwork—he was Chairman of the District, Superintendent of the large Parramatta circuit and agent for the growing mission work in the Islands. The worry became more consistent from mid-1843 and Benjamin Hurst remained in Sydney in 1844 because McKenny was unable to cope with his work. Throughout that year Hurst commented regularly on McKenny's incapacity to work and, in 1845, the District Meeting removed him to the easier Windsor circuit to reduce his load. In any case the London Committee had decided to act. In September Rev. William Boyce was appointed as General Superintendent of the missions in Australia and Van Diemen's Land. McKenny accepted this with good grace as Boyce allowed him to continue to sign papers as Chairman until the next District Meeting so that Boyce appeared to succeed rather than supersede McKenny. A year later McKenny was completely incapacitated and it was a happy release when he died on 31 October 1847.[45]

The Primitive Methodists: a tentative beginning

In 1812, when the Wesleyan Methodists of New South Wales were beginning to organise themselves into classes, the Primitive Methodists were still in the early stages of their development in

England. More than three decades passed before their church was established in the colony and the first Primitive migrants perforce associated with the Wesleyans in the various communities to which they went to live. Only in the 1840s were the first two Primitive Methodist Societies formed, one in Sydney and one on the Hunter River.

Joseph Bennett, a Primitive Methodist local preacher, arrived in Sydney in the early 1840s. He offered his services to the Rev. John McKenny, Superintendent of the Wesleyan Methodist circuit, but made it clear that if the Primitives established a cause in the colony, he would transfer to them. In those circumstances the offer was not accepted and, shortly afterwards, Bennett commenced holding services in the open air, a traditional Primitive practice, in Kent Street—though he would later move to a building in Pitt Street which was lent to him for the purpose. An early associate of Bennett in the work was Stephen Stiles Goold who migrated in 1841.[46]

In 1842 or 1843 three Wesleyan local preachers, Charles Garrett, J. Kingsbury and John Walker, along with a number of supporters, seceded from the Wesleyan Methodist Church and called themselves Australian Methodists. They met for worship in a small building in Pitt Street, probably the one loaned to Bennett. Some of these people later returned to Wesleyan membership but others were refused, except as members on trial, and eventually they became Primitive Methodists. Hon. Ebenezer Vickery later ascribed their secession to the fact that they could not have their own way, but the truth was that some of them had formerly been Primitive Methodists and it was not surprising that they rejoined their former church when it became established in Sydney.[47]

On the Hunter River the leading Primitive layman was Andrew Tulip, a native of Durham. Associated with him was William Robson, a qualified engineer from Wallsend, Northumberland. Brought by the Australian Agricultural Company to develop the coal industry, they arrived on 25 December 1841 and, for the first few years, worshipped with the group in Newcastle under the leadership of William Lightbody. In 1845 they separated to form a Primitive Methodist Society and caused some temporary disturbance to the Wesleyan body in the process.[48]

Two Primitive Methodist missionaries, Revs Joseph Long and John Wilson, were sent from England to Adelaide late in 1844 in response for an appeal for help. The Sydney Society successfully requested that one of them be sent on to Sydney and John Wilson arrived there in 1846. He commenced his ministry on 22 February by preaching two sermons at the former Hyde Park Racecourse and thus, like Bennett, he asserted the Primitive belief in the validity of open-air preaching in a new community. On the opening Sunday he issued a clear declaration that, while he was prepared to minister to the existing company of Primitive Methodists, the central purpose of his ministry was evangelistic outreach to the unchurched masses. In making this plain, he was following closely the instructions given to him by the Primitive Methodist General Missionary Committee before his departure from England. In 1846 Wilson reported that there were sixty-eight members, three local preachers and five class leaders in New South Wales.[49]

Land was acquired in Crown Street, Woolloomooloo, and on this site the Primitives built a chapel, though it was not opened until 11 March 1849. The delay was probably the result of serious problems which befell the mission and nearly ruined it. An early historian of the Primitive Methodist Church, Rev. John Petty, tantalisingly attributed the problems to the actions of certain leading laymen 'of questionable character' who later separated from the Sydney Society and greatly reduced the congregation. Only with the opening of the chapel was the Society 'encouraged to hope for better days'.[50]

Meanwhile, in 1848, Wilson changed places with Rev. Edward Tear who had worked in Newcastle since his arrival in 1847. Wilson lived in West Maitland, where he commenced his ministry with an open-air service on 2 February 1848, though he opened a Primitive Methodist place of worship in Abbott Street two months later. Henry Ikin, a devout Wesleyan, assisted Wilson to acquire and furnish a rented building before the chapel was opened and presided at the opening celebrations.[51] Not long afterwards Wilson was overwhelmed by problems in his ministry and retired from full-time work to resume his former occupation as a blacksmith and to give assistance as a local preacher in the Wesleyan church. A man of limited education and ability, though lacking in neither initiative nor energy, he seems not to have been able to cope with the demands of a ministry carried on under trying conditions.[52]

Indeed, the Primitive Church passed through difficult and disappointing days and reached its nadir in 1850 when it reported only seventeen members in Sydney and Morpeth together. Over the next few years it made a modest advance as the membership increased to 117 by 1853, but still the cause was neither vibrant nor flourishing and the discovery of gold in 1851 caused a major disturbance to its work as people rushed off to the diggings.[53]

Tear laboured conscientiously for several years before he was transferred to South Australia in exchange for Rev. William Storr who simply disappeared from the scene after a brief ministry. Another new arrival from England, Rev. Miles Moss, worked for several years then retired from full-time work, perhaps because of failing health, whilst retaining his ministerial status and continuing to serve in a more limited role.[54] During Moss's Sydney ministry, he initiated a courageous move to establish a chapel in the most difficult part of the city, Kent Street, which had become a slum and where, it was claimed, there was 'a dreadful collection of ignorance, of ungodliness, of gross sin and, as a consequence, of gross wretchedness'. It required boldness to carry the doctrines of the corruption of human nature, justification by faith, and sanctification through the Holy Spirit 'even to the very doors' of such people. In seeking in this way to maintain their traditional role of going to those who needed them most, the Primitive Methodists were seen at their very best.[55]

By the mid-1850s the situation of the Primitive Methodists was neither cheering nor reassuring: three ministers out of four had resigned and, at the very time when the Wesleyans had emerged from their 'day of small things' and were making notable advances, the Primitives were struggling for survival. In addition to the strains imposed by their circumstances, the ministers were subjected to yet further pressures from their church. Their early leaders in England had experienced a baptism of fire, had won through, and expected their ministerial brethren in the colonies to do the same. In 1846 the editor of the church's connexional journal in England declared that ministers 'who cannot bring souls to Christ will be reckoned uncredentialled of God and be treated accordingly'. Indeed, there was a general expectation that all ministers should be successful in converting sinners to God and the British Primitive Conference of 1852 exhorted missionaries in Australia and New Zealand to:

> Expect success. Do not rest satisfied without seals to your ministry and souls for your hire . . . let no motives inferior to the terrors of the Lord and the love of Christ constrain you to duty.[56]

With such high demands placed upon them, and with no senior minister near to share their particular problems and to offer counsel and encouragement, it is not surprising that these pioneer ministers lost heart.

The Wesleyans: independence

When the Wesleyan Missionary Committee appointed W.B. Boyce to New South Wales (1845) it had more in mind than McKenny's declining health and competence as a leader. It was involved in a long and difficult struggle against annual and accumulated debts which seemed certain to rob it of its effectiveness as a missionary body. It believed that while 'heathen' stations would have to remain financially dependent for a long time to come, those in British colonies should be pushed towards self-sufficiency. The Australian missions were moving towards this point and should be given every encouragement. Indeed, they should soon begin to take some responsibility for the support of heathen missions. It was made quite clear to Boyce in his letter of appointment that he was expected to lead the Australian missions towards both financial and administrative independence.[57]

W.B. Boyce, aged 40 years, was a relatively young man for the responsibility given to him, and certainly younger than many of his colleagues. Statesmanlike from the beginning, he set out to allay their fears and win their confidence. Boyce felt that although his colleagues liked him personally they would be happy to see his plans fail. Part of the problem was his lack of seniority, but some also felt that his title of 'General Superintendent' of the colonial mission was 'unmethodistical' and tended to detract from the authority of the District Meeting. He would have been much less popular had his fellow preachers known how often he wrote home asking for 'first rate pulpit men' to be sent out because most of the existing missionaries were not good preachers and were not suited to the larger congregations.

By 1850 there were local financial difficulties, and the 'old hands' were happy to see him discomforted. He was having trouble with Benjamin Hurst and Frederick Lewis who were both showing resentment of the discretionary authority he held. Boyce deliberately sent them to widely separated circuits, Lewis to Geelong (Victoria) and Hurst to Bathurst, so that they could not cause trouble. Boyce thought their opposition was related to the disturbances in favour of 'democracy' which seriously disrupted Wesleyan Methodism in England in the late 1840s and at one time he expected them to secede, though he did not think that they would take many into their rival church. This fear gradually passed and good relations were restored.[58]

Desperately anxious to achieve financial independence for the colonial church, and so relieve the English mission funds of a heavy burden, Boyce fought a long and arduous battle over the administration of state aid to the various denominations in New South Wales. The government continued to divide its aid on the basis of the 1841 census long after the 1846 census had shown this to be unfair. Although Catholics, Presbyterians and Wesleyans all suffered in comparison with the Anglicans, it was the Wesleyans who were most disadvantaged as their numbers had grown at a more rapid rate than any other denomination. (They had campaigned to get their members and adherents to record themselves properly rather than merely as 'Protestants', which led to them being counted as Anglicans.) In his view, half the people regularly attending worship joined the Wesleyans and if they had a few more plain, lively preachers they could 'carry the colony'.

So great was Boyce's annoyance with the Anglicans that, in 1851, he sought and obtained the support of the Catholics and Presbyterians in his war with the colonial government over funds, despite his well-known anti-Catholic attitudes and fear that the Roman Catholic church would gain too strong a hold over the colony. He was, however, content with a moral victory and, having gained his point, withdrew his claim.[59]

From July 1851 Boyce's letters frequently raised the issue of the effects of the discovery of gold on the colonies and the mission. Church affairs were seriously affected as the men, including class leaders and local preachers, moved out to the fields. The congregations were left leaderless and the ministers found themselves preaching only to women and children. The Hunter River District was particularly hard hit, though disturbance was also great in a 'receiving' area like Bathurst, where the circuit had to be divided into two to allow for satisfactory coverage of the increased area. Yet, if Boyce was most conscious of the derangement of the church's affairs, that was not all. The government of New South Wales moved quickly to invite the churches to station ministers permanently in the goldfields and to offer financial assistance, though only for a single minister from each of the four major denominations. Boyce sent a probationer to Sofala (under the direction of Rev. Samuel Wilkinson at Bathurst) and noted with pleasure that the Wesleyans got a quarter of the money not because a quarter of the men on the fields were Methodists but because they did more than a quarter of the work through the use of local preachers as well as ministers. The presence of local preachers on the fields gave a considerable advantage and ensured that the Methodists were able to exercise a useful pastoral and evangelistic ministry in many places.[60]

These events, and the temporary financial derangements which went with them, might well have delayed the Committee's intention to grant independence to the Australian mission. The plan went ahead largely because the disturbed conditions convinced the Committee, at last, that it was impossible to govern from afar. There had been hints of what was coming in the correspondence since 31 December 1849 and, at the end of 1851, the Committee decided to send a two-man delegation to Australia to work out a plan for the self-government of the colonial societies as 'an affiliated branch of the Wesleyan Connexion'. It was unfortunate, but not untypical, of the Committee's proceedings that the news of this decision should reach Sydney in the papers before Boyce received the letter.[61] Ultimately the delegation included only Rev. Robert Young, who was instructed to associate Boyce closely with him in his work. There is no need to discuss the detailed negotiations about the form of independence as there was complete agreement on all major principles and the delegation heeded Australian suggestions on at least some matters of important detail. Young's tact and Boyce's local knowledge and commonsense triumphed.

The plan for independence created in Australasia a 'distinct but affiliated' connexion which was required to maintain the purity of Wesleyan doctrine as found in Wesley's sermons and *Notes on the New Testament*. The Conference consisted of all missionaries in Australia, Van Diemen's Land, New Zealand, the Friendly Islands and Fiji—the inclusion of the last three groups was at the Australian request and was seen as adding weight to the Conference and as likely to stimulate interest in missions in the country in a way that would not otherwise be possible. The Conference was to meet annually and be attended by all the ministers from the colony in which it was held and two ministerial representatives from each of the other Districts. The Australians, especially Boyce, would have preferred to have had several annual Conferences created within Australia—one for New South Wales, one for Victoria and Tasmania, and so on—with a triennial Conference embracing them all. That scheme was adopted several years later and was based on an understanding of the problems of distance. The English view, which created the one ruling Conference with a series of Districts based on the colonies, lacked an appreciation of Australian distances, but seemed safer to the church fathers, who regarded the creation of several very small, self-governing Conferences in an untried area as a very risky business.

The English Conference retained three means of exercising some control over a Conference which was otherwise independent in all ways. It would appoint a General Superintendent of Missions to oversee the work in the South Sea Islands; it would have the power to disallow acts of the Australian Conference at the next ensuing English Conference after its Minutes were received; it would, until the Australian Conference was able to bear the full cost of the South Sea missions, have the right to appoint the President of the Australian Conference.[62] Boyce was quick to point out that the English Conference should not exercise its right to send out a President, as this would be regarded as an insult by the senior Australian ministers. The English Conference listened and only ever appointed on the nomination of the Australians, except that it reasonably enough required Boyce, against his own wishes, to remain as first President of the Australasian Conference with Rev. John A. Manton as Secretary.[63]

When the first Australasian Conference met in the York Street chapel, Sydney, on 18 January 1855, the Wesleyan Methodist cause in New South Wales had grown unrecognisably from what it had been forty years before. Sydney was now divided into three circuits which, with Parramatta and Windsor, made up the 'old' territory. Newer circuits were centred on Bathurst, Bowenfels and Mudgee to the west of the ranges and on the Hunter, Port Macquarie and Moreton Bay to the north. To the south were Camden, Goulburn and Wollongong. This made a total of fourteen circuits. There were a claimed 2486 full members with another 270 on trial. Including children, there were said to be 15 650 'attendants on public worship'. These were served by thirty-one missionaries and assistant-missionaries, 123 local preachers and 523 Sunday school teachers working in seventy-six chapels and 110 'other preaching places'. Bowden, Hosking, Eagar and Leigh would hardly have recognised what they had begun.

Independence marked both an end and a beginning. It indicated the attainment of a measure of maturity, but it was also a new start and much still needed to be done to spread 'scriptural holiness' throughout the land. There was a new and more aggressive spirit abroad. This was largely the result of five developments: the surge of free immigrants to the colony; the passage of Bourke's *Church Act*; the end of the unfortunate bickering which had so marred the early years; the provision of an adequate ministerial leadership under Boyce; and the growth of a substantial lay leadership which was able to take its proper place in the class meeting, the pulpit and the Sunday school. Without these, Wesleyan Methodism would have remained a backwater; with them it could challenge the other denominations and the secularism of nineteenth century New South Wales. It might even be able to 'carry the colony'!

Part 2

'Carrying the colony'

2

Spreading the Word

The story of Methodism in New South Wales in the late nineteenth century was one of expansion and buoyant enthusiasm. To the Wesleyans, in particular, it must at times have seemed that the fulfilment of Boyce's dream to 'carry the colony' was at hand. Even the much smaller body of Primitives was able to rejoice in its growing strength, at least at some periods and in some places. To some Methodists, but not all, the union of the branches was a means of consolidating the gains made over half a century by Wesley's men and women and provided a stepping stone to better things yet to be. Many had a hand in this work, but the role of the laity and, especially the local preachers was decisive.

The Wesleyans

Wesleyan expansion occurred primarily through nodes, for example Sydney. Bathurst was the nodal point for the West, Maitland for the Hunter Valley and the New England tableland, Goulburn for the Southern Tablelands and Wollongong for the Illawarra and South Coast regions. The North Coast was a partial exception. There, geographic factors forced a 'river hopping' technique before the nodal approach could come into operation.

As local preachers reached out and established new preaching places on the margins, existing circuits became unwieldy. These outlying areas then began to feel their own strength and sought independence—their increasing maturity in numbers and finances

environment. Later there followed Hay (1871), Cootamundra (1872), Temora (1880), and Wyalong (1894). An abortive Gospel Car Mission (1899) in the Riverina promised much but failed during the 1902 drought because no feed was available for the horse. A bicycle mission based in Wentworth at much the same time also failed because the work was too physically demanding. Circuits were established later in the Riverina District as opportunity presented itself. On the South Coast, Kiama and Shoalhaven were cut from Wollongong in 1859 and from there on movement continued slowly down the seaboard.

In the Hunter Valley, Methodism continued to expand as Maitland budded off Newcastle (1856), Singleton, Dungog (1859), Morpeth (1866), East Maitland (1882) and Branxton (1896), while there was an explosion of new churches and circuits as the South Maitland coalfield was opened in the first decade of the twentieth century. Methodism also moved up the Valley onto the New England Tableland to Armidale in 1860, the one circuit stretching north to Tenterfield. In 1865, a Tenterfield circuit was excised and, thirteen years later, one at Glen Innes. The area was weakly held, though, because Methodist numbers in the area were low and the church was not really 'established', even at Armidale, until the ministry of Rev. J.E. Carruthers in the second half of the 1880s.[3]

Expansion also continued in the 'old territories'. Sydney comprised three circuits in 1855—North, South and East. In that same year, Newtown separated from South. In 1860 Ashfield separated from Newtown and Balmain separated from North. Further out, Lower Hawkesbury became a separate circuit in 1860 and Penrith separated from Windsor in 1861. To the south, Stanmore opened up in 1885, followed by Rockdale in 1886. The first north-side church was opened on the later site of Ravenswood Girls' College in 1855 and St Leonards was the first northern circuit in 1870. Methodism came to Manly, the popular new 'watering place' on the north shore, in 1887. This circuit initially included Gosford!

The development of the suburban circuits was, from the 1870s, fuelled by the flight of the middle classes from the city and inner suburban circuits (York Street, Balmain, Glebe) to the more habitable areas as transport improved and industry and warehouses took over the inner city. Access to middle-class wealth allowed the construction of several fine churches: Newtown, with its high gothic facade and carved cedar panels was the first (1860), while Waverley (1889) was arguably the finest of Methodism's Australian churches. To some Wesleyans these buildings symbolised the increasing respectability of their denomination and they were proud to be able to worship the Lord in something more than the beauty of holiness; others argued that less ornate structures were better suited to a church seeking to grapple with the real problems of the people. All were pleased, though, that the land was being covered with places of worship.[4]

Wesleyan Methodism began its independent Australasian existence with a single Australasian Conference controlling all the Australian colonies and the New Zealand and Pacific missions. Each colony had its own District Meeting dealing with purely administrative matters and, at the local level, the circuits expanded in the manner previously described. This arrangement persisted from 1855 to 1873 though, in 1863, New South Wales was divided into five districts centred on Sydney, Bathurst, Maitland and Goulburn as well as the new colony of Queensland. In the early 1870s problems of growth and distance led the Australians to adopt a system very similar to that originally proposed, but not implemented, in 1855. There were to be four Annual (administrative) Conferences (New South Wales and Queensland; Victoria and Tasmania; South Australia; New Zealand) and a triennial, representative, General Conference to legislate for the whole territory. In 1893, Queensland separated from New South Wales, the last major reorganisation before Methodist Union.

More important than these organisational changes was the decision by the General Conference of 1875 to admit laymen to the Conferences, both Annual and General, for all sessions not dealing with matters relating solely to the ministry. This encouraged greater lay involvement at the highest levels of church work, though their role was still not as great as that of their counterparts in the minor Methodist branches. This change, made for pragmatic reasons but also thought to be in tune with the times, was implemented in New South Wales in 1877.[5]

The system of Conferences provided the centralised connexional framework within which Wesleyan Methodism operated. The circuits provided for self-government at the local level. Each circuit included a number of preaching places at which congregations met for worship and one or more class meetings were held for fellowship and nurture. Each was entitled to its Leaders' Meeting, though there might be only one of these for the entire circuit in rural areas. The circuit was responsible for its own affairs under the guidance of its Superintendent Minister who, along with the local preachers, and under the direction of the preachers' meeting, was responsible for the teaching and evangelistic aspects of the church's life. Likewise, he shared responsibility for the pastoral work with the class leaders. The Quarterly Meeting, chaired by the minister, managed the circuit. Circuits were grouped together in administrative Districts for oversight of the less experienced clergy by a more experienced brother who was their chairman. He could provide counsel and sympathy in personal or circuit matters, but should any man be either unfaithful or a slacker he could expect the chairman to 'deal faithfully' with him.[6]

The itinerancy of the clergy ensured the more even apportionment of ministerial talents among the circuits than would otherwise have been possible and bound the ministers into a rich brotherhood based on broadly-shared experience. Despite the considerable personal inconvenience of appointments made for one year and renewable to a maximum of three, the ministry acknowledged the advantages of itinerancy and often argued that it was responsible for the rapid growth of Methodism. Early in the Methodist experience in New South Wales, for some unstated reason, Rev. Benjamin Hurst was given a fourth year at Bathurst. The worthy laymen at Cornish Settlement (Byng) regarded this as 'unmethodistical' and refused to allow him to use their church. When he was replaced at the end of the year, his successor was welcomed and the offerings for the previous year, properly accounted for, were handed over.

Although General Conference legislated in 1890 to allow each Annual Conference to extend terms to a maximum of five years in special circumstances, subject to a two-thirds supporting vote in the Quarterly Meeting and the Conference, limited support for the measure meant that no change was made in New South Wales until 1903. Much of the support that did exist came from

Sydney and its environs and resulted from difficulties experienced in certain large metropolitan circuits and especially in the central missions. Quarterly meetings in the Bathurst, Maitland and Grafton Districts remained firmly opposed to any alteration.[7]

Several times throughout the period 1855–1914, and even beyond, the Methodists found it necessary to bring a number of young men from England to join the ranks of the colonial clergy. This did not imply failure on the part of the colonial Methodists to provide enough men. This they might have done had the population grown only by natural increase, and had settlement been confined within reasonable limits. Heavy migration, a rapid expansion of the area under occupation, and a strong evangelistic urge, made the situation impossible. It was to the credit of the New South Wales Conference that, even so, it did largely supply its own needs during the years 1885–1905. By 1900, the stream of potential candidates from England was drying up and the Australian-born contingent within the ministry (60 per cent) would increase further. It was less to Conference's credit that many of these raw 'new chums' were sent to the 'back of beyond' to serve their probationary years under conditions of such loneliness that effective study was rendered almost impossible and faith was tested almost beyond endurance as they tried to evangelise their huge circuits. Not all saw it through.[8]

The Wesleyans also did not do well in the area of ministerial training. The question of a theological institution for the training of ministers often became intertwined with the issue of the establishment of an affiliated college at the University of Sydney— to the detriment of each. The latter was forgotten for a time when it was decided that a secondary school would be of more immediate value to the church (see Chapter 3). The theological institution did not become a practical issue until 1864 when it was proposed that monies raised for the Golden Jubilee of Methodism in Australia should be used for that purpose. Education was advancing rapidly in the community, and the minister must equal his people in general attainments or he would not inspire respect for his office. Since religion was increasingly under attack, the minister needed extensive biblical and theological knowledge to be able to defend it. Insufficient funds were contributed to open a central institution and it was decided to fund the money and use the interest to train candidates in the collegiate institutions existing in the various colonies. In 1869 the collegiate institutions were formally declared to be Provisional Theological Institutions and, in New South Wales, Newington College performed that function for many years.

Discussion continued in a desultory fashion with probationary ministers pleading their case for a proper training. *The Christian Advocate* made a general case for training and Rev. J.H. Fletcher, the Principal of Newington College, occasionally pointed out the impossibility of his running the College and teaching philosophy, theology, history and homiletics to half a dozen theological students. At the 1883 Conference Fletcher pointed out that he needed an assistant to teach English, Latin and Greek to the students and that they needed the guarantee of a fixed period of study in order to undertake a planned course without interruption. Hitherto, many had received no institutional training at all, while those who had were always under the threat that an emergency might find them being used as 'President's supply' which would end or seriously interrupt their training. Conference appointed Fletcher to teach the students theology and Rev. C.J. Prescott, a new arrival from England who was a capable scholar and had experience as tutor in a theological college, to teach 'Classics and General Literature'. In 1887 Fletcher was appointed solely as Theological Tutor but, after his death in 1889, a series of ad hoc arrangements again applied for several years.

During the period 1892–1910 the theological and affiliated colleges again became entangled in debate, some holding the view that a single affiliated college could fulfil both theological and general educational needs. There were two major problems with that proposal: only men who had matriculated and who attended university lectures could live in an affiliated college which was governed under university rules and had its principal appointed by its Council rather than the Conference. No one really wanted to eliminate from the ministry all who had not matriculated, nor did anyone want control of ministerial candidates taken out of the hands of Conference. A few probably worried at the idea of theological students attending university at all.

Ultimately it was accepted that the twin purposes were incompatible in a single institution and the 1910 Conference agreed to separate the colleges. Not until 18 November 1914 was a theological college dedicated and only in 1915 did Conference appoint Rev. W.E. Bennett first Principal of Leigh College. The institution which the Wesleyans had once intended to open with funds collected to celebrate the Golden Jubilee of Methodism in Australia was finally opened with money gathered for the Centenary. New South Wales Wesleyan Methodism had not hurried over the training of its ministry and many felt that this neglect was a cause of shame to the church. The other branches of Methodism were never able even to contemplate such work before union.[9]

Wesleyan Methodism could not have succeeded without its local preachers. Prominence has already been given to the role of men like Silas Gill, Tom Brown and others as they moved out from their original homes in the Cowpastures area to other parts of the colony. In the period 1855–1914 that importance increased. By 1903 there were 1088 Methodist preaching places in New South Wales at which about 1500 services were held each Sunday. The 170 ministers (including supernumeraries) could take only about 500 of them, leaving 1000 for the local preachers. It was hardly surprising that they were seen as 'one of the glories of our Church' and one of its most distinctive features. But for these 'locals', many rural areas would have been entirely without Methodist services. In 1858 Rev. Joseph Oram noted that it was only the local preachers who enabled two ministers in Bathurst to work successfully a circuit 130 km long and 65 km wide whilst providing a regular weekly service in most of the villages. Twenty years later, at Balranald, the very young local preacher, J.A. Bowring, who in another decade would become a significant minister, provided Methodist services regularly without assistance. In 1880 the Manning River circuit had 146 appointments to divide between eight preachers each quarter. One of its preachers covered almost 800 km a quarter in this work without seeking expenses. In 1893, Armidale reported twenty-three preaching places in the circuit, with some of its men regularly taking more than two services per Sunday. The near-mythical Richard Lean, who worked in several different circuits over the years, sometimes preached twenty times in the one pulpit in a quarter.[10]

Locals were regularly involved in evangelistic effort. At Ennis in the Port Macquarie circuit in 1873, it was said that 'The Local Preachers [had] been the chief instruments' in a highly successful campaign. They played a similar role at Tenterfield in 1887 and at Molong and Garra in 1891, when the local minister actually invited a layman from another circuit to conduct a mission. In 1908 the Local Preachers' Association undertook to send out bands of eight to twelve laymen to conduct a mission in any circuit which would invite them and, in 1913, the Manly circuit sought a lay mission for Balgowlah and Brookvale. Many other similar instances might be offered.[11]

Despite the church's indebtedness to them, not every Wesleyan loved the locals. Complaints regarding their inadequacy occasionally appeared in the connexional paper in the 1860s and these became more frequent later. Most of these complaints came from suburban circuits, since country folk knew that they could not survive without the locals. In part the problem was educational. Many of the locals were rough diamonds and sometimes both their grammar and their theology were inadequate. Local effort might help in individual cases but it could not overcome the wider problem and connexional attempts to form a Local Preachers' Union met with only limited success until 1906 when the energetic efforts of Fred Over gave them life. But some locals were as well educated and preached as well as any minister, and education was never the whole problem. There was also a prejudice which sprang from the increasing pretensions to 'respectability' of some members of the Wesleyan church. To such objections there was no answer, especially as the very people who cried out for a professional ministry also complained frequently that the professionals were out of touch with the ordinary person's life.[12]

Other churches occasionally attacked the systematic use of local preachers, but these attacks could be dismissed easily, especially as the system was achieving so much for the Methodists. It was a different matter when, under the new *Education Act*, regulations were made which threatened with dismissal any school teacher who acted as a local preacher or Sunday school teacher. The first bitter complaint against this gross abuse of personal liberty came from the Windsor circuit in 1883 but the problem remained until

1911. The Methodists, who suffered more severely than other denominations, never received much support for their complaints and this may explain why it took so long to rectify the situation.[13]

During this long period many local preachers continued the work of their spiritual forbears. James Graham travelled throughout New South Wales for seventeen years at his own expense and without fee preaching to shearers and conducting missions; William Burgess of Bolwarra was welcomed all over the Hunter Valley, from Newcastle to Singleton and from Paterson to Sugarloaf, for fifty years; while John Delves spent forty-eight years as a preacher, first in the Hunter Valley and then on the Manning River. In the Sydney suburbs John Bowmer laboured for fifty years at Ashfield and Rockdale. Besides these, John Graham and John Vidler in the Illawarra, Silas Gill on the North Coast, William Tom in the West, and George Everingham on the Lower Hawkesbury each continued during this period the work he had begun earlier.

A number of women were involved in the work towards the end of the century. In particular, the Sydney Central Mission Sisters of the People were constantly and heavily involved and one of their number, Sister Laura Francis, developed into a successful travelling evangelist early in the twentieth century. Others, like Miss Raward of Goulburn, also contributed where they lived.[14]

The local preacher had a status given to no other layman in Methodism. He belonged to the Connexion as well as to a circuit and carried his status with him when he shifted. He had a lifelong right to a seat at the Quarterly Meeting of the circuit in which he resided and, without any special training, acted as the almost regular preacher to many congregations. Furthermore, because the only route to the ministry was through their ranks, the local preachers provided an unbreakable link between the clergy and the laity generally. The local preacher might not have been ordained by the laying on of human hands, but Methodism believed that ordination by God was sufficient warrant for a person to occupy this unique office.

One peculiarly valuable piece of machinery developed by the Church to aid it in its task was the body known originally as the Wesleyan Methodist Church Sustentation and Extension Society

(CSES). This passed through a number of name changes until, well beyond the present period, it became the Home Mission Department. Ultimately it became almost a state within a state, but in the period to 1914 its status remained that of an instrument. Boyce had tried to transplant to Australian soil the old British Chapel and Contingency Funds to assist with chapel building and to meet urgent needs. This move failed and collections in New South Wales were so meagre that the colony was largely reliant on the declining grants from the government under the *Church Act* to meet its needs. Led by the Rev. William Hessell, the New South Wales District Meeting of 1858 resolved to establish a new Church Sustentation and Extension Society to replace the two existing funds. This was authorised by Conference in January 1859 and inaugurated in March that year.

The object of the Society was to stimulate and co-ordinate efforts to extend the work of the church and to promote the spread of scriptural holiness through the land. In particular, it was to provide assistance to maintain ministers among scattered or neglected populations and to aid in the erection of new chapels, parsonages and schoolrooms and the liquidation of old debts. Local effort would be stimulated because the CSES would provide only a proportion of the total cost of a building. The Society had no illusions about the magnitude of the task before it given the existing state of spiritual negligence in many parts of the colony.[15]

The great weakness of the Society to 1914 was that it lacked any remotely adequate representation in many circuits. Wesleyans generally remained ill-informed about the purposes of the Society and, at the local level, were not urged with any persistence to contribute to its work. Since many did not take the connexional paper they did not see there the very extensive coverage which it gave to the Society. Many circuits contributed little or nothing to funds. In 1866 the giving averaged only four shillings and four pence per member or nine pence per year per adherent. In 1880, collections were made from only 150 of 500 possible congregations and only 60 of 260 Sunday schools. Contributions from circuits passed £2000 for the first time in 1882, rose sharply for a year or two, then fluctuated again before declining equally sharply through the depressed 1890s. They remained low early in the twentieth century but rose to record heights in 1913.

The Wesleyan Methodist Church Building Loans Fund was set up by the Society in 1860 and made its first loan in 1864. Interest free loans to circuits for chapel building, and to allow small congregations to overcome the problem of 'settled debts', were intended to be repaid over not more than ten years. Much later the funds available for this purpose were greatly boosted by the Schofield and Bright Bequests which provided large amounts of capital for use. But the loan funds suffered problems because of the unwillingness of trustees in many places to take seriously their duty to repay the capital sums. At 31 December 1890 almost 30 per cent of the total capital in the Methodist Loan Fund was in arrears with obvious effects on other circuits seeking assistance. A Special Help Scheme introduced by Rev. James Woolnough in 1896, and extended in 1902, assisted the circuits to overcome many of these old debts and enabled the property problems associated with Methodist union to be faced with some equanimity.

If the difficulties of the CSES were many so were its achievements. On several occasions the Society financed the passages of young Englishmen to supplement the ranks of the ministry and make possible the occupation of many additional stations. In a sense, this enlarged its problems since many of these men went to weak circuits and required support for years, but this had to be undertaken if the perceived problems of spiritual destitution and moral degeneracy were to be overcome. Not every occupancy of a new area resulted from the Society's efforts. Some would have occurred in time anyhow but other thinly settled areas would have remained deprived of Christian worship for many years had not the Society stepped in and supported an appointment. The CSES also financed a ministry to the armed forces and to merchant sailors and supported Rev. J.A. Bowring when he was appointed Connexional Evangelist in the mid-1880s and Rev. A.E. Walker in the same role from 1910.[16]

The failure of a pre-independence scheme delayed until 1889 any attempt by New South Wales to copy the Victorians in employing single, untrained 'home missionaries' to pioneer the backblocks. A plan devised by Revs J.E. Carruthers and J.B.

Waterhouse saw W.H. Thompson go to the Tweed River as the colony's first home missionary in July 1889 while J.J. Boyd followed him to Narrandera in September. A third, Mr Lund, went to Gosford in February 1890. The availability of finance limited the extension of the scheme but eight stations were occupied by the end of 1891 and Narrandera had already developed into a full circuit.

The burden cast upon these young men was enormous. Thomas Walker was sent to Collarenebri in 1898 to care for its 250 people, a similar number at Mungindi 100 km down the track and a 'very small' population at Angledool 110 km away. At Nyngan, in 1906, John Perry covered over 7700 km^2 in the face of difficulties posed by fire, flood and sticky black soil. In 1910, the Society sent Herbert Green to Nyngan immediately on his arrival from Leeds!

Despite the permanent state of financial stringency, the key men of the CSES, Revs George Hurst, George Lane, George and James Woolnough and Hon. Ebenezer Vickery, succeeded beyond their dreams. The going would have been even more difficult had not Wollongong businessman John Bright, Rev. W. Schofield (a wealthy minister) and Vickery given more than half the total income of £300 000 in the Society's first half-century. Had financial supply been limitless, the Society could not have found the men to occupy the whole field. Nevertheless it was a key instrument in the attempt to 'carry the colony'.[17]

Primitive Methodist and other minor Methodist groups

The Primitive Methodists were never strong enough to share the ambitions of their Wesleyan brothers. Although their pattern of development was essentially nodal as far as it went, it was patchy and confined to limited areas and their organisational structures lacked the complexity evident among the Wesleyans. They established causes in the working-class suburbs of Sydney, the goldfields (briefly), the coalfields, and a few rural districts, including Goulburn on the Southern Tablelands, Mudgee in the West, Nundle (another goldmining centre) on the Northern Tablelands, and the Macleay River on the North Coast, but failed to take root elsewhere.

When Rev. John Sharpe arrived in Sydney in 1854, he found the only Primitive Methodist minister, Miles Moss, in ill-health and the cause struggling. A man of strong will and inexhaustible energy, Sharpe, who had already served in several English circuits, brought an experience previously lacking and provided a leadership which revived the church and enabled it to advance.[18]

During the remainder of the century, Primitive Methodism moved out of central Sydney as first the Kent Street chapel closed (1883), followed by the 'mother' chapel in Crown Street (1884) and a later one in Albion Street, Surry Hills (1901). But, in the same period, they built fifteen chapels in the suburbs of Sydney, extending from the inner suburb of Pyrmont to Leichhardt, 6 km west, and Canterbury, 13 km south-west. Always this expansion led to the subdivision of existing circuits to form new ones as was the case with the Wesleyans. The first of the new circuits so formed was St Peters (Newtown) in 1861. The strongest suburban churches were undoubtedly in St Peters (where over 6 per cent of the population of the municipality claimed Primitive Methodist allegiance), Annandale, Forest Lodge and Dulwich Hill. Thus their ministry was restricted to the strong working-class localities on the edge of the city and in the nearer western and south-western suburbs. Attempts to establish causes on the north shore and in the eastern suburbs of Sydney were unsuccessful despite the existence of small Primitive populations there. Where they had churches, Sunday school enrolments far exceeded the number of Primitive Methodist children available, suggesting a measure of success in gathering children from non-churchgoing families of the working class.[19]

Many laymen and laywomen played a significant role in the early city and later suburban churches. Stephen Goold raised large sums of money in the attempt to keep Kent Street open and he was also widely used as a local preacher. Goold joined the political Protestant Association in 1868 and campaigned for political and municipal candidates. In 1870, he became Grand Master of the Orange Lodge and was responsible for organising many lodges in country districts. He also became an alderman of the Sydney City Council in 1870, Mayor in 1874 and was elected member of Parliament for Mudgee in 1874. Another major figure was Henry Carruthers, brother of the prominent Wesleyan. As a youth, he joined the Primitive Church and was instrumental in opening a Sunday school and church in Forest Lodge where he lived—he also bore most of the financial burden associated with the church.[20]

The establishment of Primitive Methodist causes in rural areas depended mainly on the initiatives of laymen who settled in the various localities. Morpeth circuit was established before 1854 and maintained a ministry until union, though sometimes the minister resided in East Maitland. The Primitives were established in Camden and Greendale (1856) by Charles H. Harrison, a shoe-maker and local preacher. The cause spread to many nearby places under the leadership of men like Simeon Brown and his brother Thomas, David Doust and John Wilson. A Primitive cause also began in Goulburn in 1856 under the guidance of Daniel Kadwell, William Townsend and others. From both Camden and Goulburn, further causes were established in what became Bowral circuit as the progress of the southern railway led to development. The ministers at Goulburn undertook further work to the south-west and west, at Jerrawa (1857) and Crookwell (1871). The pioneer Primitive laymen on the Macleay River on the mid-North Coast were George Tredgett and James Jeffery. After working with the Wesleyans for several years, they formed Primitive Methodist societies in Euroka and elsewhere about 1867 and invited Rev. E.C. Pritchard of Newcastle to visit them and form a circuit. Tredgett and Jeffery, each of whom died in 1899, continued to play a leading role in this circuit for almost the whole of its existence prior to Methodist union. The Mudgee cause was commenced in 1873 after Rev. James Studds of Hill End responded to a lay invitation to visit the town.[21]

The real strength of Primitive Methodism in the colony was to be found in the coalfields, particularly in the Newcastle district. There they outnumbered the Wesleyans in a number of mining townships. From 1856 to 1901, the percentage of Methodists in the Newcastle district increased from 10 per cent to almost 22 per cent or twice that of the colony as a whole. More signifi-cantly, during the thirty years from 1871 to 1901, while the population of the district increased threefold, the total Methodist component increased by 50 per cent. In the mining townships, which were then quite separate from Newcastle, the total Methodist share of the population was 31 per cent while, the Primitive proportion was 19 per cent. Concerning the latter, E.M. McEwen wrote that 'It was the Primitive Methodist Church which was most responsible for the unique religious character of the colliery townships'.[22]

Rev. Henry Green, en route to England from New Zealand in 1858, was persuaded to cut short his journey and become the first Primitive Methodist minister in the Newcastle circuit which had become independent from Morpeth in 1855. In time, the one circuit became a cluster covering Wallsend, Burwood (Merewether), Wickham, Stockton, Charlestown, Lambton, Minmi and Catherine Hill Bay as well as the city. Many able men served in the area, including E. Cook Pritchard, John Penman, George James, James Blanksby—a man with a passion for social justice—and the scholarly Theophilus Parr. At the time of Methodist union there were six circuits served by four ministers and two home missionaries compared with the two circuits and three ministers of the Wesleyans.[23]

As elsewhere, so much depended on the work of devoted laymen. Richard Hall was utterly faithful to the total discipline of his church and over a period of fifty years held almost every office in it, his name becoming a byword for liberality. The army of local preachers included some with little education, some who were eccentric, and many who were outstanding orators, passionately concerned to win men and women for Christ. Prominent among them was John Dixon who came with his father to the Newcastle district in 1857 where he worked in the mines. Over the years he rose to become the first Inspector of Collieries in New South Wales; he preached in every Primitive pulpit in the district and in many of those of other denominations. In 1893, when the Primitive Methodist Church in New South Wales was divided into two districts, he was elected President of the Northern District Assembly, the only layman to be accorded this honour.[24]

The Primitive Methodist cause was established in the Illawarra district from Camden in 1858 by Rev. Jabez Langford and John Howard, a hired local preacher, was appointed to work the area. With the development of the coal-mining industry this work became concentrated in the mining areas rather than the rural areas. Until the appointment of Rev. James Spalding in 1880, the work was maintained for long periods by laymen without ministerial assistance. Rev. Thomas Davies, who spent two terms in the circuit (1884–86 and 1898–1901), was important for his work as a builder of churches and as a forthright speaker on social issues. At Lithgow, the centre of the western coalfields, the Primitives anticipated the Wesleyans. Initially an outpost of the Parramatta circuit, it became independent soon after the opening of the first church in 1880.[25]

Although there is evidence of Primitive Methodists on the various goldfields from 1851, the connexion did not establish a society on any field before the 1860s and the only one where it maintained a cause until union was Nundle. Causes were established at Young (1864) and its neighbouring centres, Grenfell and Cootamundra, and at Hill End but, with the exception of Young where the Primitives continued for twenty years, they were of short duration. The goldminers were too nomadic and there were never enough Primitive Methodist settlers in the centres to maintain a permanent cause. Nundle, east of Tamworth on the Peel River, and the neighbouring goldfields of Bowling Alley Point and Hanging Rock, first experienced the witness of Primitive Methodists around 1869. Although the area became a circuit, for much of a period of thirty-three years it had no minister and the man at Morpeth superintended the work.[26]

Primitive Methodists were few in number and, in general, belonged to the working class. Consequently their circuits experienced constant financial troubles and, in the 1890s, their problems were accentuated by strikes and the trade depression. Many of their churches were exceedingly plain, but in a few centres more durable and ornate buildings were erected. To some extent the Primitives depended on the generosity of well-wishers from other denominations to supplement the sacrificial giving of their own members to pay for these churches. Their ministers were much more poorly paid than those of other denominations and frequently they left circuits with a part of their stipends unpaid.[27]

The Primitives depended on England for the supply of ministers until about 1870 but thereafter sent their own men into the ministry. Of the sixty-nine men who served either a part or the whole of their ministry in New South Wales, thirty-one came from England, thirty-five from the colony, and the other three from Victoria and New Zealand. One-third of these men did not remain in the Primitive ministry, though several transferred to one of another denomination. A few resigned over issues relating to doctrine and church government, but it is probable that many more left for economic reasons.[28]

Among the lay people, there was considerable mobility between the Primitive Methodists and the Wesleyans. Not all Primitive Methodist migrants were able to link with Primitive Methodist churches in the colony. Most of those who lived in communities without a Primitive cause joined the Wesleyan Methodist church, though the 1891 census shows that they often continued to think of themselves as Primitive Methodists. Detailed analysis is impossible but numerous published accounts relating to individuals show that the Primitives won many who belonged nominally to other denominations. Some Primitives also joined other denominations, especially in the 1880s when the Salvation Army made its appearance and some of them saw its noisy, aggressive evangelism as a revival of earlier Methodist practices. Yet Primitive expansion had been considerable over the years. In 1854 they had possessed only two chapels and a few other preaching places in Sydney and on the Hunter River and their minuscule membership of 116 was served by two ministers. By 1902 there were twenty-seven circuits and 2036 members, though the church had peaked in 1894–95 with twenty-nine ministers, 142 local preachers, 2187 members and 7296 Sunday school scholars.[29]

The final seven years of the Primitive Methodist Church in New South Wales, from its Jubilee in 1895 to union in 1902, were a time of frustration and stagnation, with little or no progress in terms of membership. In its early years the church had struggled to establish itself and, at the end, it could barely maintain its position. In 1899 their Missionary Committee attributed this problem to 'the decay of spiritual life, prevalent worldliness in the church, and lack of the aggressive spirit and work of our fathers'.[30] The imminence of Methodist union probably also had much to do with it.

There were two other Methodist 'splinters' in New South Wales: the United Methodist Free church, which originated in

England, and the Lay Methodist church, a splinter formed in Newcastle from the Primitive Methodist church. The interplay between authority and freedom in the constitutional history of Methodism produced a number of divisions in England in the first half of the nineteenth century as laymen sought greater participation in the decision-making processes of the church but were resisted by the conservative force of Rev. Jabez Bunting and his associates. This led to the defection or expulsion of some 100 000 members from the Wesleyan Methodist church. Resultant 'splinters' were the Protestant Methodists (1827), Wesleyan Association (1835), Wesleyan Reformers (1848) and others.

A series of reunions brought into being the Wesleyan Methodist Association which united with the Wesleyan Reformers in 1857 to form the United Methodist Free Churches (UMFC).[31] This church was established in Victoria in the 1850s and had a small following in Queensland and New South Wales but a negligible presence in South Australia. For many years, all UMFC churches in the Australian colonies belonged to the Australian District with its headquarters in Melbourne. In 1892, the British Conference granted the Australian churches a greater measure of autonomy, enabling them to hold annual Assemblies as two separate Districts, one for Victoria and Tasmania and the other for New South Wales and Queensland.[32]

In New South Wales the first congregations were, surprisingly, formed from a Primitive Methodist 'splinter'—the 'Independent Primitive Methodist' chapels formed by Rev. Jabez Langford after his quarrel with Rev. Robert Hartley in 1863. As a consequence of this serious difference, Langford was appointed to New Zealand but refused to go. Instead, he established four churches, which he designated 'Independent Primitive Methodist', in St Peters and its neighbourhood. In 1868, he handed them to the UMFC and himself entered the ministry of that church, accepting appointment in Melbourne. At that time, they had sixty-two members and seven local preachers but within a few years, they dwindled to one congregation in Wyndham Street, Waterloo (Alexandria). Later, congregations were developed in West Botany, Rockdale and Balmain and these constituted the Sydney circuit.[33]

In the Newcastle district the church commenced operations in Wallsend in 1870. Later, further congregations were built up in

Merewether, Lambton, Minmi, Adamstown, Newcastle, Belmont, Wakefield and Thornton. These were formed into two circuits with ministers at Wallsend and Merewether, though ministers also resided at Belmont and Minmi for a short time. In 1891, of the 11 210 Methodists in the Newcastle area, almost 3 per cent (325) belonged to the UMFC. In the mining districts one-third of all the adherents of the UMFC became full members. It thus enjoyed a deeper commitment from its followers than any other denomination.[34]

At union the UMFC in New South Wales had ten churches, fifteen local preachers, eight class leaders, 272 members and 770 attendants at worship. Most of its members belonged to the working class and, throughout its history in New South Wales, the church had experienced acute financial problems. There was a constant need to hold special efforts to raise the finance needed to pay the ministerial stipend which was, in any case, small.

The three circuits in New South Wales had been served by a considerable number of ministers and home missionaries, some of whom had very little education. Most appointments were of short duration. The church in New South Wales did not have any institution for the training of ministers. Prior to ordination, they were required to pass annual examinations during a four year period of probation.[35]

According to J.S. Werner, 'Ranterism', or Primitive Methodism, began as a lay movement and long bore traces of its origin.[36] This characteristic resulted in the establishment of several large and vigorous Lay Methodist churches in the Newcastle district in the 1880s and 1890s. With their rise, some Newcastle districts were presented with the spectacle of four branches of Methodism in close proximity to one another. On 24 November 1889, four members, three of whom were local preachers, resigned from the Lambton Primitive Methodist Church and formed a Lay Methodist church. According to John Hughes, son of one of the four, they left because a depleted Circuit Quarterly Meeting (depleted because some of its members were attending a miners' meeting) resolved to take a second minister, despite financial difficulties which had resulted from the intermittent working of the mines. This may have been the proximate cause, but it is likely that some who became Lay Methodists were anticlerical and were exemplifying Werner's view that 'this tendency towards fissipa-rousness was a natural adjunct of the Ranter emphasis'.

This movement was immediately joined by a group which had broken away from the Adamstown Primitive Methodist church in 1885 and had established a United Methodist Free church. The following year they had severed their connection with the Merewether UMFC circuit and remained separate until the Lay Methodist movement was formed.[37] The Movement spread rapidly across several of the mining townships and these congregations were formed into a circuit with a layman as President. Ninety-four per cent of the membership were miners or labourers and their families, thus giving this small denomination a higher percentage of working class members than any other denomination. As with the early Primitive Methodists, their religion was passionate and enthusiastic and they paraded the streets with bands and singing groups before their camp meetings and services to draw in outsiders.[38]

In 1890 the Lay Methodists drew up a Declaration of Faith and Order which stated that they did not accept any 'human standards and Creeds' and that they would declare 'what is taught by the inspired word as a Divine authority and the foundation of Christian faith and practice'. On polity they emphasised that their ministry was 'purely voluntary and unpaid'.[39] The Lay Methodists were not involved in the Methodist union of 1902 and they continued to expand after that date. Indeed, some Primitives joined them rather than enter the union. This occurred at Charlestown which only had a Primitive Methodist church before union but which had a Lay Methodist church and a United church thereafter. Miners in Kurri asked the Lay Methodists to establish a cause there in 1908.

After the Great War the Lay Methodist church went into decline and died in 1951 when the few remaining members attached themselves either to the Methodist church or to another denomination. Their failure to maintain themselves was attributed to a lack of sufficient leaders, feeble youth work and an unsound financial structure.[40]

Overseas missions

Foreign missions provided a further field for expansion in the nineteenth century although only the Wesleyans were able to concern themselves with it. The story of mission work in the islands is too large and too different to be told here and we can only consider the support given to the Pacific missions from within New South Wales.

At independence, while it was realised that the Wesleyan Missionary Committee in London would have to supplement the income for mission work for a time, the Australian Wesleyans requested that the island missions be put under the control of the Australasian Conference in the belief that the responsibility would quicken interest in the work in a way that nothing else could. It was thought that the Australian church would soon raise the whole cost and provide the men. That hope found support in the fact that, in 1854, New South Wales alone had contributed £3200 to mission work out of a total expenditure of less than £8500.

New South Wales collections rose to £3558 in 1855, but it was many years before they approached that figure again. Figures for the colony are not always available, but there were several years in which they were under half that sum and the total figures for Australia were no better. Even with burgeoning receipts from the islands themselves, the English Committee often found itself bearing an unwanted burden. The £1268 of 1855 became £5973 in 1864 and, though it fell away thereafter, the Committee's responsibilities continued to be significant until the 1880s, long after everyone had expected that the Australian church would have assumed full responsibility. These financial problems had many causes. The rapid advance of the work involved the church in an ever-increasing expenditure. The opening of the New Britain field in 1876 and the New Guinea field in 1891 were major steps forward, but other smaller advances also required more staff and increased the financial burden. Yet the church rejoiced in these events for membership was growing more rapidly in the islands than in Australia and it was there that the favour of God towards Wesleyan Methodism was most clearly shown. While the parent society was prepared to make up the deficit, the Australian church could not be expected to allow such a field to 'waste ungathered into former desolation'.

Financial problems also had less happy explanations as collections in the colony were often poor. Sometimes this was the unavoidable consequence of natural disaster or financial depression; sometimes it was the result of poor organisation or lack of interest in the circuits. In 1905, only 145 Sunday schools out of a total of 467 contributed. In the 562 New South Wales churches, not to mention other preaching places, there were only ninety-nine collectors at work. In the same year the Women's Auxiliary for Overseas Missions (WAOM) could raise only £60. Often, circuit missionary meetings were held late in the year, leaving the missionary committee to borrow money at interest to pay its way in the early part of the year and repay this at a later date. This was wasteful and inefficient.

The existence of real interest in overseas missions was also confirmed by the men from the NSW Wesleyan church who served in the islands. The best known of these, but by no means the only ones, were Revs Stephen Rabone, John Watsford, George Brown, Benjamin Danks and R.H. Rickard, each of whom served faithfully for many years. On their return to New South Wales such men were often leaders in the missionary effort on the home front.[41] Nevertheless it is difficult to avoid the conclusion that missionary interest was fairly narrowly confined among the clergy and the idealistic young. The laity generally preferred to concern themselves with local projects.

Methodist union

In the second half of the nineteenth century Methodists in New South Wales clearly perpetuated the differences and divisions which had grown up among them in Britain. Migrants to the colony brought their particular brand of Methodism with them and, if they could, continued to practise it. However, for three decades, the Wesleyan church had no Methodist rivals and even after the minor bodies commenced their mission the Wesleyans continued to display little interest in their poorer and weaker sister churches. For their part, these smaller sisters, for they regarded themselves as 'sisters' rather than 'daughters' of Wesleyan

Methodism, frequently sought some acknowledged relationship with 'big sister' by inviting a Wesleyan minister or layman to preach or preside at some special function in the life of their church. Otherwise each Methodist branch went its own way, fulfilling its particular ministry.

The practice, already noted, of members of the minor bodies joining with the Wesleyans in thinly settled localities which could only maintain one Methodist church brought about a de facto union by absorption in those places, despite the tendency of the people concerned to regard the change in allegiance as merely temporary and to maintain a nominal adherence to their original branch, at least at census time. In some centres, after a period of coexistence, one body vacated the field and left the other in undisputed possession. At Hill End, Young and Cootamundra, residual Primitive Methodists became Wesleyans wheras the Wesleyans gave way to the Primitives at Parkesbourne and Nundle. Indeed, by 1888, there was no second Methodist church in seventy-three out of the ninety-eight Wesleyan circuits in the colony, a fact which may explain much of the Wesleyan indifference to the question of Methodist union.

In most circuits where there were rival Methodist bodies, the Wesleyan church had been first in the field and had by far the largest body, except in those Newcastle mining townships where the Primitives predominated. Wesleyan members were usually people of greater community prestige and financial resources. Where two or more Methodist bodies coexisted relations were usually amicable, though occasionally there was a slight undercurrent of chagrin and ill-feeling if a family transferred its allegiance from one body to another (there had been such an incident in Newcastle in the 1840s). Overall, by the time the minor bodies reached their peak in the mid-1890s, the Wesleyans claimed about three times as many members, children and local preachers as did the 'other Methodists' combined and about four times as many ministers and churches.[42] The latter fact was an indication of their superior financial strength and social standing.

The first person publicly to advocate Methodist union in New South Wales was the Rev. F.W. Ward, formerly a Primitive minister, and then a very junior Wesleyan minister. In 1871 he argued the similarity of doctrine and polity in the various branches of Methodism and the wastefulness of having two or three branches operating in close proximity. There was no response. Six years later, as editor of *The Weekly Advocate*, he noted 'growing cordiality between various sections of Australian Methodism', but wondered 'whether organic union [would] ever take place'. By 1880, however, a new editor, Rev. George Martin, felt able to call for rationalisation and co-operation, a development which might lead to union.[43]

Several factors contributed to the growing desire for union, for example, the increasing awareness that sister Methodist churches were competing to establish viable congregations in communities where the population was too small to support more than one Methodist church and the institution of ecumenical conferences of Methodist churches, the first being held in London in 1881 and the second in Washington in 1891. A third factor, the importance of which must be emphasised, was the example of the various Methodist bodies in Canada, where union occurred in 1883. After a lively debate on a motion initiated by the Victoria and Tasmania Conference, the 1884 Wesleyan General Conference resolved that the union of the Methodist churches was desirable and that 'the basis of union that has taken effect in Canada will be found generally suited to the circumstances of Methodism in these colonies'. It further directed the Annual Conferences 'to open communications with the other branches of the Methodist families in their respective colonies' and to take other necessary steps to achieve union and to report to the next General Conference (1888). Significantly, no New South Wales delegate contributed to the debate.[44]

Two months later the New South Wales Conference adopted the General Conference minute and then passed an innocuous resolution authorising the President and Secretary to 'receive any overtures from other Methodist body' and 'to correspond with any officials of any such Methodist bodies'. There was no suggestion that the Wesleyans initiate any move and it is unlikely that any action was expected.

In 1888 Conference appointed five ministers and five laymen to confer with similar committees appointed by other branches of the Methodist church but it is not known whether they took similar action. Conference further decided that 'in view of the absence of any manifested general desire for union on the part of other Methodist Churches of this colony' it believed that there was 'no strong feeling for Methodist Union'. For some time thereafter, while other colonies pursued the cause of union more actively, New South Wales did nothing and, despite an 1888 General Conference direction to consider ways of avoiding the needless multiplication of Methodist churches in the same locality, competition actually increased in New South Wales. About this time the Primitives began in Granville and Penrith where the Wesleyans were already established, the UMFC opened in Stockton and Belmont where the Primitive Methodists were at work, and the Wesleyans built churches at Leichhardt, Lithgow, Greta and Carrington where the Primitives had causes.[45]

In 1892 Rev. W. Woolls Rutledge charged the Wesleyan Conference with failure to carry out the express direction of General Conference to open communications with other branches of the Methodist family arguing that, had it done so, it would have found little support for the opinion that there was no general desire for union on the part of the smaller bodies. The Conference was stirred into activity and established an enlarged committee (thirteen ministers and fourteen laymen) to confer with similar committees from the other Methodist churches on 'the advisability and practicability of organic union'. The Joint Committee was authorised to prepare a draft basis of union should it be deemed desirable and such a basis was received by the ensuing Conference and remitted to Quarterly Meetings and District Meetings for consideration and report to the following Conference.[46]

A series of joint meetings of representatives of the three Methodist bodies was held, beginning on 28 June 1892, and resolutions were carried relating to the desirability of union, doctrine, worship, finance and the name of the new church.[47] At the close of 1892, it appeared that Methodist union in New South Wales would be attained before long but this was not to be. Soon the widespread indifference in the Wesleyan church was replaced by determined opposition from a significant minority which continued to claim that there was 'no sincere desire on the part of other (Methodist) bodies for union'.

The 1893 Wesleyan Conference resolved that organic union

was desirable provided a satisfactory basis could be agreed and it remitted the matter to Quarterly Meetings and District Meetings for report to next Conference. Quarterly Meetings were to be asked whether they were in favour of organic union and whether they approved generally of the basis of union drawn up by the Joint Committee. After a frenetic debate in *The Methodist*, 67 per cent of Wesleyan Quarterly Meetings voted in favour of organic union and 61 per cent in favour of the proposed basis of union, but most of the ensuing synods, where the ministerial vote equalled the lay vote, did not think that the time for union had arrived.

The editor of *The Methodist* argued that the people were not ready for union and that the other Methodist bodies had failed to respond sympathetically on that issue. Rev. Elias Crozier denied this and pointed out that the Primitive Methodist Conference had approved of union unanimously, Quarterly Meetings voted heavily in favour, and the Intercolonial Conference held in October 1893 had also voted in favour of union. The UMFC Conference also unanimously approved the basis of union. In fact the 1894 Wesleyan Conference merely approved the establishment of a Methodist Federal Council whose functions were not spelled out, though subsequent correspondence suggested that the proponents of the idea did not intend that it should be more than a forum where the representatives of the various Methodist bodies could meet and talk to one another without achieving any organic change.[48]

In 1896 a vote was taken among Wesleyan members and adherents and there was a second vote in Wesleyan Quarterly Meetings. In the latter, the vote for union was only marginally higher than before (68 per cent), but only in twelve circuits did the adherents vote against it while four were evenly divided. No pattern can be detected from the voting figures and there is no clear evidence that ministers opposed to union unduly influenced the vote in their circuits. In areas where only the Wesleyan Methodist church existed, three circuits provided the highest of all votes against union while another six supported it unanimously. Lismore adherents voted strongly against union, but in nearby Ballina they were almost unanimously in favour. In Lithgow, Kempsey and Gladstone circuits, where the Primitive

Methodists had active causes, the pro-union vote was in excess of 90 per cent. In twelve circuits, the adherents supported union while their Quarterly Meetings opposed it. Although the adherents' vote indicated strong support for union, the 1897 Conference decided to defer action 'until the spirit of union was more largely developed'. Clearly, opposition to union in the Wesleyan church was strongest among ministers and church officials, not the generality of members and adherents, 70 per cent of whom had supported union.[49]

During 1896, the Methodist Federal Council of New South Wales, which arose from the Joint Committee appointed by the three Methodist bodies in 1892 and was very different from the similarly named body referred to above, produced a highly practical plan for the reorganisation of the human, physical and financial resources of the churches. The Wesleyans, however, still had many who were vociferous in their opposition to union and who advanced many and varied reasons against it. For example, they claimed that the spirit of union was absent, that many Primitive Methodists would not enter the united church and that each church could do better work separately.[50] Whilst the first claim was certainly true for a minority of Wesleyans, there was no significant evidence to support the second and third claims.

The real reasons, which were not always stated clearly, had much to do with the conception of the pastoral office held by Wesleyan ministers. Financial issues and the generally conservative Wesleyan attitude to social and political questions were also important. Wesleyan ministers enjoyed both status and authority far exceeding that of the ministers of the other Methodist churches and a number of Wesleyan ministers found the polity of the minor Methodist bodies too democratic for their liking. Rev. C.E. James complained that there was less kinship between the Primitive Methodists and the Wesleyans than between the Wesleyans and the Church of England. He instanced differences relating to ministerial privilege and to the order of worship and expressed particular concern about the Primitives' use of 'concert room accessories' and of a 'free and easy style'. On the other hand, some Wesleyan churches were opting for more liturgy in their services, a development which the Primitives regretted.

The debate in Wesleyan circles continued through the years

of acute depression and opponents of union referred with increasing frequency to 'insuperable difficulties' in financial matters which would occur if union were effected. The poorer paid ministers of the minor bodies would be entitled to receive the higher stipends already paid to Wesleyan ministers and circuits would not be able to afford them. The entitlement of Primitive Methodist ministers from the Supernumerary Fund would be less than that of the Wesleyan ministers. The Wesleyans would have also to assume responsibility for the heavy property debts of the smaller bodies. The 1890s also saw the emergence of the Labor Party with which many Primitive Methodists were identified. Although some Wesleyans sympathised with it, the party's political stance was repugnant to most of the more conservative among them.

For seven years a number of Wesleyan ministers and a few laymen brought forward variations on these same themes in Conference debates and in lengthy correspondence in *The Methodist* and, despite protestations from members of the minor bodies, they continued to maintain that there was no sincere desire on the part of those bodies for union. The main ministerial opponents to union, William Clarke, Benjamin Meek, Joseph Spence and Charles Prescott, had all received their training in England at a time when there was little sympathy for, or co-operation with, the minor Methodist bodies and this may have affected their attitude. There is no evidence that any of them was influenced by his experience with Primitives or other Methodists in the colony. Prescott was once accused of preferring union with the Church of England to the Primitives on social grounds. The leading Wesleyans in the cause of union, Rev. W.W. Rutledge and William Robson, MLC, were both born in the colony and Robson's father had been a Primitive Methodist in his youth.[51]

Unlike the Wesleyans, the ministers of the minor Methodist bodies did not divide over union. In the absence of debate there was no occasion for them to take sides either for or against and there is no surviving evidence of a minister expressing opposition to union (although, in 1892, the Rev. John Penman confessed that he was a recent convert to the cause). Some Primitive Methodist laymen, including some officials in the Parramatta church, were not favourably disposed towards union, but the only one known to have expressed strong opposition was William Puddicombe, a local preacher of many years standing. When the vote on union was taken in the Primitive Methodist Conference in 1895 he was one of only two dissentients. He told the Conference that he was not prepared to give anything away. Ultimately, conciliatory words and actions by both minister and officials averted his resignation and he continued as a local preacher in the Methodist church, but he was nearly lost.[52]

In spite of the declared attitude of the Primitive Methodists in favour of union, the 1899 Wesleyan Conference, in an effort to delay or, as some hoped, defeat union, insisted that the Primitive Methodists and the Free Methodists take a vote among their members and adherents. The Primitive Methodist Conference in 1900 expressed resentment at the attempt of the Wesleyan Conference to interfere with their affairs but agreed to a vote being taken 'conditionally upon the Wesleyan Conference pledging itself to the consummation of Organic Union at an early date'. The vote among Primitive Methodists resulted in a vast majority (90 per cent) supporting the proposed union and only one circuit (Waterloo) voting against it. The UMFC also registered a large majority vote for union.[53]

The Wesleyan anti-unionists maintained their opposition and Prescott requested that the matter rest for a further three years, but such rearguard action could no longer delay union. After years of agitation, opposition and struggle in Wesleyan circles, the 1900 Conference voted for union by 107 to 53 and even the strongest opponents accepted this with reasonable grace.[54]

New South Wales was the last State to enter Methodist union. The three denominations synchronised their Conferences in 1901, which enabled them, after holding separate sessions, to have a United Conference on 6 March. The sole business of this session was to consider the Plan of Union, which was unanimously accepted and adopted. At midnight on 31 December 1901 the three bodies became the (united) Methodist church. That event was celebrated throughout New South Wales in various ways. In a number of centres watchnight services were held. In Sydney, a meeting of prayer and praise was held on 1 January 1902. In Newcastle, there was a Camp Meeting attended by more than 2400 people. This was followed by two Tea Meetings, after which two public meetings were held. The main event for the State took place when the first United Conference was held on 25 February 1902 with over 4000 participants.

Rev. James Colwell wrote that in New South Wales organic union had been achieved without the loss of a property, the secession of a minister or the resignation of a church officer. That was correct but, as we have seen, only just. Despite fears in Wesleyan circles, there was no reason for them to resign for they had the least to lose. Some Primitive Methodists, and maybe a few Free Methodists, chose to join another denomination. Within a few years many congregations were amalgamated and many properties were sold. For a number of years old attitudes persisted in some centres and kept congregations apart. This was most noticeable in the Wallsend circuit where the Metcalfe Street congregation (ex-Wesleyan) and the Devon Street congregation (ex-Primitive) did not amalgamate until the 1960s. It took time before the members of the separate Methodist bodies grew into a truly united body, but most Methodists agreed with Theophilus Parr that 'God was in the movement'.[55]

In the event, Methodist union was more an absorption of the smaller bodies by the Wesleyans than a true union. In 1895, Sir Samuel Way, Chief Justice and Lieutenant Governor of South Australia, and a member of the Bible Christian church, addressed a great United Demonstration held in Sydney. Seeking to allay Wesleyan fears and dampen opposition to the projected union, he told them that 'The basis of union is the Wesleyan Constitution unaltered, except in the one permissive addition of laymen to the stationing committee, and in restoring to Methodism its right name'.[56]

He was absolutely correct: Wesleyan funds absorbed the other funds; Wesleyan properties remained (apart from the occasional Primitive Methodist church which had no occasion to amalgamate with another congregation); the Wesleyan newspaper continued under the same name (admittedly the appropriate one) and editorship; and the Wesleyan structure of government continued unaltered. The Wesleyan Committee appointed to gather and preserve historical church records also continued unchanged, without the name of one person from any minor body being added. No attempt was made to preserve the newspapers or printed minutes of the smaller bodies although all such Wesleyan records were preserved.

Yet Methodist union was long overdue and, when it came, its importance was recognised by the *Sydney Morning Herald* which noted that 'The immediate result [of union] may be expected to be a great development of the resources and power of the Methodist Church, and that cannot but make for the public welfare'.[57] Certainly the united Methodist church was able to witness to the Gospel and to serve the community in the new century more effectively than the divided Methodist bodies could have done.

Growth and composition of the Methodist body

Since the period 1855-1914 was one of significant development for the Methodist churches in New South Wales it is necessary to consider the extent of that growth and its social composition, as far as possible.

Wesleyan Methodism reflected fully Phillips's view that Protestant religion in the late nineteenth century was 'largely a middle class affair'. All the groups represented among Renate Howe's Victorian Wesleyans were replicated in New South Wales. Ken Cable located the strength of the Methodists in the suburbs of Sydney, the small townships and the adjacent farming areas. Urban Wesleyans were from the commercial and retail groups, not the working class, while rural Wesleyans were farmers rather than pastoralists. The census of 1901 showed Methodist breadwinners to be under-represented among pastoralists, bankers, merchants, men of independent means, refuse collectors and domestic servants, but over-represented among farmers, miners, educators and skilled tradesmen.

These census figures included minor Methodists, and some special mention must be made of them since they stand out from the overall, Wesleyan dominated, pattern. In the main, Primitive Methodists came from the mining and agricultural communities of England, with smaller numbers from Wales and Scotland. Those from the mining counties usually settled in the northern, western and southern coalfields. Migrants who settled in Sydney and its suburbs were usually working-class people from many different parts of England. Migrants from the rural communities settled mainly in country districts. The Primitives thus tended to provide much of the Methodist segment among the miners and the unskilled and semi-skilled workers, both rural and urban. The UMFC contributed even more strongly to those categories from its small numbers.

In the last decade of the nineteenth century, while the total population of 'good' suburbs like Burwood and Stanmore increased by 40 per cent, the number of Methodists of all kinds in the area increased by 76 per cent. In working class Newtown, the total Methodist increase was slightly below that for the population at large. Together, these facts corroborate both the middle-class status of the majority of Wesleyans and the observed stagnation of the Primitive Methodist church between 1895 and 1902. In an 1865 article on education, *The Christian Advocate* boldly proclaimed this general Wesleyan middle-class status and reinforced the point by noting that the kind of education Wesleyan people sought for their children was one which would equip them for 'the actual business of life' with 'a fair chance of success' and which would guard them from youthful vices. The rapid spread of the archetypal middle-class organisation, the Mutual Improvement Society, in the church at that time further substantiates the point. Especially from the 1880s onwards, many of the churches built by the Wesleyans reflected their social aspirations as did their behaviour in church, especially over the class meeting. It will be shown later that the Wesleyan church's loss of contact with the working class of the inner city was a major failing.

Yet, if Wesleyans were largely a middle-class group, it must be admitted that, at least until late in the nineteenth century, there was a certain fragility about this social status. The clearest evidence for this view lies in the frequency with which office holders were temporarily disbarred for insolvency and, sometimes, if the brethren thought their account-keeping inadequate, even 'dismembered'. Further evidence may be found in the obviously self-taught nature of many local preachers. All this applies *a fortiori* to the middle-class people among the membership of the minor bodies.[58]

That the expansion of the Methodist bodies, both Wesleyan

and minor, more than kept pace with population growth until the end of the century, though not thereafter, is obvious from census figures. Methodists of all types comprised 5.3 per cent of the population of New South Wales in 1851, but had reached 10.2 per cent in 1901 to decline to 9.3 per cent in 1911. This made New South Wales the State with the lowest percentage of Methodists in the Commonwealth. R.B. Walker shows clearly that total Methodist growth cannot be accounted for by natural increase and that while migration from overseas undoubtedly helped at times the percentage of Methodists among migrants was not consistently high enough to provide a complete explanation. Part of the answer lies in the fact that, in the early years, many people in outlying areas of the colony were unchurched. Wesleyan Methodism, through its policy of extension, brought many of these within its fold and cared for them spiritually. Of those who were not Methodist by tradition, many later returned to their own denomination, though some doubtless remained with the church which had come first to their aid.

The process of evangelism, described in detail in a subsequent chapter, added many to the membership of the church, though the fact that a large percentage of all converts came from within its own bounds suggests that few were added to the Methodist share of the population by that means, especially since converts at Methodist missions who had a spiritual home elsewhere were normally referred to their own pastor. In 1895, the Wesleyans of Moree, in the midst of a revival, proudly proclaimed that they had not drawn away a single adherent of any other denomination.

Phillips rightly points to the substantial migration of Methodist miners from South Australia to Broken Hill and the Lower Hunter in the 1880s as a major contribution to this expansion. The sharp increase in the number of Primitive Methodists in the colony through the 1880s, and the extraordinarily high percentage of this group in the Newcastle population at the time, substantiate his argument. He also shows that when religious decline set in late in the century, it was in the city and suburbs of Sydney rather than overall. At the very time when Sydney and its suburbs were providing a higher percentage of the total population, its citizens were becoming less likely to attend church. The Wesleyans were conscious of this weakness. The Sydney Synod took up the issue in October 1889 noting that, in 1888, attendants at Wesleyan churches in the metropolis were only 1:28 of the inhabitants compared with 1:17 in 1871. Later, in 1901, J.E. Carruthers raised the question vigorously with respect to the suburbs, which he thought needed to be considered apart from the city proper where the Central Methodist Mission was by then well established. In the decade 1891–1901 the total suburban population had increased by 96 000, but Methodist ministerial provision was up by only three, two in the north and one in the south; other suburban areas had gained 50 000 people with not even one additional Methodist minister among them. Even the number of church buildings had not kept pace and major suburban areas were inadequately provided for.

Carruthers's forceful advocacy led to some central planning for suburban advance and some determination to use the opportunity provided by Methodist union to increase the number of agencies available. For the next three or four years, *The Methodist* wrote with pride of the advances being made. Yet, by 1912, it had again to admit that Methodism was falling behind and that suburbs like Randwick, North Sydney, Mosman and Neutral Bay, which had undergone enormous expansion, were no better off than they had been ten years before and had only small and inadequate churches. It suggested a policy of concentration on strategic areas, naming Randwick, Mosman, Balmain and Redfern-Waterloo. All that could be done before the war was for the Church Sustenation and Extension Society to set up a fund to acquire sites in new neighbourhoods. The problem was still a long way from being solved.

More important to the Methodists than their raw census numbers was their church attendance record since that better reflected the activity of adherents. In this respect, Methodists were conspicuous among the major denominations. The Methodist share of all regular church attenders was never less than double their proportion of the population. No other major denomination had a record even approaching that. Nevertheless, the disparity between the two percentages did decline substantially over the period.[59]

Despite the fact that Methodist expansion in the period was strong in both absolute and comparative terms, by the first World

War it was certain that Boyce's dream of 'carrying the colony' would never become a reality.

3

Living and worshipping the Methodist way

A major function of any church is the pastoral task of nurturing Christians, of encouraging the growth to mature manhood and womanhood of those who have entered the Kingdom of God through the process of conversion and of bringing its young people to the point of conversion. In the second half of the nineteenth century, the Methodists of New South Wales were concerned to do far more than bring sinners to repentance. It was also their purpose to spread 'scriptural holiness', or 'sanctification', across the land.

This characteristic Methodist concept is not easy to define and is not to be confused either with 'justification' or with the 'second blessing' of the modern charismatic or with the mere absence of 'worldliness'. According to a contemporary catechism, 'Entire sanctification is that state in which the heart is cleansed from all unrighteousness, and in which God is loved with all the mind and with all the soul and with all the strength, and our neighbour as ourselves'. It involved the scriptural notion of being 'filled with the Holy Spirit', living close to God day by day and having perfect confidence in Him.[1]

Methodists used many means to pursue these ends: public worship and fellowship, private devotion for adults, and the provision of education and fellowship for children and young people. Margaret Reeson, in her fine historical novel, *Certain Lives*, provides useful insights into the public and private spiritual lives of nineteenth century Methodists, both urban and rural.

Worship, fellowship and holiness

The foundation of the sanctified Christian life was to be built on regular personal and family devotion. Conference and *The Christian Advocate* constantly called Wesleyans to commit themselves to this higher devotional life of open communion with their Lord and to participate eagerly in the fellowship of believers. To be a Sunday Christian only was a sign of spiritual degeneracy. The mid-week service, the prayer meeting, the love-feast and, above all, the class meeting also called them. As the 1855 Conference advised, 'The more extensive and urgent your worldly business, the more need you have of fellowship with God'.[2] The minor Methodist bodies were equally insistent on the spiritual life and the means they recommended to attain this were identical.

Earlier we saw how Methodists in new communities sought each other out, formed societies and met for the class meeting and for services wherever they could, in homes or even in hotels and billiard rooms. It was only natural that, as soon as possible, for convenience and as an expression of their devotion to God, they built a chapel. At first such chapels were plain, humble structures of wattle and daub, upright slabs or weatherboard, but within a few years they were replaced by equally plain but larger and more durable churches of brick or stone. A rostrum or large pulpit usually dominated the front and in some places a choir sat behind the pulpit. The now ubiquitous symbol of the cross was not then used in their buildings though in many a scroll with a text such as 'O worship the Lord in the Beauty of Holiness' hung on the back wall.

The buildings reflected the nature of the worship for which they were intended, for preaching, singing, praying and sharing fellowship were the vital elements of Methodist worship. Whenever and wherever Methodists united in these activities, whether in homes, halls or chapels, they exemplified the biblical precept, 'Whatever you are doing, put your whole heart into it'. Always more evident among the minor bodies than the Wesleyans, more common in the humble places of worship than in the finer ecclesiastical buildings, and everywhere declining in importance as the nineteenth century progressed, enthusiasm, intensity and a lack of inhibition nevertheless characterised the worship of all Methodists.

'Old Tom Brown' was typical of many: 'When he preached, every faculty and muscle was called into play; when he sang, every expressive quality that he possessed was drawn upon, and when he prayed, devils feared and trembled'. This was serious business, for his soul and those of his hearers depended on it; there could be no perfunctory performance, no half-hearted worship. Strong emotions were generated and communicated, binding the worshippers into a united company of Christians who sang fervently:

And if our fellowship below
In Jesus be so sweet,
What heights of rapture shall we know
When round His throne we meet.[3]

Differences in worship between the Wesleyans and the minor Methodists were less evident in the colony than in England because of the pioneering situation in which they lived. Little emphasis was placed on balanced worship and preaching predominated, the other elements often being referred to as 'preliminaries'. Much of this preaching was of the simple Gospel type aimed primarily at the conversion of sinners, though it often had the additional purpose of building up Christians.

Congregations generally supported their preachers in that ministry with exclamations such as 'Amen', and 'Glory be'. When John Gilbert, in the Adamstown Primitive Methodist church, announced his text, 'This is a faithful saying and worthy of all acceptation, that Jesus Christ came into the world to save sinners', a member of the congregation called out, 'She's a good 'un; let her go, Johnny'. Gilbert knew that he had the support of the congregation and that encouraged him to preach with power. Some also preached at length. It was generally believed that powerful preaching would fill churches and preachers rejoiced in the privilege of proclaiming the Gospel. In time, the old habit of exclamation during worship declined and older preachers, like Rev. J.H. Fletcher, retiring President-General in 1888, bemoaned 'the silence which has crept into our worship, instead of the soul-stirring responses of earlier days', and regretted that 'The

Arctic chill of indifferentism' was telling against the attendance at public worship.

Quarterly preaching plans were published in all circuits indicating times and places for all ministers and local preachers to take their services. If they failed to keep their appointments or to attend the preachers' meeting, they were disciplined. Depending on the nature of the dereliction, the penalty might be a loss of seniority among the preachers or removal from the plan either temporarily or permanently.[4]

Next to preaching came singing. Methodists knew that 'the true liturgy of Methodism [was] to be found in its hymns' and the Wesleyans found the hymns of Charles Wesley, together with those of Isaac Watts and a few others, adequate to express all their emotions and experiences. To these, the Primitives added more exuberant hymns of their own creation. Later, when the Primitives gave up their lively, uninhibited style of worship, the Lay Methodists revived it. Methodists who sang with zest and enjoyed powerful preaching and fervent prayer did not welcome the more liturgical form of service which Wesley had bequeathed to his followers and, in the early years, there was no such service in any chapel in the colony, although they were introduced later at York Street (Sydney), Ashfield, and one or two other churches. Some thought such liturgy 'a piece of senseless mummery' and opposed even the chanting of the Lord's Prayer. One such person wrote:

> Fancy a joyous Methodist who 'rejoices in God his Saviour' having to repeat in every public service, 'O Lord have mercy upon us miserable sinners' . . . The strength of Methodism consists in a simple form of service, good hearty congregational singing, and in the power of the pulpit, both mental and spiritual.

Yet the same person would sing, with tears running down his face, the penitential hymns of Wesley. Of course, even this 'simple form of service' in time developed its own stereotyped 'hymn-sandwich' order which some found deadening. Sometimes, too, the freshness and spontaneity of worship was dulled by the over long continuance of traditions beyond their usefulness, such as the 'lining out' of hymns once made necessary by illiteracy and a lack of hymn books.[5]

Methodists also proclaimed the Gospel and sought fellowship

beyond the walls of their churches. Open-air services and camp meetings were held regularly by all four branches of Methodism, though the Primitives did so with more enthusiasm and for a longer period than the Wesleyans. Open-air services frequently preceded the Sunday evening service as well as being held on week evenings. In the 1880s the Sydney Central Methodist Mission and some other churches livened up these meetings by introducing brass bands.[6]

The camp meeting was Methodism's open-air meeting *par excellence*. Such meetings in New South Wales were usually confined to a single day, either a Sunday or a public holiday, unlike their American equivalents which were often conducted over several successive days. In England, the Primitives pioneered camp meetings and the Wesleyans opposed them; in the colonies all branches of Methodism used them, though the Wesleyans did so to a lesser extent. The first Wesleyan camp meeting in the colony was held at Pitt Town on 26 December 1843, well before the appearance of a separate Primitive body. Another Wesleyan meeting, 'enormously attended', was held in Sydney on 26 January 1848, and another at Chippendale in the same year. Thereafter, all Methodist bodies regularly held such meetings at which many people experienced conversion. Often, camp meetings were forerunners of a series of revival meetings which might continue for weeks.

What such meetings meant to Methodists may be better appreciated from the report of the camp meeting held at Wisemans Ferry on 26 December 1860. Twenty-five boats brought people from all parts of the river while others rode or walked. Under a large canopy covered with green branches a two-hour morning service was held during which several people came to repentance and one who had long sought sanctification was filled with the Holy Spirit. After lunch the services continued until 5.00 p.m. when separate prayer meetings for men and women began. Many were in distress for salvation and the meeting eventually adjourned to the nearby home of a local preacher where it continued until 11.00 p.m. by which time ten to twenty persons had 'found peace'.[7]

In many places, services of Holy Communion or the Sacrament of the Lord's Supper were held infrequently and the first Conference after Methodist union in 1902 felt it necessary to urge a more frequent observance, though much of the problem was undoubtedly due to the irregularity with which ministers conducted service at many rural preaching places. Few churches had communion rails and in most the minister served the elements to communicants in their seats. Despite the popular conception that Methodists always practised 'open communion', inviting 'all who love our Lord Jesus Christ' to participate, nineteenth century Methodist law specifically restricted communicants to members of the Methodist church, though devout persons who were not members might also be invited. Among the minor Methodist bodies, with their stronger emphasis on total abstinence, unfermented grape juice was used, but in a number of Wesleyan churches fermented wine was retained until late in the nineteenth century. Likewise, the chalice was not finally replaced by the use of individual glasses until near the century's close.[8]

In addition to Sunday worship, spiritual nurture and fellowship were sought through a variety of meetings. Weeknight services were sometimes simply a means of allowing ministers to visit regular preaching places which could not be reached on a Sunday. Elsewhere, until it was discarded late in the century, the regular weeknight service was a supplement to the Sunday service and an opportunity for additional teaching and fellowship. Methodists regarded the prayer meeting as a 'spiritual powerhouse'—an essential ingredient in the life of a congregation. Such meetings were invariably held after the evening service during which people were often converted. They were lively meetings which sometimes continued until midnight with passionate expressions of feelings and aspirations in song as well as prayer. In many places, there was also a weeknight prayer meeting and sometimes an early Sunday morning meeting when prayers were offered for the conversion of sinners during the day. Evangelistic campaigns and other special efforts required additional purpose-directed prayer meetings.

Akin to the prayer meeting was the love-feast which was usually held quarterly and after a camp meeting. After a simple meal of bread and water, members sang, prayed and gave testimonies. For many, these were times of spiritual enrichment and the characteristics of such meetings were said to be 'life, soul, (and) fire'. Sometimes a love-feast was held in connection with the annual Conference.[9]

In practically all established Methodist societies weekly class meetings were held. These were formally structured groups with appointed leaders and roll books where members were assigned to a particular class. Class leaders included the ministers and appointed lay men and women. Ideally, a class comprised twelve members but groups were often larger because of insufficient leaders. The class meeting was a particular source of strength for Methodists and an opportunity for fellowship, prayer and praise, but above all for testimony. The victorious soul inspired others by recounting the Lord's goodness in the week gone by; the struggling soul expressed its fears and doubts and was helped by the faith and love of classmates and the spiritual wisdom of the leader who bore the brunt of initial pastoral care. The class was held by its supporters to mould Christians of all conditions, ages and levels of experience into a wonderful spiritual brotherhood— though this 'levelling' tendency eventually ceased to appeal to the more upwardly-mobile Wesleyans. It also provided an environment within which discipline could be exercised over members. The dreaded words 'expelled' or 'dismembered' in the class book indicated a soul lost through active wrongdoing as surely as the phrase 'ceased to meet' suggested one grown careless in spiritual matters.

The value of the class meeting was acknowledged by the leaders of other churches. Dr R.W. Dale, a leading Congregationalist, described it as 'a striking and original contribution to the institutions of the Church' but, as the nineteenth century progressed, it was less and less accepted. As early as 1856 the first appeals were made to maintain the system, a sure sign that weakness had been detected. Time made the problem worse and many regular church-goers ceased to attend class. It was described as 'inquisitorial', people were unwilling to speak openly about their spiritual experience, the quality and number of lay leaders declined sharply and leadership passed largely into ministerial hands, something which had never been intended. Those who loved the old ways were hurt by this and could not understand why people who participated actively in Holy Communion and other means of grace no longer attended class. Among the

Wesleyans, one problem was their increasing concern with 'respectability', for public discussion of one's spiritual state was no longer acceptable to people who saw themselves as members of a church rather than a sect. Unity and enthusiasm were early casualties of this attitude. By 1914 it was no longer 'the', or perhaps even 'a', characteristic Methodist meeting.[10]

The two other significant services which persisted for a longer period, perhaps because they were less demanding, were watch-night services held on New Year's eve and Covenant services. The latter were held at various times of the year, but especially on the first Sunday of the New Year. This service remained important in the lives of Methodists, for the renewal of vows to God, through to the union of 1977. Less important overall, but still significant in the life of a congregation, were the local special occasions, the church and Sunday school anniversaries, the missionary meeting, the harvest festival and the Sunday school picnic.

Methodists saw nothing intrinsically wrong with the pursuit of wealth through business and they were not surprised when men made upright and hard-working by their faith succeeded in their enterprises. But such men were warned to be on their guard and not to be dominated by a love of wealth. Borrowing and speculation were condemned outright while businessmen were urged to keep the hectic activity of their professional lives in perspective by regular attendance at public worship and the class meeting, especially the latter. Entertainment and relaxation were recognised as necessary, though some forms, for example the theatre and dancing, were considered to be completely out of keeping with the Christian character. Others, while not in themselves evil, might entail a less than optimal use of a Christian's time. Such activities must be judged against the same standard as business activities: would they advance your Christian life and could you seek Christ's blessing on them? Thus Methodist opposition to many forms of entertainment, of which dancing was perhaps the most important, should be traced not to a negative approach to life but to the positive desire to 'put first the Kingdom of God'.[11]

The combined Methodist churches of Sydney held a joint camp meeting in the interests of holiness on 9 November 1885 which was attended by 1200 persons. This initiative led to a further meeting in the York Street church two days later, a three-day convention (also at York Street) on 9-11 December and also to the formation of an Association for the Promotion of Christian Holiness which thereafter met monthly (usually at York Street in the early days, though it later became peripatetic). The movement reached out to such distant parts of the State as Wagga, Kempsey and the Upper Hunter.

W.G. Taylor had much to do with the establishment of the Association though the presence in New South Wales of the American evangelist and holiness teacher, Miss Leonard, must also have been important as her teaching made a considerable impression on the church. At the very least, her presence at the early conventions must have contributed greatly to their success. The movement had its own paper, *Glad Tidings* which, after an existence of twenty-five years, claimed a circulation of 11 000— considerably more than the connexional journal and higher than the number of active Association members. (This was probably because many who did not necessarily subscribe to the Association's views were still prepared to buy a good quality monthly church paper for one penny.)

While the Association had its strongly positive aspects—the co-operation between Primitives and Wesleyans, the paper and the renewed emphasis on the need to deepen the spiritual life—it also displayed some negative aspects. Those problems typical of groups claiming elite experiences arose from this one too. As early as 1892, at the Sydney Ministers' Meeting, it was said that 'some who were forward in expressing their enjoyment of this blessing (sanctification), were by no means the most devout and lovable of Christians'. The fear was expressed that this crowning experience of the Christian life was being discredited by the springing up of 'a talkative, self-assertive counterfeit'. More importantly, the fact that such an association was believed to be necessary suggests strongly that its progenitors felt that New South Wales Methodism was weak in the area and that its spiritual life was in need of strong medicine.[12]

From the 1880s through until his death in the late 1920s, William Hall Pryor, a farmer of Deep Creek and later Branxton, was typical of the truly committed 'ordinary' Methodist. Born in

November 1851, this young Sunday school teacher was converted at Lochinvar on 30 November 1871 after an inner struggle lasting some three months. For several years he continued his work, participating regularly in the class meeting which gave him special joy. After his move to Branxton in 1881 he started a cottage prayer meeting in his own home and another at the church after the Sunday evening service. An entry in his diary soon after this move reveals the earnestness typical of many:

> I thank God that He ever led me to seek His mercy and feel His pardoning grace . . . and earnestly pray that He will baptise me more fully with His Holy Spirit. Truly living for Heaven is the greatest happiness here below and nothing is worth a thought beneath (comparatively) but how we may escape the death that never, never dies.

In January 1882 his minister arranged for him to be appointed class leader, though the introspective and self-deprecating Pryor hardly felt himself fit for the role as he was only self-educated. Pryor was an ardent evangelical, willing to walk miles to every mission service in the circuit and to work there at saving souls until the early morning if necessary. On one such occasion in mid-August 1883, between one and two o'clock in the morning, Pryor experienced entire sanctification. Thereafter, he began to speak occasionally at open-air meetings and, in time, became a local preacher, an office which he filled faithfully and well for more than forty years. He was a tower of strength to his minister, working hard to organise special meetings in the cause of both evangelism and sanctification. He read *Glad Tidings* from its inception and was its agent in his area. It almost goes without saying that he was also an Orangeman and a temperance worker.[13]

Pryor's diary leaves the reader wondering what he thought of the debate over the criteria for church membership. This was a growing problem for many Wesleyans, though not for their brethren in the minor bodies. When Methodism had been a sect within the Church of England, attendance at the class meeting was the only possible test of membership of the Methodist Society. Once the break was made, and Wesleyanism assumed the mantle of a complete church, the role of the class meeting necessarily changed, but strangely no one foresaw that its future as a condition of membership was limited. In New South Wales the class meeting was already losing favour and attendants among the Wesleyans by independence. One consequence of this was the decline in the ratio of members to adherents from 1:5.7 (1861) to 1:8.1 (1891), with the change being most rapid in the period 1871–81, the time at which dissatisfaction with the class meeting was growing apace. This created a practical difficulty as many devout Christians who attended church regularly and participated in means of grace other than the class meeting were not eligible to be officers. The Wesleyans were not making good use of the talent available to them and some of those excluded were offended.

Those who wished to develop new membership requirements invariably assured their opponents that they did not wish to abolish the class as a fellowship meeting; their only objection to it was as 'the' rather than 'a' test of membership. Most would have been prepared to allow it as one such test among others. Agitation led to periodic discussion of the possibility of a change in the rules, as at the 1873 Conference, but part of the problem was that the only people involved in the discussion and voting were those who had grown up in the class meeting. Much distress and disturbance was caused, but neither settlement nor compromise was reached for many years.

Some unfairness resulted from the fact that, with the decline of the once strict Wesleyan discipline, some who ceased to attend class, including some local preachers, continued in office. In the last fifteen years of the century the view was occasionally expressed that rules were enforced with less rigour for the better-off, 'liberal', upwardly-mobile adherents than for others. If true, and it is impossible to be sure, that was an unacceptable position and the church had either to apply the old rules fairly to all or change them for all. A vote taken at the September Quarterly Meetings of 1889 showed that a substantial minority wanted change. Although the New South Wales Conference recommended to General Conference that there be no change in the rules, other Conferences were less conservative and it was evident to all that the 1890 General Conference would have to reach some kind of compromise. In fact, the law was amended to allow membership by attendance at a monthly fellowship meeting as an alternative to the class meeting. The latter ceased to be a test of membership at all in 1904 when that status was granted on confession of faith and the evidence of consistent Christian living. An immediate change in the ratio of members to adherents became evident and, by 1914, it had reached 1:4.6, its highest ever level. Methodism was coming into line with the other major denominations, but membership was now probably a smaller step to take and marked one out less as a person of deep piety than it had previously. Little of this would have pleased a simple conservative Methodist like Pryor.[14]

Along with the other major denominations, the Wesleyans prospered under the State aid to religion given by the *Church Act* in the 1830s. From 1862, when salary assistance was confined to those clergy who already had an established right to it, the church as a whole faced the gradual decline of assistance with equanimity, but individual circuits must often have regretted it. Wesleyan circuits rarely enjoyed comfortable circumstances and some might not have survived without the rule, convenient to them but less so to their ministers, that when a man left a circuit any shortfall on his salary was his loss and did not constitute a continuing obligation. The decline of the class meeting involved a reduction in related income and other means had to be found to supplement funds. The traditional tea meeting was useful but could not bear the whole burden and pew renting was gradually becoming less fashionable and would continue to do so as the century drew to its close.

By the mid-1870s, *The Christian Advocate* was lamenting that New South Wales was slow to follow the example of the other Australasian colonies which had turned to weekly collections which it saw as the way of the future. Before the decade was out, the need for consistent weekly giving was being argued and the envelope system was promoted in a number of circuits. Rev. James Woolnough was its most fervent advocate and he introduced it wherever the itinerancy took him. Yet such was the conservatism of Wesleyanism in New South Wales that the scheme took decades to become widespread in the colony and, in some circuits (Manly, for example), it failed more than once before it was finally successful. Even so, circuit records continued to indicate many deficits and an unremitting struggle to balance the books. If this was true for the Wesleyans, it was the more so for the Primitives and other minor groups. As well as generally attracting a membership of a lower socio-economic status, they had always taken a principled stand against State aid and so were heavily reliant on sacrificial giving and the generosity of their few wealthy members.

Among Methodists, only the Wesleyans dared to attempt to raise special connexional funds at times of major significance in the life of the church and these were never fully subscribed. There were three main extraordinary collections in the present period. The 1864 Jubilee of Missions Fund fell well short of its target of £10 000 and was considered a failure. At the end of the century, the Century Commemoration Fund was pursued with vigour in the hope of paying off local trust debts, and the debts on Centenary Hall, Newington College and Ladies' College (Burwood). Anything left after that was to be used for home and foreign missions. The aim was to raise 50 000 guineas (£52 500) but the final result of £42 000 was claimed as a success. (Certainly it was closer to being one than were the equivalent funds of other churches—except the Presbyterian church). The Methodist Centenary Fund (1914) was collected over five years, but raised only about two-thirds of the £52 000 sought. No one called it a success and it certainly did not meet all the needs of the Theological Institution and the Affiliated College as had been intended.[15] Yet it is difficult to know whether the failure occurred because, for many, the hip pocket was the last part of their person to come under the divine influence or whether the church simply misjudged the capacity of its adherents to give. A detailed rationale for the target figure chosen was not given.

Over the years, the Methodist churches in New South Wales had developed and used many and varied 'means of grace' to strengthen their fellowship, make vital their worship and 'build each other up'. Some they shared with many Christian groups, others were distinctive. At their best, they had ensured a warm and vibrant spiritual life centred on the local congregation and linked to the wider connexion. Yet by the Great War there was little doubt that it was a system in decline. An increasing number of references note the ebbing of the freshness, vitality and joy which had once characterised love-feasts and class meetings, while the 'paralysis of the prayer meeting' was becoming increasingly apparent. Second and third generation Methodists simply did not experience the same thrill of spiritual change that their forebears had once known. The nature of the inner life was changing and to many the change did not seem to be for the better.

Schools, Sunday schools and youth groups

In the nineteenth century, neither education nor youth work attained its later prominence, but the Methodist churches were conscious of their responsibility to children and young people and fulfilled this by creating day schools, colleges, Sunday schools and a limited number of other organisations for them. The Wesleyans, as the largest group, made by far the most extensive provision.

In earlier times day schools were opened on local initiative wherever they were practical and, by 1849, such schools were educating 1657 children and were largely financed by a government grant of £570. But, while Wesleyans preferred their own denominational schools on the ground that education should be founded on religion, they understood that colonial conditions made a single national system necessary. Over the years, therefore, the Wesleyans generally supported the colonial governments in their effort to introduce a more satisfactory general system of education and thought that Catholic and Anglican opposition had more to do with 'ecclesiasticism' than with Christianity. Indeed, they found those aspects of the debate which related specifically to State aid a heaven-sent opportunity to attack the Catholic church. *The Christian Advocate* also supported the formation of the Teachers' Association and attacked the Education Council for its antagonistic attitude to that body. It was only consistent that the Wesleyan church should support Parkes's Act for 'free, compulsory and secular' education though, like Parkes, they did not see that as excluding either general religious education or even dogmatic teaching given by clergy.[16] Minor Methodist bodies, being strongly voluntarist, were of necessity supporters of a national system.

More important to the Wesleyans was the opening of a

grammar school for boys. In 1853 a government offer of land and a building grant to any church which would build an affiliated college on the site of the University of Sydney turned Wesleyan thoughts in that direction. Insufficient money was raised to allow building to begin. Many in the connexion either disliked the very idea of a Wesleyan college affiliated with the secular university or, more commonly, argued that the greater need was for a secondary school and that the university college (already named 'Wesley') should follow that. Boyce voiced this view first in January 1856, though the most notable fighter for the grammar school was Rev. John A. Manton. The affiliated college was long delayed and did not open officially until 1 December 1917.

The Education Committee of the New South Wales (Wesleyan) District began in December 1861 to seek donations and information on the number of boys likely to attend the school, to be called 'The New-South-Wales Wesleyan Collegiate Institution'. After some delay, Newington House, the old Blaxland home on the Parramatta River, was leased as a school building and the 1863 Conference approved the school. It opened in July 1863 with Manton as President and T. Johnstone as Principal. The 'nineteen miserable boys' in residence increased to fifty-nine by the end of the first year, though among them were two theological students sent there in the hope that Manton could find time to prepare them for their future role. The college, which quickly became known simply as 'Newington', was open to all boys but was to be 'decidedly Wesleyan in its character'. Its curriculum was to be commercially oriented, though provision was also made for classical and mathematical studies. This ordering of priorities suited the middle-class ethos of the Wesleyans. The successful businessmen and professionals who would send their sons there had no doubt that education was first and foremost for practical ends. At least Newington also provided the religious element on which the church placed so much importance—Bible classes, preaching and public and family worship were part of school life.

The death of Manton after little more than a year might well have led to the collapse of Newington had it not found in Rev. J.H. Fletcher a man able to continue and consolidate the work. Fletcher's long reign included not only the decision to move to

Stanmore (June 1869) but also the actual move many years later in 1880. Thereafter, apart from a temporary and unavoidable set-back in the depression of the 1890s, Newington continued to prosper throughout the period to the Great War and, in time, provided its fair share of men to bear arms in that conflict.[17]

By 1883, *The Weekly Advocate* was supporting firmly the idea of a girls' school because a woman needed a good education rather than learning the superficial accomplishments and house-keeping to which girls were often limited, if she were to be a proper 'helpmeet' for her husband and to enable her to contribute properly to the physical and mental development of her children. She also needed a means of earning a living should she not marry. More liberally, it also 'generally supported' the attempt of J.S. Mill to open up the full range of employment for women 'without necessarily wanting to go quite so far'.

Burwood Ladies' College was opened with undue haste in January 1886 in premises formerly used for a school by a Miss Lester. This ill-advised haste ensured the school a difficult begin-ning, despite the ability of its outstanding President, C.J. Prescott. Numbers were low and financial losses were incurred at the start suggesting that the school had been opened less to meet a need than to create one. The Connexion did not give Burwood the support it needed and which Newington had enjoyed. The building of the better organised Presbyterian Ladies' College near it, and the financial disasters of the 1890s, almost led to its demise though it found a good friend in the generous and wealthy Mrs Schofield. As late as 1912 there was still a possibility that the school would close and its buildings be used for a theological institution, and it was only after the Great War that its situation brightened.[18]

The Wesleyans were much more interested in the progress of their Sunday schools—something that the early missionaries had emphasised from the beginning. The mid-1830s, under Orton, had been a time of rapid development and had witnessed the founding, largely at the instigation of the lawyer, George Allen, of the Wesleyan Methodist Sunday School Society of Sydney (superseding an almost defunct Sunday School Union). The number of schools increased rapidly, though that was the conse-quence of general expansion during the 1840s and the growing efficiency of Methodist work. Despite Colwell's extensive claims on its behalf, there is no surviving evidence that the Society had long-term success even in its basic purpose of creating a con-nexional link between the schools. On 15 February 1849 a meeting of Sunday school teachers in the Sydney South Circuit was held at Chippendale 'to protest against this Committee not exercising the supervision expected of it' and to set up its own committee to co-ordinate the work of the Sydney South schools. This work lasted until 1865, when the schools again separated and went their own way.

To combat problems caused by the loss of experienced teachers during the gold-rushes, Sydney South established its own Teachers' Quarterly Improvement Meeting to provide at least a limited training. This meeting, which continued from 1854–1872, was more enduring than most Mutual Improvement Societies, probably because it was based on a shared interest in a matter of real importance.[19]

By the end of the 1850s the purpose of Sunday schools was changing. Originally they had existed as much to teach reading and writing as scriptural knowledge, but by 1860 that need had declined and they had, instead, become a nursery for the church. Yet the church was never really satisfied with its schools which, it was said, 'both fulfil our hopes, and disappoint them'. The greatest disappointment was that so few of their scholars became church members, though more must have become adherents without taking the extra step of membership. Major problems existed. Few schools were adequately equipped or accommodated and their efficiency was impaired. When the Rockdale school, which fifty years later was to become one of the most up-to-date and efficient in the country, was founded in 1855 it was in an enclosure formed by ti-tree bushes and roofed over with calico. The floor was earth and the furniture, a few tables and stools, had to be shifted to a neighbouring house each week. There and elsewhere trained teachers were few and often those who offered themselves were either too young or had not been converted. This concern led to the appointment of a committee in 1870–71 to look into the matter. Its report led the 1872 Conference to approve a set of rules by which Wesleyan Sunday schools were to be governed. Each of the twenty-five rules was eminently sensible, though it is unlikely that many were capable of full implementation even in the larger city schools.

It was not really surprising that the carry-over from Sunday school to church was so slight. This problem caused particular worry in the late 1870s when the rate of school growth slowed dramatically and the schools were not keeping pace with population growth. There were many suggestions regarding what might be done, but no cures were found and the problem persisted though the discussion died down for a time.[20]

To improve the standards of the Sunday schools, which it thought were not even moderately effective, and to create the long sought connexional link between them, the Conference of 1877 resolved to form a Wesleyan Methodist Sunday School Union. When it was finally formed in June 1879 the Union had high ambitions but only a handful of schools joined and it collapsed almost immediately. For the next eight years, the only help available for teachers was that given from time to time by the ablest superintendents of the day. Men such as H. Capey of York Street, J.A. Cainfield of William Street and the greatly beloved John Corbett of Bourke Street, who sought to pass on the experience of a lifetime.

A further attempt in 1887 to reorganise the Union achieved little. But in 1889 Rev. W.H. Beale became secretary. Beale's particular contribution, apart from improved organisation, was the introduction of competitive examinations for scholars throughout the Connexion. At the time this was regarded as a major step forward and certain to lead to better teaching and a surer knowledge of the scriptures and the catechism. The view persisted for many years despite the considerable potential of the examinations to disrupt teaching. The enormous drop-out rate between entry and sitting the examination, around 30 per cent in the early years, suggests that either the teachers or the scholars had decided that they had little chance of passing and that it was wiser not to sit. The most likely implication is that many of the schools were not particularly efficient at inculcating even basic scriptural knowledge in their charges.

Possibly the most important fruit of the Union was a greater awareness of the need to train teachers adequately. Yet little was achieved and, at the end of the century, it was still possible to list among the faults of the schools: the lack of training among teachers; unsuitable buildings and equipment; the inability to retain older scholars; the exaggerated importance attached to preparation for the yearly anniversary; and the tendency for the school to be regarded as an institution separate from the church.

A Sunday School Department was set up in 1904 to oversee the whole range of work associated with youth and especially to assist with the attainment of 'greater spiritual results' and the better training of teachers in the Sunday schools. This Department tried to assist schools to establish libraries and circulated books to small outback schools. It introduced the idea of holding a 'Decision Day' for scholars once each year, an indication that the spontaneous evangelism of the nineteenth century was becoming less a part of the life of the twentieth century church. A full-time head, Rev. Harold Wheen, was appointed in 1912.

The early twentieth century saw big changes in the organisation of Sunday schools as the larger ones were divided into departments according to the ages of the various children and as new teaching methods were introduced for the youngest children. Rockdale, under the superintendency of C.C. Jones, became a model for New South Wales and, indeed, for the whole of Australia as workers came from all States to study its organisation and methods. By the Great War, its eighty-two staff and 383 attending scholars were divided into Adult, Institute, Junior, Primary and Beginners (with a subdivision for Little Beginners). In addition, it provided for a further ninety through its Cradle Roll and Home departments, the latter providing material and occasional visits for those who were unable to attend for some reason. It established a Young Worshippers League in 1914 to involve its children more definitely in worship and it gave them work to do for the Church. The school was fortunate to have a scholar–teacher ratio of a little over 5:1, a luxury that probably could only be envied by most.

Surviving records are most concerned with the problems of the schools because both the Wesleyans and the united Methodist church recognised the vital importance of this work and worried about its many weaknesses. At no stage did they feel that the work was truly efficient and making the contribution to the life of the church which it might have. But it would be superficial and inaccurate to accept that view of the schools at face value. It would also be unfair to scores of unknown men and women, some very young, who gave much time and effort to this work. A few names have been mentioned, and others might be, like A.F. Davis of Manly who was enthusiastic in the work of teacher preparation early this century, the Hon. Jacob Garrard, MLA, who spent thirty years as a Sunday school teacher and superintendent (continuing in this work even when he was Minister for Education in the 1890s) and William Davies, the parliamentarian from Goulburn who travelled back to that city each weekend to take his place in the Sunday school. These and others showed both faith and commitment.

The Church was rightly concerned about the many scholars who never became adult members, but it remained true that the main source of church members and adherents was the Sunday school. Many of those members owed much of their scriptural knowledge and understanding of the faith to the school; never again were they to receive such consistent teaching. Church statistics suggest that the Methodist schools were teaching about 42 000 scholars by 1914. The proportion of children in Methodist Sunday schools was always far higher than the percentage of Methodists in the community. Methodist Sunday schools fell far short of the ideal in every respect, but they did face a problem which was incapable of satisfactory solution and, without their achievements, the Methodist Church in 1914 would have been incomparably weaker.[21]

The nineteenth century church made even less adequate provision for youth than it did for children. In this it was probably reflecting society at large. Among Wesleyans, the Mutual Improvement Society, usually for young men, was the characteristic society for much of the second half of the century. Possibly the first in Wesleyan ranks was that already noted in the South Sydney circuit from 1854. This was unusual in that it included both males and females and was specifically directed towards Sunday school teachers. General societies mushroomed in the 1860s and were formed in Surry Hills in 1862 and in Sydney North and Wollongong in 1863. Other places followed quickly. Usually membership was available to non-Methodists of good character. The primary purpose was educational: essays were written, speeches given and lectures attended. At Kiama in 1865 a young man, J.E. Carruthers, surprised his listeners with the excellence of a speech on the subject 'Success in Life—how to attain it'. Since Carruthers later became President of the New South Wales Conference and President-General of the Australasian Conference, it may be assumed that the content as well as the style of his speech was good. Only occasionally were specifically Christian objectives spelled out in the rules of the societies and they sometimes failed to meet the religious expectations of the church. The problem was that if the societies were too strongly religious in intent they found it hard to attract and hold the youth; if they made entertainment and intellectual improvement too prominent their role as a church society became questionable.[22]

Apart from the Bands of Hope, which are dealt with elsewhere, the other body which deserves mention here is Christian Endeavour. This interdenominational organisation reached Sydney in 1881 and was taken up enthusiastically by the Wesleyans. By its twenty-fifth anniversary, more than half of all the Endeavour groups in New South Wales were within the (united) Methodist church. While Endeavour lacked the ability to attract young people beyond the Sunday school age group, it was overtly Christian, sought to inculcate scriptural teaching, effect conversions, provide fellowship and lead young people into service for the church. That the organisation served a valuable purpose is clear from its ability to attract the support of leading ministers, including P.J. Stephen, Joseph Woodhouse and Woolls Rutledge.[23]

4

Church and community

Until the late nineteenth century the Protestant theological tradition remained excessively concerned with the question of the salvation of the individual and was inclined to separate the spiritual and secular aspects of life, allowing a heavy emphasis on the former in its thinking. The first priority of the church was perceived to be the proclamation of a pietistic gospel of individual spiritual salvation. Out of this would flow a morally reformed society, since better men and women must make for a better society. Individual acts of philanthropy would also occur as the consciences of Christians led them to offer personal assistance to the less fortunate among their brethren and sisters. The remaking of society was not within the purview of a church which had still to recover the largely submerged Gospel concept of the Kingdom of God.[1]

Despite Wesley's own greater emphasis on social reform, noted by J.R. Green and J.W. Bready among others, his nineteenth century followers in the Wesleyan church were generally conservative in politics and complacent in the presence of glaring social wrongs and shared fully in the common Protestant failing.[2] The minor Methodist bodies, especially the Primitives, displayed greater reforming zeal and were pioneers in both the temperance and trade union movements. With a passionate love of men, and a like passionate desire for justice, they were appalled by many social and industrial conditions which militated against human well-being and they worked for a more just society.

In New South Wales, for more than thirty years, only the Wesleyan church existed, and it could not be expected to take a different approach from that followed by its parent body in England. Indeed, conditions in the colony did not encourage changing the charter. From the colony's inception, intemperance and a disregard for Sunday as a day of rest and worship were features of life. The imbalance of the sexes, and the predilections of the convicts, led to considerable sexual immorality. Those in authority valued clergy as moral policemen and those Sydney Wesleyans who pleaded with the Wesleyan Missionary Committee in London for a preacher apparently shared the view as they wrote, 'Drunkenness, adultery, Sabbath-breaking and blasphemy, are no longer considered even as indecencies . . . Send a faithful servant of the Lord to us'. Methodists, over the years, were appalled at the situation and were glad to be exhorted continually to avoid those and other sins to which they had little inclination and to maintain a high standard of personal ethics. They sought, by faithful witness, to remedy the situation and were pleased when the proclamation of the Gospel did transform human lives and change communities as when it was claimed in mid-century for the region around Dalton that 'The character of the whole neighbourhood has altogether changed . . . and religion *alone* has done it'.[3]

In the early years Leigh sent his supporters to visit the sick, the poor and the dying in the Rocks area of Sydney, notorious for its squalor and vice. The discovery of abject penury led to the formation, already noted, of the Sydney Asylum for the Poor, later to be known as the Benevolent Society, which provided accommodation for fifty indigent people who were fed and given medical aid. He was prevented from further involvement by his lack of resources, the internecine strife with his colleagues and the injunction of the Missionary Committee not to engage 'in any of the civil disputes or the local politics of the colony'.[4]

Against this kind of background it was to be expected that in the second half of the nineteenth century the Wesleyans, at least, would move slowly on social reform, attending first to what were essentially personal moral issues with social implications—like temperance, gambling and Sunday observance—and attending only later to genuine social, economic and political issues. Few of the earlier ministers would have felt comfortable with the view expressed by Rev. James Blanksby at the 1895 Primitive Methodist Conference that 'the task of the Church is not only to reclaim from sin, but to work upon the conditions of life, with a view to minimising the causes of evil and the influences which induced wrong'. A few Wesleyan ministers, like Wools Rutledge and P.J. Stephen, were beginning to adopt similar views and to argue that the church had a moral duty to work for the eradication of social wrong as well as to exhort members to eschew such evils in their own lives.[5] Without question, it was the Primitives who gave the lead; most Wesleyans were far more cautious.

Moral issues

The temperance movement began in England in the 1830s and soon made its appearance in New South Wales. At that time Sydney had 500 hotels and it was claimed that 'the drinking habits were ruining a large class of inhabitants'. Thirty years later John Sharpe claimed that there were 1421 public houses in the country and 511 in the city and he asked, 'Can we wonder that our prisons are crowded? that our benevolent asylums and madhouses are crammed? that our cities, towns and districts swarm with vice and crime?'. Sharpe was an enthusiastic temperance advocate and he promoted the cause in distant centres like Newcastle and Goulburn. Many churches, Methodist and other, had active Bands of Hope and other temperance organisations. For some, temperance meant moderation, but Rev. Thomas Davies declared that the Primitive Methodist church was a 'total abstinence Church'.[6]

The Wesleyans came more slowly to that position. In 1859, after referring to the 'beastly intemperance, unblushing lewdness and shameless profanity' prevalent in the community, the editor of *The Christian Advocate* called for 'effective legislation to check the prevailing crime of drunkenness'. The Australasian Wesleyan Conference of 1860, in its pastoral letter to members, referred, for the first time, to the 'evils resulting from *ardent spirits*' and urged them to 'exercise caution'. In 1864 the President and Secretary wrote in the Pastoral Letter: 'We ever look on the habits of intemperance as among the greatest obstructions to social progress, one of the most formidable hindrances to the spread of true Godliness, and a destroyer of the happiness of mankind'.

They argued that conversion to Christ was 'the grand remedy for moral evil', but at the same time they welcomed the work of temperance societies, especially among the young people.

The first Australasian Wesleyan General Conference, meeting in 1875, declared that the Methodist church was 'itself a temperance society' and, echoing that phrase, the New South Wales and Queensland Annual Conference of 1878 recognised the work of the various temperance societies, approved the establishment of the Bands of Hope in connection with Sunday schools, and petitioned for the reform of licensing laws. Such steps, taken over two decades, indicate the gradual involvement of Wesleyans in the cause of temperance. Henceforth, all branches of Methodism were at one in advocating temperance education and appropriate legislation to curb intemperance. Methodists were also active in such new organisations as the Good Templars and the Women's Christian Temperance Union.

In 1886 the Wesleyan Conference established a Temperance Committee. Wesleyans and Primitives had temperance meetings in connection with their annual Conferences and one Sunday in the year was designated Temperance Sunday when the cause of temperance was advocated in all church services. Joseph Cook, Primitive Methodist local preacher and member of Parliament, tried to bring a Local Option Bill before parliament in 1896. In the 1901 election, for which the Temperance Alliance selected seventy-one candidates, it was claimed that from 80–90 per cent of Methodist members and adherents had 'voted steadily on Alliance lines', though it is not clear how that was known. In 1902, Methodists vigorously opposed a government proposal to adopt a system of public control of hotels in the Rocks area of Sydney.

While the cause of temperance featured so prominently in the latter part of the nineteenth century that Bollen averred that it was 'the' Protestant reform of the period, it was far from being the only issue of interest to Methodists. In 1899, the Wesleyans indicated the increasing range of their social concerns by changing the name of their Temperance Committee to 'Temperance and Public Morals Committee'. Nevertheless, temperance continued for many years to be a major area of concern for the united Methodist church and was one of the few areas where the church had no doubts that political action was justified. It also helped to give the impression that Methodism was aligned with the conservative political forces rather than with those of Labor because of the latter's equivocal stand on temperance and local option (see below).[7]

Gambling was endemic in the colony from the beginning but, possibly because it was much less extensively and thoroughly organised in the nineteenth century than it was later, it did not draw the constant fire that was directed at the liquor traffic. However, the Methodist bodies consistently opposed all forms of gambling, which they regarded as a pernicious social evil with serious ramifications in the lives of the people, and refused to allow members to participate in any form of gambling, including raffles. Methodists considered it a major weakness in the Roman Catholic church that it used raffles to raise money. In 1899, the Wesleyan Conference declared that gambling was 'immoral' and opposed the introduction of the totalisator on racecourses as 'demoralising to youth, and destructive to the good order of society'. Methodists played their full part in the general Protestant attack on gambling in the early years of the twentieth century.

There was one weakness in this stand: Methodism had a narrow understanding of gambling which failed to take proper account of those forms of gambling confined to the better-off. In mid-century, the Wesleyan Conference condemned business speculation, though without specifically identifying it as gambling, and in the midst of the crash at the end of the century, C.J. Prescott commented cryptically that 'a good deal of the depression . . . was due to the spread of gambling in quarters where few would look for it'. In general, however, Richard Broome's judgement that the clergy failed to appreciate the involvement of gambling in business is soundly based. What is less clear is whether they genuinely did not understand the situation or whether they merely found it impolitic to include the church's wealthier supporters among the gamblers.

James Blanksby was one of the very few who tried to explain the fascination of gambling. He argued that it was caused largely 'by the tyranny of monopoly which [was] widening the breach between the very rich and poor'. No doubt he was right to believe that, in part, the poor gamble in the hope of being delivered from poverty, but his explanation did not offer any understanding of why the rich also gamble, nor did it take into account factors like the desire for excitement to brighten a drab existence which may also have affected the poor.[8]

From the outset Methodists protested against 'Sabbath desecration', or the misuse of Sunday. For them Sunday was 'the Lord's Day', to be kept as a time for public worship and related religious activities and for rest. Methodists were expected to refrain from all sport and work, except that which was absolutely necessary, and this prohibition even included church business meetings (except in those places where members had to travel so far to attend that a mid-week meeting was impractical). Buying and selling was forbidden, except medicine for the sick or necessaries for funerals, as were all pleasure parties and all travel by public transport.

Many Methodists were sabbatarians who believed that the biblical legislation dealing with the Jewish Sabbath in the Ten Commandments was transferred to the Christian Sunday and was binding on everybody and they sought to impose their views on the community by moral suasion and legislation. But many also took this action because they believed it was in the best interests of all members of the community—it gave even the humblest of them an opportunity for rest and refreshment after long hours of toil during the week. Rev. George Woolnough remarked that even if the Sabbath was not divine, it was humane.[9]

Methodists readily united with other Protestant denominations in 1856 to form The Society for Promoting the Observance of the Lord's Day, later revived as The Lord's Day Observance Society. In 1859, they helped form a Council of Churches the primary objectives of which were the promotion of the proper observance of the Lord's Day and opposition to inroads into such observance by sporting bodies, employers, shopkeepers and publicans. As early as 1858, the editor of *The Christian Advocate* expressed opposition to a Bill designed to open hotels from 8.00 p.m. to 10.00 p.m. on Sunday evenings, mainly on the ground that it would be a sin against God who decreed that this should be a holy day kept free from all trade. They opposed the opening of public libraries, museums and galleries and advocated legislative measures to preserve 'the sanctity of the Sabbath'. In 1877 *The*

Weekly Advocate protested against the transport on Sunday of Messrs Bailey, Cooper and Co.'s circus from Sydney to Orange. Even their support for the early closing of shops was, to some extent, prompted by their desire for a proper observance of Sunday. They believed that a Saturday half-holiday would encourage people to participate in worship the following day. The Wesleyan Conference of 1899 urged Methodists to refrain from secular employment on Sunday and to elect men to parliament who would preserve its sacredness and oppose the opening of hotels. Their antipathy towards 'Romanism' and towards the liquor trade, and their sabbatarian attitudes, were inextricably interlinked and mutually reinforcing because the Catholics held much less strict views on each subject than did the Methodists.[10]

Travel by public transport on Sunday was held to be wrong, even to fulfil preaching appointments. In 1859, the Newtown Local Preachers' Meeting requested the Superintendent Minister, Stephen Rabone, to give no more appointments to Ralph Mansfield because he travelled by omnibus to fill them. Rev. J.S. Austin, recalling his own ministry, said that he never travelled by public transport on Sunday, except to take funerals, while the Wesleyan Conference in 1871 expressed disapproval of Sunday travel by public conveyance and urged ministers and people to 'discountenance it'.[11] There was no difference of opinion between the various Methodist groups on this issue.

This strictness affected many seemingly minor aspects of life. John Gale spent a Saturday evening at the home of Thomas Southwell of 'Parkwood', near present-day Canberra, before preaching in the little Methodist chapel nearby on the Sunday morning. At the breakfast table Gale mentioned that he had taken an early morning walk in the garden. 'What! have you been walking in my garden on the Sabbath?' was the stern and unexpected response. 'That's Sabbath-breaking. I allow no one in my garden on Sundays.'[12]

John Waters of Wollongong was employed as an engine-driver on the train which travelled from Mount Kembla to Port Kembla. In October 1888, when the Mount Kembla Coal Company organised a free return trip to Sydney for all its employees to celebrate the opening of the railway line from Sydney to Wollongong, Waters refused to avail himself of the pleasure of a free trip because it occurred on a Sunday.[13] Even in the late nineteenth century it was difficult for these earnest sabbatarians to maintain their more extreme claims. That difficulty increased with the passage of time, as many people sought refreshment not in rest and worship but in the more vigorous outdoor activities to which the environment seemed to call them irresistibly. At the time it did not to occur to Protestant Christians that legislation provided a shaky base in matters of public morals.

In 1886, Wesleyans were encouraged by the Conference Committee for Guarding Our Privileges to oppose the Divorce Extension Bill because it would make divorce easier and destroy 'all sense of the sacredness of the marriage tie'. *The Weekly Advocate*, while acknowledging that there were many situations where there was, for one partner, 'an intolerable burden of an unfaithful or unkind husband or wife', thought that, rather than facilitate escape by divorce, there was need 'to tone up the heart and conscience on the question of marriage', and for Methodist pulpits to speak more clearly on the subject of marriage. The Primitive Methodist, Ninian Melville, claimed that the Bill was a secularist plot. However, the Conferences did not pass any resolutions on the subject. In 1890 when Rev. Hans Mack, a consistent opponent of any extension of the provisions for divorce, attempted to introduce a resolution in the Wesleyan Conference, he was told that the Privileges Committee had considered the question and had encountered such a division of opinion that it had decided to take no action, thus making it appear that at least a significant minority of Wesleyans recognised the difficulty of dealing humanely with so complex a question of personal relations.[14]

Intellectual and emotional issues

The second half of the nineteenth century saw a continuing controversy over the apparent conflict between science and the Bible. For most this meant the 'Genesis versus geology' controversy, though that was not the whole story. After a less liberal beginning, *The Christian Advocate*, and its successors, tended to argue that religion had nothing to fear from science, though it did deplore the attitude of a scientist like Professor Huxley who, it claimed, often wrote as if he had a brief against the churches. It had little patience with those church people who opposed evolution and creation and it argued that 'we should never lose sight of the fact that Evolution is not a cause, but a mode'. Not all Wesleyans took so liberal a view and many letters criticised the journal's stand and those of Christian scientists like Professor Drummond in his book *Ascent of Man.*

The higher criticism, dealing with the origin and character of biblical texts, which caused such a stir in Europe and America in the late nineteenth century, did not greatly trouble New South Wales Methodists much before 1890. After that, however, there was considerable debate which continued well beyond the present period. The debate may have been slow in developing because Wesleyans, ministers and laity, were 'protected' by their relative lack of theological sophistication. In 1895 the retiring Wesleyan President, Rev. J. Spence, lent support to this view by remarking that:

> Fortunately for us as a Church, we have not been much troubled with the speculations of higher criticism. Our labours have been too practical and absorbing, for that which is merely theoretical and speculative. The fact is that we have no time for the discussion of these questions . . .

While the church, before and after the 1902 union, was divided on the issue into modernists and conservatives there was a disinclination to accept any new thinking which could not draw a substantial consensus among the best overseas scholars. Methodists generally seemed to regard the increasing worldliness of members as more potentially damaging than any question relating to biblical scholarship. *The Weekly Advocate* argued that nothing, not even the Bible, must be put before Christ: 'He is the one great centre of our faith'. Thus, more than anything else, the most basic teaching of Methodism, the theology of experience and of 'the warmed heart', protected it against such intellectual controversies.[15]

The least attractive feature of nineteenth century Methodism was its militant anti-Romanism. The connexional paper regularly carried articles which, in the context of the times, were not seen as mere criticism of fellow Christians but, rather, as part of an attempt to overpower one of Satan's instruments for the destruction of souls. *The Christian Advocate* summed it up neatly in 1860:

> We believe that Popery is the greatest evil, as well as social and religious enemy of mankind, that the world has ever seen, and that it is so because it is a *false religion*—a huge and complicated system of blasphemy and superstition.

Catholics were seen as 'famous for immorality and crime' and the poverty which many experienced elicited no sympathy as it sprang from the idleness and low moral life which their religion bred. Most damning of all was their disloyalty to Queen and Empire.

Protestants who gave any comfort to Popery were roundly condemned, as Rev. A.J. Webb, minister at Bathurst, and William Kelk, one of his leading laymen, found when they visited St Stanislaus College for no more evil purpose than to view an exhibition of x-ray equipment. Scientific enlightenment bought at the expense of enhancing the position of Romanists was had too dearly. In 1900, when the Governor attended the dedication of St Mary's Cathedral and remained there during attacks on Protestantism, there was a huge demonstration in the Town Hall by Protestants and *The Methodist* devoted three pages and three columns of its next issue to an account of the demonstration and to criticism of the Governor.

There were many causes for this bitter sectarianism, and it must be remembered that the Catholics gave as good as they got; the blame did not all lie on one side. One major cause of tension was the Catholic position on education which opened that church to the charge that it was 'political' in nature. Methodists also perceived Catholics to be erroneous in doctrine, given to actual idolatry and eager to dominate the colony. Worse, the two churches were not only rivals for the hearts and minds of the people but lived in different moral worlds, for (as we have noted) the Catholics refused to support the Protestants in their efforts to protect Sunday, enforce total abstinence and oppose gambling. Indeed, many Catholics were involved in the drink traffic and the Roman Catholic church itself profited from certain forms of gambling. There seemed to be no common ground on which they could meet and coexist.[16]

So much was loyalty to the Empire an article of faith that Rev. E.J. Rodd (an Englishman) had no difficulty in demonstrating from the New Testament that such loyalty was the near ally of religion. God was the source of civil authority and, because of this, the Christian must be more loyal to his country than his fellows. Respect for, and obedience to, the national constitution was the foundation of good order and stable government. However, the Christian's obedience should not be blind and he should not submit to proven wrongs but should be prepared to advocate change where it was necessary, though presumably without compromising his basic loyalty.

The British Empire deserved the Christian's loyalty because it was the champion and promoter of the Christian religion. When the Boer War broke out Conference expressed its loyalty to the throne and person of Her Majesty and its confidence in her advisers; it approved the steps taken by the government of New South Wales and 'devoutly recognise[d] the hand of God in ordering events in connection with the war, so as to consolidate the Empire and deepen in the national mind a sense of dependence upon God . . .'. The 'arrogance' and 'ambition' of the Boers had caused a devastating war which Britain had tried to avoid.[17] Such unquestioning loyalty to Empire and ready acceptance of such a morally dubious war might be presumed to indicate Methodism's complete acceptance of the necessity of war, but this was not altogether true. After the Franco–Prussian War of 1870–71, *The Christian Advocate* drew the conclusion that providence may bring good out of evil but that force alone could never make a nation enduring. Civilisation and culture alone were unable to put an end to the world's woes; only Christianity could terminate war.

While it later argued that war was sometimes unavoidable, a regrettable necessity, and that in the existing state of human affairs defence preparation was necessary, *The Christian Advocate* commended the aims of the Peace Society and supported the concept of disarmament and the settlement of international disputes by arbitration, admitting that:

> Very likely it will be said that any great reduction in national armaments would involve the reconstruction of European society. It is highly probable that it would, but the voluntary

reconstruction of Europe on a peace basis would be an advantage to the whole world.

In 1895, Conference expressed 'profound regret' over the Sino–Japanese War and hoped the time would soon come when disputes could be settled by arbitration. Two years later it issued its first ever 'peace resolution':

> That this Conference desires to record its sorrow at the attitude of Christian nations armed for the destruction of their enemies and believes that a National [sic, International] Court of Arbitration would best adjudicate on matters of dispute.

Conference continued to argue for this development throughout the Boer War while *The Methodist* turned jingo and informed its readers that 'war has been one of the greatest civilising agencies in the progress of the human race' and that the courage of our soldiers should inspire the 'soldiers of the Cross'.[18]

Racial, social, industrial and political issues

In 1868, John Sharpe argued that it was the duty of ministers to try to direct public opinion on all matters of interest to their fellow men. Many of the interests he had in mind related to personal moral issues—such as drunkenness, dishonesty, hypocrisy—which his Wesleyan colleagues would have endorsed fully, but he also had other, wider, concerns which included the welfare of Aboriginals and the abolition of capital punishment. Concerning the latter he said that the existing law was not good for it did not reform the criminal, protect society, or prevent crime 'but was evil always and altogether evil'.

Sharpe was not the first Methodist to speak out on behalf of the Aboriginals. From the time of Samuel Leigh onward, Methodists were solicitous for their welfare and anxious to protect them from the baleful influence of European society. In the 1830s Joseph Orton was trenchant in his criticism of the white man's ill-treatment of them.[19]

However, from 1851 racism became evident in the community in a virulent form. The discovery of gold brought thousands of Chinese to the colonies and their presence, together with the prospect of the continued influx of coloured immigrants, kindled racist attitudes in the white community which sometimes resulted in acts of violence against the Chinese. In 1878, a petition with 15 000 signatures favouring the limitation of Chinese immigration was presented to the Legislative Assembly. *The Weekly Advocate* regarded this as a legitimate act but did not believe that the 'people of a professedly Christian country' were entitled either to act violently against those Chinese already present in the country or to attempt to drive them out. Thus the Wesleyan connexional paper opposed cheap Chinese labour which adversely affected the employment of others and was also opposed to a 'Mongolian flood' of migrants, but it did not support either the expulsion of Chinese or the curtailment of all such immigration. It favoured the migration of whole Chinese families. It called on Christians to love foreigners, to show genuine charity, and to share the Gospel with them. This call bore fruit a few years later when a Chinese catechist, Rev. J. Tear Tack, was appointed to exercise a ministry among the Chinese population in Tingha and Inverell from 1884–1896. In the latter year, he was transferred first to Darwin and then to Cairns to exercise a similar ministry.[20]

In 1888, *The Weekly Advocate* took a more definite stand against Chinese immigration, stating that the continent must be preserved from 'the evils that would assuredly result from the free immigration of Mongolians—the conflicts of different civilisations, races, and religions'. Not all Methodists adopted this attitude, however. After the Legislative Council had passed a Bill (1897) to exclude coloured races, the Governor refused to sign it, considering the Bill to be anti-British. Supporting his stand Josiah Parker, a well-known Methodist local preacher, raised two objections to the Bill—one civil, the other moral and religious. The British nation comprised many races whose rights must not be taken away. The Bill would also hinder Christian missions. By the time the Commonwealth passed its *Immigration Restriction Act* in 1901 (the so-called 'White Australia Act'), there seemed to be little to choose between the view of *The Methodist* and that prevalent in the community at large. The connexional journal shared a conservative fear of possible damage to both 'imperial interests and obligations' and to the economy if white men were forced to work in industries for which they were not suited. It had a vague but undefined concern for 'international amity and brotherhood', but it shared the widely felt desire to preserve 'racial purity' and protect 'the morality of the people'. It saw little need to discuss the question at length.[21]

Methodism had few answers to offer to the problems raised by the changing social and industrial conditions of the second half of the nineteenth century. It was true, of course, that in England some Methodists were involved in the early stages of union development and that the famous Tolpuddle Martyrs were a group of Methodists who linked England and Australia in the industrial struggle. Within New South Wales, as elsewhere, industrialisation crowded workers together in cities and workplaces in a manner inimical to their physical and psychological well-being. It robbed them of their traditional skills, their sense of creativity and their satisfaction. Those who lived in slums and tenements and who worked long hours in insanitary factories found little enough cause to praise their Maker, especially as the immature capitalism of the day was unable to protect them against the rigours of 'boom' and 'bust' in the industrial cycle.

As in England, many Methodists, especially the Primitives, were actively involved in trade unions, seeking a reduction in the long hours of employment and an amelioration of wretched working conditions. Prominent among such men were John Dixon and James Fletcher on the northern coalfields, Joseph Cook on the western coalfields, and John H. Cann and Josiah Thomas in the Broken Hill district. In 1898 and 1899, some Methodist ministers supported those advocating the early closing of shops, in which some employees were working 70–80 hours a week. *The Methodist*, in several issues, offered strong support for the Early Closing Movement, arguing that 'It is the duty of the Church to go on crying against oppression and injustice. It is not right that human beings should be kept behind counters to late hours, to the detriment of their health'.[22]

Ultimately, the creation of unions led to serious conflict between capital and labour, and the Wesleyan journal, *The Weekly Advocate*, was usually to be found on the side of the former. In the very early 1880s, for example, during the serious strife on the Newcastle coalfields, it opposed the selfishness of the owners' cartel called the Vend, but condemned the miners' strike because it hurt the community at large. It held precisely the same attitude regarding the wharf labourers' strike of 1882.[23] The industrial strife of the last decade of the century severely tested the church's attitude to the workers. In 1890, the editor of *The Weekly Advocate*, Rev. Paul Clipsham, apportioned blame for industrial turmoil between employer and employee, stating that the causes of such disruption were 'about equally attributable to the inconsiderateness and greed of employers, and to the envy and aggressiveness of employees'. The community was the loser in strikes and he accused the unions of using 'tyranny'. Taken as a whole, his editorial leant heavily against the working man and his equal apportionment of blame to both parties seemed to be little more than a not particularly skilful attempt to avoid accusations of unfairness. Other ministers, Rainsford Bavin and Henry Wiles among them, made it clear that their sympathies were not with the workers. It was a considerable step forward in 1897 when Rutledge and Stephen spoke in support of the right of the men at the Lucknow gold mine to strike against injustice because there was no effective system of arbitration.[24]

The financial crash, depression and consequent suffering of the 1890s also found Methodism inadequately prepared. It was true that there was general agreement that the victims of these disasters must be assisted as individuals by individual Christians. However, the Pastoral Address from the 1892 Conference asked sententiously, 'Have not commercial disasters, sickness and death followed because sin preceded?', while the President, Charles Stead, wrote to the leader of the Unemployed Deputation to Conference that while it regretted the distress caused to deserving families, it could do no more. Individual ministers would try to provide whatever relief they could to those who approached them. It seemed not to matter that those who sinned and those who suffered where often not the same people. The dominant individualistic, pietistic theology of the day could go no further. In 1894, Rev. M. Maddern asked Conference to affirm its belief 'that it is the mission of Christianity concurrently to promote the material and spiritual interests of the people . . . and [remove] the preventable ill-conditions of life', but all it was prepared to do was to affirm its 'unabated sympathy' with the poor and needy and pledge itself to render whatever personal assistance it could.[25] Throughout this difficult period, then, the Wesleyan church continued along its individualistic and unsatisfactory way, though some—like Maddern—were beginning to realise what Ninian Melville, Alfred Edden and Rev. John Foggon had known for many years, that a church which had no answers to the physical and social needs of the people accomplished little.[26] A different response was, of course, being offered by the Sydney Central Methodist Mission, and that will be discussed later.

Some Methodists, mainly Primitives, who had been active in the trade unions also saw the need for the direct representation of the working class in parliament and when the Labor Party was born in the early 1890s a number of its members were Methodists. Several were local preachers, including Joseph Cook, Alfred Edden, John H. Cann, John G. Gough, J.L. Fegan, Jacob Garrard, Josiah Thomas and George W. Smailes. *The Freeman's Journal* exaggerated provocatively when it said in 1896 that 'The Labor Party is largely composed of pulpit-punchers and local preachers', but the statement did point up the significant role of Methodists in the new party. Methodism also sent into the Legislative Council such men as James Blanksby and William Robson. Their hope was to enshrine in legislation Christian principles, particularly those of the Sermon on the Mount, and Blanksby campaigned directly on the 'gospel of social reform'. Even *The Methodist* expected its constituency to send such men of 'conscience, integrity and honour' to parliament in the place of the 'dishonest, immoral, and unworthy'.[27]

Some Wesleyan ministers publicly championed the principles for which the Labor Party stood, among them W. Hessel Hall, Woolls Rutledge and P.J. Stephen. Others contended that politics should not be brought into the pulpit. *The Weekly Advocate* had, in 1890, been critical of the Christian socialists whom it dubbed 'political and religious faddists' with their 'loose preaching of brotherly love and a sort of Christian communism'. Rev. William Clarke took the same stance in his opposition to those whom he called 'preaching demagogues'. Defending the right of ministers to address themselves to the economic and political issues of the day, Rutledge accused Clarke of failing to distinguish between politics and party politics. The editor of *The Methodist* contended that a minister's duty was 'to preach the Gospel to all, and not to entangle himself with party politics', but he was prepared to make exceptions on the questions of legislation relating to 'the Sabbath and the abolition of the drink traffic' and later pontificated that 'It [was] right for ministers to be active fighting for righteousness and temperance, but not on political subjects which are matters of opinion and not of conscience'. Yet some Methodists contended that these so-called 'matters of opinion' were also 'matters of conscience' and that in pursuing them they were 'fighting for righteousness'.[28]

By the first decade of the twentieth century, there was a noticeable change in the policies of the Labor Party which led to the disenchantment of many Methodist supporters who concluded that the majority in the party were anti-Christian. Methodists ceased to support the Labor Party for many reasons. In 1894, Joseph Cook refused to pledge himself to support decisions arrived at in caucus but continued to serve in parliament for many years in association with more conservative parties. Many withdrew support because of the perceived growing influence of Roman Catholics and because of its equivocal stand on temperance issues, particularly the local option. This disquiet was expressed by *The Methodist*: 'In so far as [the Labor Party] has allied itself with Romanism and Drinkdom . . . it has become a menace to pure government and the general good'. [29]

Methodist Labor members resented such opposition to their party. J.L. Fegan and James Blanksby in 1904 complained of discrimination against it by the Australian Protestant Defence Association (with which some Methodists were associated). In 1907, Frederick Flowers, who claimed that until the last few elections his own denomination 'had done much for the masses', said:

> . . . he was sorry to see a number of ministers attached to the Methodist Church who had been urging the Reform Association to do as it liked . . . one could come to no other conclusion but that the Reform [Liberal] Party had captured the Methodist Church in the same way it had captured the so-called Temperance Alliance.

The Methodist issued 'a most emphatic and unqualified denial'. Despite such protests, many Methodists in 1906 found the 'combination of Labour, Liquor and Romanism' unacceptable. One year later, the terrible threesome had become the fearsome foursome in the Labor Party of 'Rum, Romanism, Socialism and Gambling', against which they felt compelled to wage unremitting warfare. Because of this perception, Methodists turned against Labor in increasing numbers.[30]

This deep division was also manifested in their varying attitudes to 'Christian socialism'. The phrase was ill-defined but many agreed with the British Wesleyan minister, S.E. Keeble, that 'a purified socialism is simply an industriously applied Christianity'. Many Primitive Methodists, acutely aware that much was amiss in industrial and social relations, shared 'a divine discontent' (the words are those of Rev. Theophilus Parr) and advocated Christian socialism. To James Blanksby, 'The greatest problem of the day was the equitable distribution of the wealth which was produced. The question was not how to relieve poverty, but how to do away with it'. Rev. John Metcalfe said that 'Christianity and socialism both condemn the present social order, and both look forward to brighter and better conditions for the great mass of the world'. He urged Christians to work for the removal of grievances and the establishment of just laws.[31]

Most Methodists believed that a prerequisite for a Christian society was the regeneration of individual men and women. Metcalfe saw the difference between Christianity and socialism at this point: socialism placed the emphasis on environment but the Christian emphasis was on character. A change of character would soon express itself in changed surroundings. The more conservative Wesleyans wrote disdainfully about 'the sort of communism when everybody is to have everything at the expense of nobody'. One of these conservative Wesleyans, Rev. Richard Sellors, deplored that 'development of the democratic spirit' in the Primitive Methodist church which led numbers of their ministers and laymen to seek to enter parliament with the express purpose of effecting change. But, as James Blanksby pointed out, they did it because 'human law must be made harmonious with Divine law, the laws of the Sermon on the Mount'.[32]

Not all Wesleyans opposed socialism. Rev. Paul Clipsham said that, in its best sense, socialism was 'a war against classes and class distinction', and was 'the very spirit of Christianity', though two years later he took a different line and argued that the claimed socialist incident in Acts, chapter 4, should not mislead the church as it was without divine sanction, did not last long, and was never repeated.[33] Division was also experienced over a further specific aspect of this general question. In 1890 Henry George, the American champion of the 'single tax' visited the colony and a number of Methodists accepted and proclaimed his teachings. Indeed, in 1882, long before the arrival of George, the Wesleyan minister in Singleton, Rev. James Woolnough, preached a sermon dealing with the land question, using the story of Joseph's administration in Egypt as the basis of his message. He prefaced his sermon by saying that he was mindful that this was a religious service and not a political meeting. He believed the pulpit to be 'one of the most powerful educators of the public mind', and he felt responsible to God and the community to undertake to speak on the subject he had chosen.[34]

When the Henry George [Birth] Centenary celebrations were held in 1904, Rev. W.W. Rutledge, ex-President of the Methodist church, preached on 'The Bible and Land Tenure'. This produced an animated debate in the Parramatta synod which, almost to a man, condemned the introduction of politics into the pulpit. The debate was taken up in other synods, in the correspondence columns of *The Methodist* and in the 1905 Conference, where it raged for seven hours. Conference decided that 'indulgence in party politics was disastrous for the peace of the Church' but it agreed to sweep the problem under the carpet, withdrawing all charges and obliterating all minutes. Believing that this would end strife, members of Conference 'heartily sang the Doxology'.[35]

The first Methodists in New South Wales had readily adhered to the Missionary Committee's injunction against involvement in political parties and social disputes. Many of a conservative outlook, especially Wesleyans, continued to follow their practice in succeeding generations. Others, especially Primitives, whose tradition favoured involvement, took the view that loyalty to Christ's Gospel required a different stand. Conditions and circumstances at the turn of the century forced these differences into the open and generated conflict within the church. Methodists would continue to be divided by such issues, but actual conflict would only be occasional, not endemic.

Social outreach: the central missions

Once the Industrial Revolution produced the new phenomenon of the industrial city, that locale provided the Protestant Christian churches of many lands with their main threat and their major missionary challenge. As the city proper was taken over by factories, warehouses, bond stores and the like, the middle-class proprietors of businesses withdrew to the suburbs to live. Only the working classes remained in the inner city, living in buildings which had been subdivided to gain a better return and which became more crowded, noisome and slum-like each year. Unless the churches were to retreat from the cities, admitting their incapacity to deal with the major problems of the day and the irrelevance of Christ to the most vital growing points of modern civilisation, it was imperative that they find an answer to this challenge. In the United States, the Social Gospel theology and the institutional church were developed to tackle such problems; British Wesleyan Methodism developed the concept of the Central Methodist Mission as the favoured form of urban ministry.

In Australia the British approach was adopted and, in 1884, Rev. W.G. Taylor inaugurated the Sydney Central Methodist Mission in faithful but unacknowledged imitation of his friend, Charles Garrett of Liverpool. This form of urban ministry was developed particularly strongly and successfully in the Australian environment and some attention must be given to the evolution of this concept in the period before World War I.[36]

'Old York Street', the 'cathedral church' of Sydney Methodism, went into an irreversible decline in the early 1870s and, although several experiments were tried, nothing could counterbalance the inexorable demographic change which was robbing the church of the good middle-class people who had previously formed its backbone. The question of the sale of the premises was taken to the 1884 Wesleyan Conference and this course would have been adopted but for the intervention of an elderly supernumerary, Rev. George Hurst, who appealed successfully for an evangelistic solution to York Street's problem.

When Conference appointed William George Taylor, a minister with a reputation for ardent and successful evangelism, it was seeking a conservative solution to its problem: it simply hoped that he could win enough people from the surrounding streets to enable the church to pay its way once more. There is no evidence that Conference was looking for a more radical solution or even that it expected the conservative one to succeed. Taylor understood this and his initial plan was for a well-organised evangelistic mission. His services were advertised by distributing handbills in the boarding-houses which crowded his district and in the ships which visited the port. The only new feature for Sydney was a regular street corner ministry which eventually had the assistance of a brass band. Early success strengthened him in this approach and led him to do everything possible to prepare his team of helpers for their work both spiritually and mentally. During his first appointment to York Street Taylor did not stray far beyond the usual nineteenth century church structures and organisations except for the introduction, at the Princes Street church, of free mid-week social evenings to compete with the hotels and billiard saloons.

At the end of 1886 the York Street building had to be closed so that it could be demolished and replaced by the larger Centenary Hall. Taylor himself took a year off to recover his health, which had suffered considerably, and went to England to study the work being done there in the mission-type ministries. When the Centenary Hall opened there were many who did not want to reappoint Taylor to the church and who were even more unwilling to declare it formally as a connexional mission. Nor were all attracted to the new ideas which Taylor had gathered in England and which would turn York Street into a genuinely different enterprise. They could see no need for 'spiritual novelties' and considered that the usual Methodist circuit approach was adequate to deal with the needs of the working class.

It has been argued that the ministry of the Methodist central missions in Australia was built around six concepts, each of which was present from the beginning. These concepts have been defined as: the centrality of worship and the sacraments; the idea of the 'servant church', with the worshipping congregation at the heart of a group of service agencies; the church as a community and fellowship centre for people on a seven-day-a-week basis; the importance of using the mass media to make contact with the people outside the church; the involvement of the church in the debate on social issues with the intention of fashioning a Christian conscience in the community; and, finally and most importantly, the centrality of a vigorous evangelism.[37] The identification of these principal concepts is undoubtedly correct, but the suggestion that all were equally present from the beginning greatly underplays the potential of the central mission ministry for growth and development. It would be more correct to say that the first, second and sixth concepts were fully developed from the beginning of the Sydney Central Methodist Mission, the third developed there rapidly but the fourth and fifth were virtually unknown until much later. The pattern of development was sometimes different elsewhere in Australia. This notion of evolutionary development, which accepts the role of human agency and of circumstance as well as the will of God, poses no theological problems and answers more historical questions than the view that all six concepts were present from the beginning.

The role of circumstance in the development of the Central Methodist Mission is indicated by the early stress placed on its mission to seamen which had its own separate agent and hall. This work had important social and philanthropic commitments as well as its evangelistic aspect and the emphasis put on it was not surprising since Taylor claimed that Sydney was visited by 45 000 seamen each year, of whom 30 000 were English, many with Wesleyan parents.

The central mission opened an evangelists' institute to prepare young men to become candidates for the Methodist ministry and to give them experience in visitation and street preaching. There was a considerable volume of general philanthropic work and the inception of the order known as 'sisters of the people' contributed to both the evangelistic and service ideals, since the sisters became heavily involved in the children's home (Dalmar), the homes for 'fallen and friendless women' and the Medical Retreat which sought, with some success for a time, to save men and women who had become dependent on alcohol. A boys' club and, briefly, a workingman's club were attempts to contribute to the fellowship concept, though they were only very temporarily successful. The Pleasant Sunday Afternoon (PSA) movement was partly educational and partly recreational. From an early date, the

Mission had its own periodical, *Our Weekly Greeting*, to spread its message. Any expenses in relation to this not met by advertising were paid by Hon. Ebenezer Vickery, the mission's most prominent early supporter.

The move in 1908 to occupy the old Lyceum Theatre premises in Pitt Street gave the Sydney Central Mission the physical facilities to expand its work on all fronts and by the time of Taylor's retirement in 1913, Methodism in Sydney no longer had a void at its heart. Indeed its city ministry had become a vital part of its ministry throughout New South Wales, though there continued to be some who preferred the concept of a solid middle class (and probably much less successful) 'cathedral church', on the model of Old York Street instead of the vigorous assault on sin, suffering and secularism that was carried on at the Lyceum.

The Lyceum was not the sole home of the Methodist city ministry, however. Once the Sydney Central Mission had passed the experimental stage it was natural that the concept should spread. The Balmain Quarterly Meeting of 4 October 1889 requested Conference to create a mission there. Since it was estimated that some two-thirds of the 27 000 persons then living in the area never attended any form of religious worship it seemed an ideal area in which to try the newer methods. P.J. Stephen was made Superintendent Minister of the new Montague Street mission in 1890, though it remained a part of the old Balmain circuit until 1893. Stephen, with the energetic support of a devoted lay leader, W. Druce, quickly over-filled the old church and had to shift to the Town Hall where his evening congregation reached 850. When the local government authorities doubled the rent, the Wesleyans bought a disused skating rink and converted it into a mission hall, thus providing more adequately for their other activities as well as the Sunday evening service. Balmain rapidly developed the usual religious, social and philanthropic services and ran its own paper, though its most interesting activity was probably its Wednesday lunchtime open-air service at Mort's Dock. This was said to be responsible for the high proportion of men attending the Sunday services.

The Helping Hand Mission at Rozelle, which developed as a direct result of the United Tent Mission in the area in 1902, later became a regular central mission. 1906 saw the additional development of a mission at Leichhardt, again inaugurated by P.J. Stephen. Each of these missions had a hard time in a hostile environment and though each did good work in terms of both religious and philanthropic effort, neither added anything import-ant to the central mission concept.[38]

From 1904, the Bourke Street church, which for thirty years had been one of the strongest centres of Methodism in Sydney, began to move towards de facto mission status as it introduced first a mid-week 'people's entertainment' for the poor and also a Benevolent Society managed by the church ladies. The formal change of status did not occur until 1911. This mission introduced the idea of after-church film services in the new Olympia Theatre. These often attracted as many as 1250 people but broke down because the supply of religious films was inadequate at the time. Just before the Great War a free kindergarten was introduced which was popular with parents in the area.

A further mission was formed in the South Sydney district at a huge camp meeting in Redfern Park on 21 April 1907. This involved the amalgamation of the former Wesley church, Hay Street, Pyrmont, Mount Lachlan and Cleveland Street circuits, each of which was suffering from the usual effects of the changing nature of the population in the area. The continued existence of seven churches, all with small congregations, caused a dissipation of energies and serious financial problems which would only be overcome with the consolidation of the mission work on a centrally located property beyond the period currently under discussion.[39]

The development of the central mission style of ministry was ad hoc and unplanned, but it need not have been so. In mid-1897 Rev. J. Woodhouse suggested that the circuit system had broken down in Sydney and in other great cities and that Methodism must move away from it and its cherished itinerancy in the city. He suggested a great Metropolitan Mission in imitation of the policy pursued in Manchester and sought to include York Street and Balmain missions along with the William Street, Bourke Street, Cleveland Street and Chippendale circuits, and any others which might be considered advisable.

The 1898 Conference set up a committee to study the urban problem and to suggest a solution. This body prepared a scheme for the District synods and eventually for the 1899 Conference which was superficially very like that proposed by Woodhouse. It sought to amalgamate six circuits for 'mission' purposes (philanthropic activity, evangelism, the training and employment of evangelists and sisters) while leaving them separate for ordinary 'circuit' purposes, administrative and financial as well as spiritual. The scheme was accepted by Conference with one alteration of substance: whereas the Committee had proposed that if the Metropolitan Mission failed for any reason, its assets would pass to the York Street central mission, Conference determined that both assets and liabilities would be passed on. In the view of the York Street mission, the scheme which it had once regarded as 'inspired' had been rendered totally unacceptable by this change, though it seemed logical enough to many. Without York Street there could be no worthwhile Metropolitan Mission and no action ensued.[40] In fact, the Committee's final proposal was too administratively complex: there had to be either a total amalgamation or none at all. But the breakdown was unfortunate because the Sydney problem would not mend of its own accord and Methodism never solved it completely.

The second city in New South Wales, Newcastle, also had its urban problem and it is necessary to see what happened there. In 1863, the Wesleyans built a church in Tyrrell Street on high ground overlooking town and harbour. Probably the Wesleyan love of 'respectability' made them build above the town and among the wealthier sections of the community. But the location was remote from the common people and inaccessible to all but the physically fit. Work among the sailors and the non-attenders at church fell by default to the Primitives who were better located in Brown Street. Methodism as a whole seems to have reached its zenith in Newcastle city around 1880 and then to have followed the population into the suburbs mirroring events in Sydney on a smaller scale.

Union in 1902 brought a strong 'forward movement' in the second city. Part of that movement was the decision to create a central mission in the city by the amalgamation of the Tyrrell and Brown Street congregations and the building of new premises in King Street right behind the shops and wharves and down on the flat where it was easily accessible. Rainsford Bavin, a prominent evangelical who had spent three years as superintendent of the Sydney Central Mission was sent to plan for and inaugurate the Newcastle mission. Despite a serious cost escalation which created a millstone for the young mission, the new building, constructed in the elegant 'federation' style of the day, opened on Sunday 24 January 1904. It boasted a central hall seating 1200, a Dorcas room, a basement gymnasium of massive proportions, a lecture hall seating 1000, together with the necessary offices, committee rooms, a waiting room and quarters for a house-keeper.[41]

The luckless Newcastle Central Mission lost two superintendents by death before the Great War (Bavin in 1905 and W.F. Oakes in 1913) and was plagued by the large and growing debt with which it began. There were, however, three characteristic aspects of its work which deserve some attention: the seamen's mission, the Door of Hope Rescue Home, and the work among men. It was argued that the large number of sailors visiting the port made each of the first two institutions necessary. Surprisingly for a church where the need for a seamen's missionary had been recognised for thirty-five years, there was no quick move to appoint one and this important work was carried on by ad hoc methods until early 1909 when H.D. Gilbert, already well-known for his work in Sydney and elsewhere, was appointed to the task. This led to an immediate improvement in all aspects of the work, including the number of sailors being converted during their stay in the port.[42]

Mrs Bavin suggested the introduction of rescue work not long before the death of her husband and remained long enough after that to see it under way. The work was then undertaken by a mission sister and was initially under the control of a Ladies Committee. By the latter part of 1907 the Door of Hope Rescue Home, as it was called, was in difficulty and the Ladies Committee was anxious for the mission General Committee to take over its management. Problems of management, of finding an efficient matron who would remain in the work, and of meeting the changing government requirements for such institutions, continued to plague the Home and while rescue work at Newcastle was done in love and kindness, it experienced so many unresolved difficulties before the war that it cannot be considered to have been a success.[43]

Two aspects of the work for men may be dealt with briefly. Lunch-time factory meetings were held regularly at Arnott's biscuit factory, Davies' sweets factory, Morison and Bearby's and at the railway and Dyke workshops and these provided an important contact between the employees and the central mission. The Downeys, an evangelistic father and daughter pairing, did good work at these places during their extended mission in Newcastle in 1909, though no one was so beloved by the workers as Rev. R.C. Oakley in the period immediately preceding the Great War.

The Newcastle Central Mission began its first Men's Brotherhood in mid-1906 during the superintendency of Rev. Frank Duesbury. At least initially, this seems to have been effective, but it must have failed later as a new start was made in mid-1912 by Rev. W.F. Oakes with a fellowship breakfast at 9.00 a.m. Sunday. This grew rapidly and little more than a year later, on special occasions, the attendance sometimes reached 200. No one was barred, not even atheists or agnostics. Apart from the monthly Sunday session, there were associated clubs and the men were involved in practical work for the mission. For many years it remained one of the central mission's most effective organs and a vital part of the outreach to men in what was essentially 'a man's town'.[44]

By the outbreak of the Great War in 1914, the central mission concept was well-established in New South Wales and was certainly the favoured form of Methodist urban ministry. It was more capable of reaching the unchurched urban masses than any other form of ministry offered by that church, though it was still heavily dependent on the interest and goodwill of the middle class. In Newcastle, the mission tended to rob the suburban churches to the benefit of its own evening congregation, but in Sydney that characteristic was less obvious though it undoubtedly existed. The situation was necessarily different with the Sydney inner suburban missions. But central missions were far from a complete answer and Methodism was not taking either Sydney or Newcastle by storm. Each of the missions provided an 'ambulance' ministry, picking up the wrecks of broken humanity at the foot of the cliff and trying to help them piece their lives back together. No one in the missions sought to remake society so that it would break fewer people, nor would any attempt this much harder task for many years to come.

Evangelism

For the first sixty years of its independent existence, Wesleyan Methodism in New South Wales never doubted that its primary task was evangelism. It was an aggressive evangelistic agency pursuing religious revival, (which it understood to include the strengthening of the saints as well as the winning of sinners) with a constancy and a determination difficult to comprehend a century later. In its view political science and human philanthropy were of limited usefulness in the world, the religion of Christ alone could eliminate the moral evils so prevalent in a community adrift from God:

> This [S]ociety proposes to apply the sovereign remedy, and to seek the regeneration of society by securing the spiritual salvation of individual men . . . the corruptions of communities are the result of individual depravity; and hence the way to improve society is to make men good.[45]

The connexional paper regularly reported evangelistic effort wherever it occurred, rejoicing in every sign of revival and lamenting when progress seemed slow. Methodists everywhere, clergy and laity alike, prayed, preached and worked for revival. Itinerant evangelists were assisted and local evangelists encouraged, though the level of enthusiasm varied with time and place. There was no great revival but there were three occasions when substantial renewal occurred and it was legitimate to believe that a major breakthrough was near. These and other occasions must be investigated more closely.

In 1858 and early 1859 there were notable revivals in both the United States and Britain as well as 'gracious awakenings' in Victoria, Tasmania and South Australia. New South Wales hoped that it too might share in the blessings so freely given elsewhere and sought to stimulate revival. There was no general breakthrough though there were significant local revivals in Windsor–

Richmond, under Rev. Charles Creed, and West Maitland, under Rev. John Watsford. In the former the revival occurred during the second half of 1860 and large numbers of converts were gathered into the class meeting for nurture. At West Maitland the revival period was much shorter, from late September to late October. More than one hundred professed conversion. There was no general flow on from these successes and *The Christian Advocate* wondered whether economic depression in New South Wales had hindered revival, though earlier it had seemed to doubt whether the church in the colony was really ready for it.[46]

The first significant renewal occurred in June 1864 when the Rev. William ('California') Taylor, a tall, bearded, handsome American with a fine voice, came to Sydney to raise money to pay off a debt on his Methodist mission in San Francisco. The visit became a triumphal procession of evangelistic witness across the suburbs and countryside of New South Wales. Professions of conversion were counted by the hundred. Joseph Oram, newly arrived at Newtown when Taylor swept in to claim 132 conversions, was convinced that the effects of the visit continued throughout the remainder of his three-year pastorate in the area, though membership figures for the period do not support his view strongly. Even Newcastle, more spiritually depressed than usual because a hurricane had extensively damaged its newly built chapel, was excited and uplifted by the vibrant American. More than one hundred were converted, new classes were formed and an 'earnest spirit' pervaded the Society. So it was everywhere he went.

Taylor's second visit at the end of the 1860s was equally successful but reference to one locality will suffice to illustrate the lasting effects of his work. At Orange, membership, including members on trial, leapt from 179 to 295 as a result of his visit (mid–1869) and continued to grow thereafter to a peak of 336 in October 1870. Three years after the visit membership was still 282, or 103 above the pre-visit level. Further growth cannot be attributed to Taylor but, in sharp contrast with the all-to-frequent consequences of superficial evangelistic campaigns, Orange did not experience a temporary gain followed by a rapid decline back to or below the original level. Other evidence for the lasting nature of his work can be found in the number of his converts who became local preachers and ministers. Australia-wide the membership of the Wesleyan church leapt by 21 000 (net) over the seven years covered by Taylor's two visits and, with some justification, he has been linked with John Watsford and W.G. Taylor as one of the greatest evangelists to work in Australia in the nineteenth century. No one at the time described his work as a general revival. Yet, in the multiple senses that it brought many into the church and that it gave new life and purpose to the church itself, it certainly was. The only serious limitation was that there was a tendency for the ministers of churches other than the Methodist to stand aside, though their congregations often benefited from his work.[47]

Subsequent years brought a string of travelling missioners from the United States and Britain, but none had more than a passing influence. More important were the scattered local revivals which occurred in the period 1877–80 mainly in the Illawarra and South Coast, spreading to the southern suburbs. Only in 1879–80 did the movement affect the north or west to any extent. But this proved to be a false dawn and New South Wales had to wait until the early 1890s for a taste of something approaching real revival. But one local effort, at West Maitland in 1880 under Charles Olden, does illustrate well the pattern of such evangelism.

The campaign was carefully planned by the minister and leaders and began with an attempt to quicken the spiritual life of the Church before going outside. As part of this, 'an unbroken concert of prayer' was developed. When all was deemed ready the special services began in Largs, the place thought most likely to crack, and continued in a planned fashion around the circuit. Ultimately over 160 'sought mercy' and of these only about twenty were thought to be 'doubtful cases'. New classes were formed to train the influx of new Christians.[48]

The year 1892 must have seemed like the *annus mirabilis* for which Methodists had so long hoped and prayed. The first report of revival appeared in *The Methodist* on 23 January that year. Such a thing was almost unheard of as revival campaigns usually began in mid-year to avoid major church festivals and the turn of the Methodist year at the beginning of April with its consequent removals of ministers from circuit to circuit. Such timing also avoided the heat of mid-summer and the harvest in rural areas.

But in January 1892, Rev. J. Gardiner of the Ashfield circuit had reaped a harvest of another sort at his Lewisham church, especially among the young people. Sisters Francis, Fuller and Thompson did likewise in the Auburn–Rookwood area, then the spark leaped to Manly where three women and two laymen had good success at a camp meeting. Revival then spread apparently at random around most parts of the colony, slowing in 1893 but not dying down until close to the end of that year. *The Methodist* was ecstatic, declaring that there were strong indications of 'a flood in the tides of spiritual life' in the colony and that it was close to a great and widespread revival because 'By hundreds, church members and penitent sinners have crowded the communion rails in search of pardon and purity'.

The only common thread running through these various movements was that, with very rare exceptions, they were all local efforts, the result of local prayer and of preaching by the circuit minister and the local preachers. Often revival was not even the result of special services but, rather, the regular services or the annual camp meeting were the occasion for unusual results.

People both inside and outside the church frequently ask whether the effects of evangelism are enduring. Although a legitimate question, it is often incapable of being answered. We have already seen that converts endured at Orange after 1869 and it would prove so again in the suburbs in the 1890s. Seven years after the events of 1892, a member of the Balmain circuit indicated that a group of young men from the Darling Street church, who had been converted in the 1892 revival, had been brought together by the minister and a layman to work for the church and Sunday school. They had also decided to meet together regularly for praise and prayer. That was still happening and resulted regularly in further conversions. They, and a young woman converted at the same time, continued to be active in Christian Endeavour work, Sunday school teaching, open-air preaching and prayer meeting work.

Undoubtedly the Balmain group, and most of the other converts, were won from among the young people within or on the fringes of the church—from the older Sunday school classes or the youth groups—a fact which would help to explain the outstanding success in retaining and using these young people

122

on a permanent basis. That does not detract from the success of the work, since it was and is a part of the evangelical faith that no one is born a Christian and that all must be converted.[49]

It was another decade before anything happened to equal or surpass the events of 1892. The wanderers from overseas continued to come, the Rev. Thomas Cook experiencing considerable success. Limited local revivals continued to occur, such as that at White Rock, 10 km from Bathurst. This meeting was more emotional than most Wesleyan revivals by the end of the century and had 'big farmers weeping like children and calling to God for mercy. Young fellows, hitherto utterly godless, boldly coming out to the penitent form to plead for salvation'. There were fifty-seven converts in the tiny district, and hardly a family without at least one. The church was totally revitalised and had to be enlarged.

Late in 1901 the combined evangelical churches held a Simultaneous Mission in forty to fifty locations around Sydney, many of them in tents. This proved an enormous success with 4500 enquirers and the churches were ecstatic. The Wesleyans were already planning a campaign of their own on the South Coast in 1902, in connection with their Century Commemoration Fund, with the aim of winning 50 000 souls as well as raising 50 000 guineas for church work—this was now extended to include the whole State and was to be financed by Hon. Ebenezer Vickery. It also became a joint campaign by the evangelical churches, though it always looked more like a Methodist campaign with assistance from the Salvation Army and Congregationalists wherever they existed. The Presbyterians often assisted while the Anglicans did so occasionally. In Newcastle, the United Tent Mission, as it was called, really became an extension of wonderful celebrations for Methodist union at the beginning of 1902. Novocastrian Methodists had very properly decided that, the inevitable tea meetings aside, there was no better way to celebrate union than in evangelism.

The Tent Missions, which extended from January 1902 until March 1904, were a truly State-wide event and it would be tedious to enumerate them. The number of places visited in the campaign, some of which were very tiny, was amazing. The larger localities were usually allocated a mission of eight to ten days duration and some areas were visited more than once. Much of the time, five tents were used, each with an evangelist, one or two assistants and sometimes a tent manager. The two main clergy associated with the work were Revs Robert Robertson and Dan O'Donnell. H.D. Gilbert of the central mission, A.E. Walker, at the beginning of a long and able evangelistic career, and lay evangelist J. Allison were involved throughout while others assisted from time to time. In April 1903, it was reported that 122 campaigns had been conducted and 17 374 converts had been registered. Broome claims a final figure of 25 000 converts, but does not support it.

A mission was only allocated to a locality if adequate physical arrangements were guaranteed, prayer preparation undertaken, the town canvassed at least twice beforehand, adequate advertisement undertaken and counselling assistance provided at the meetings. Nothing was left to chance and the organisation must have been an education for those used to muddling along more in hope than in confidence. In return, clear guidance was offered from the central administration.

The most successful missions were those on the South Coast, the North Coast and in the Balmain–Waterloo district of Sydney. There were 2735 enquirers at the various Illawarra missions, but better accounts exist of the work in the other areas. In Lismore–Clunes, formal preparation began in June 1902. Cottage prayer meetings were held in three or four centres and weekly united services allowed Christians of various denominations to get to know each other better. There was an 'abundant' response to a call for visitors and it was clear that revival was underway in the hearts of members long before the preparation concluded. Both homes and places of employment were visited. Local preachers began evangelistic work in the out-churches with good success before the mission proper and there was an air of high expectancy by the time the mission began on 31 August. Early morning prayer meetings were conducted throughout. Attendances varied from 800–1350, with people travelling from Casino, Coraki and Woodburn. More than 600 converts were claimed, many from outside the church.

A preliminary skirmish in Balmain led to the conclusion that an extraordinary effort was required there. On 26 April 1903 there began something more like a military operation than a mission in the intensity of its planning. Two large tents were used and twenty open-air preachers occupied four selected locations each night within a mile of the tents which were erected at 'Devil's Corner', where the 'wicked elements' congregated in numbers. Meetings suffered dislocation and the ropes of tents were cut, but a flock of 450 was won from the anti-Christian mass and when the tents moved on Vickery kept it together in a building until a mission hall could be planned and built in Evans Street Balmain West. This became known as the Helping Hand Mission.

The co-operative nature of the tent missions was important, even if the Methodists did bear a disproportionate share of the work. The intensity of the planning, the combination of active local participation with the interest aroused by an outside speaker, and the use of a novel and neutral setting all helped. Never before, nor probably since, has there been so successful an evangelistic campaign in terms of number of enquirers, while coverage of the State was unequalled in pre-radio days. As usual, most enquirers were previously unconverted persons from within the church, though Broome suggests that about 1000 persons a year over the average sought membership of the Methodist church at this time so the impact outside must have been considerable.[50]

There were no more major movements before the 1914 war. Foreign evangelists continued to find the ready assistance of the Methodist church and local effort continued to a degree, but the environment seemed to be less friendly to evangelism. *The Methodist* thought that this was largely because the church was out of step with the democratic temper of the times and too little interested in the problems of ordinary folk, despite the fact that the Gospel had always stood for popular rights. Surprisingly, the most successful field for evangelism over the next few years was the South Maitland coalfield, where Sister Francis began work at Kurri in 1906 which spread through Weston and Pelaw Main, a new church having to be built at the latter place.[51]

Part 3

A boiling pot and a rod of almond

5

Challenge of a changing world

New South Wales Methodism was about to enter the twentieth century and be subjected to intense and constant tests of which it had no previous experience. The war of 1914–18 was itself a boiling cauldron but in its wake there came other powerful challenges, including class-based industrial strife and a new and extensive community cynicism about a world which seemed to be getting out of all control. The Depression tested the church's resources further and led to the even deeper probing of World War II. While the church was trying to meet these extraordinary challenges, it also had to carry on its every day tasks: spreading scriptural holiness across the land by evangelism; extending the physical and other facilities of worship into outback areas and the newly developing suburbs; providing fellowship for its adherents and training the young; and continuing to fight the traditional moral battles relating to temperance, gambling and Sunday observance. The years 1914–45 were a time of unremitting contention. Yet, as in Jeremiah's scriptural metaphor so in the reality of New South Wales, the warning of the 'boiling pot' was balanced by the almond branch of hope, in this case the infant ecumenical movement.

The Great War

In 1911, when the Australian government acted to enforce the compulsory military training of boys and young men it aroused some opposition within the Methodist church. *Glad Tidings* led that opposition, declaring that the nations were arming themselves in 'heathenish' fashion and that Australia was needlessly following suit. The Christian churches must raise a united voice against the 'lust for war' and must try to abolish conscription because camp life would have an unwholesome effect on the moral life of young men. Rev. F.W. Walker believed that the effects of military power were 'continually evil and invariably pernicious' and asked the church whether it could believe 'that it is part of the Divine plan that the human race should only develop the virtues attaching to discipline, and should only become bodily fit by cultivating arts and practices entirely different from those taught by the Prince of Peace'?

Conference itself came close to performing a remarkable act. The elderly and highly respected W.H. Beale moved a motion expressing 'grave and emphatic disapproval' of the compulsory clauses of the *Defence Act* on the grounds that 'If they were to interfere with the character and conscience of their youth there would be nothing worth defending'. Seconded by the equally respected W.G. Taylor, a firm supporter of Empire and loyalty, the motion was lost only on the casting vote of the President, Rev. J.E. Carruthers. Convention justified his vote but, as we shall see later, there can be no doubt that it also expressed Carruthers's personal convictions.[1]

But the limited debates of 1911 and 1913 in no way prepared the Methodist church for the coming war. It had no theology of war and peace and, for the most part, neither clergy nor people had thought deeply about the relation of the Gospel to international affairs. Nor was a church which was only slowly emerging from the intensely individualistic religion of an earlier day well-placed to take so large an intellectual step. All it had was a resolution, passed at the 1914 Conference, which committed Methodists both to defend the Empire and to pray that the time would come speedily when 'nations shall learn war no more'. In any case, New South Wales Methodists, like their fellow citizens of all faiths, were imperialists to the core and unlikely to do other than support Britain in its hour of need. Loyalty came naturally to them, at least partly because of the perceived link between Empire and Gospel referred to in the last chapter.

Yet it seemed necessary to the preachers to buttress their support for the war by spiritualising it and arguing that God permitted it as an opportunity to redeem national life and restore it to a higher plane. War came because man rejected God by being indifferent to the development of the military spirit, by sabbath-breaking and other sinful acts; through it God might bring man to see the error of his ways, though he should not have needed the lesson.[2]

In January 1915 *Northern Light*, published monthly by the Newcastle Central Mission, described the war as a struggle between civilisation and Christianity on the one hand and 'a barbarism unsurpassed in the worst records of the past' on the other. A month later it reported Rev. W.A. Murray as saying from the Newcastle mission pulpit that 'we are fighting the most spiritual conflict we were ever engaged in' and, later, the central mission superintendent, Rev. S.V. Cock (later Cocks), described the war as 'a crusade' with every soldier 'pledged to all that is right and true'. So belligerent was the *Northern Light* that when its comments on the good character of the Australian troops were belied almost immediately by their serious misconduct in Egypt, it did not even pause to blush. The Merewether Quarterly Meeting of July 1915 expressed its 'utmost pleasure' that the Australian soldiers had proved themselves to be 'British fighters, of the most approved Bull-dog breed'. Later, Cock expressed disquiet that the people at home had not returned to God in penitence as had been expected, but his shallow theology could offer no answer to this dilemma. Early in 1916, despite its origins in possibly the most unionised city in New South Wales, *Northern Light,* running true to form in its comments on a strike, declared itself 'not interested' in the justice of the men's claims because of the 'larger issues' at stake. Men who put their own interests before the nation's in an hour of dire peril were traitors.

Conference 1915 accepted that the Empire and its allies had been 'forced' into this 'dreadful war', pledged its 'unswerving' and, perhaps, unthinking loyalty, admired the courage and patriotism of the volunteers and expressed 'its abhorrence of the anti-Christian teaching of much of the modern philosophy which

[had] contributed to the creating of the spirit which has found expression in the present war'. Rev. G.C. Percival at Drummoyne believed the war had struck a death blow 'to the old, long-persistent fallacy of materialism' and brought people's attention back to 'the inner and spiritual realities'. Japan had allied itself with Great Britain because it recognised the latter's 'soul' and Russia had 'found impetus' by discovering the spiritual principles which motivated Great Britain!

In June 1915 *Northern Light* offered the first public Methodist advocacy of conscription after which there was little opposition. J.E. Carruthers, editor of *The Methodist*, saw it as comparable with compulsory taxation and vaccination, though he did allow for conscientious objection. Few did so publicly, though at least one young man lacked the assurance of the editors and sought spiritual guidance from the President because he was troubled that it was 'in opposition to the law of Love when our great nation was spending millions of money in [sic] men-of-war'. His letter concluded sadly, 'The Germans are wrong we know, but I am afraid we are wrong too'.[3]

One Methodist minister was not content to follow the official pro-war line. At Hay, B. Linden Webb expounded a different and more costly view. From January to March 1915, he preached three pacifist sermons at monthly intervals and later published them as a pamphlet entitled *The Religious Significance of the War*. Webb was concerned not with the legitimacy of any particular war but with the moral quality of all war. He began from John 18:36, 'My kingdom is not of this world', and argued the complete separation of the 'Kingdom of Christ' from the 'kingdoms of this world' in bases, ideals and methods. The underlying principles of these kingdoms were fundamentally different and mutually exclusive; humans had to make their choice between them, they could not accept both. As a consequence of this, war could not, as so many argued, bring spiritual improvement for it made devils rather than saints and 'gave the lie' to the concept of universal love. Germany was the aggressor in the existing conflict, but the 'relative justice' of one cause over the other was not the question, rather, whether 'as a Christian Church we should advocate or discountenance participation in the warfare of the "kingdoms of this world"'. Already there were signs that the

Rev. Samuel Leigh: first Wesleyan missionary
to NSW (by courtesy, Mitchell Library)

'The Sparrow', Bankstown: an early rural Methodist Church (by courtesy,
Uniting Church Archives)

Rev. William B. Boyce: organiser of Wesleyan Methodism in NSW (from Colwell, *Illustrated History of Methodism*)

George Everingham, first Australian-born local preacher (from Colwell, *Illustrated History of Methodism*)

John Sharpe: prominent early
Primitive Methodism minister (from
Kendall, *History of the Primitive
Methodist Church*)

Central Mission Sisters of the people, ca. 1905 (from CMM Annual
Report, 1905)

Waverley Church: Bondi Junction (from *Jubilee Souvenir*, 1859–1909)

Rockdale Sunday School: Primary Department at work ca. 1905 (from Jones, *An Australian Sunday School At Work*)

Rev. W. H. Jones: long-serving
Home Mission Secretary (from
The Methodist)

'On the road': Rev. G. A. Bailey on outback mission work, 1919–20
(from Home Mission Report, 1919–20)

Rev. John W. Burton: overseas missionary, Mission Secretary and President-General (from *The Methodist*)

Rev. F. T. Walker: founder, The Men's Own Movement (CMM Annual Report, 1916)

Crusader Movement: first youth camp, 1929 (from Hyde, *Lo Here is Fellowship* by permission Board of Education, UCA (NSW Synod))

Alan Walker preaching at the First National Youth Convention, 1955 (courtesy Alan Walker)

'A new beginning': Inaugural Assembly, Uniting Church in Australia, 22 June 1977 (by courtesy, Uniting Church Archives)

'jarring discord' between Christianity and war was causing a loss of faith to many. The answer was not easy, but God had already given us a 'sufficient revelation' in Jesus and Christians must be absolutely true to Him.

Webb's sermons aroused considerable comment, though most of it was of a lamentably low calibre. Reviewers of his pamphlet in *The Methodist* and *Glad Tidings* simply did not understand his message. The latter paper decided that 'Neither the law of Sinai nor the teachings of the Sermon on the Mount [overrode] the law of self-preservation'. Christ's injunction, 'Resist not evil', meant that in dealing with selfish or brutal men we should allow our patience to be strained to the limit before striking back—no more. Carruthers, soon to become President-General of the Methodist Church of Australasia, exhibited a level of expediency and an inclination to discount the meaning of the Sermon on the Mount which his readers should have found hard to accept. Only two ministers wrote in support of Webb and neither was prepared to give his name. Webb received a better hearing at Hay where his church officers, with a single exception, stood by him loyally whether they agreed with his views or not.[4]

In the conscription debate, again it was only Linden Webb who was prepared to pay the price for supporting a principle. There was a poignant correspondence between him and the President, Rev. William Pearson. Webb was anxious to learn the church's position on the moral issues involved in conscription. Pearson could see none and, thinking the subject merely political, advised his younger colleague to keep away from it. In any case the people preferred to hear about something other than the war when in church. Eventually Webb, who felt his position on 'the moral implications of Christian doctrine' was greatly at variance with that of the church, sought resignation but, under advice, accepted the designation 'without pastoral charge' for a year or two. Ultimately he returned to the active ministry though ill-health marred his later service.[5]

An interesting theological question was raised during the war over the salvation of unconverted soldiers. The doctrine of salvation by faith, as usually understood, implied that they remained unsaved, but many who supported the war naturally wished to be convinced that God would make a special case for them. A contributed article in *The Methodist* argued that even those who died guilty of the 'paramount vices of the age' (drinking, swearing and gambling) would find salvation because the love which had led them to give their lives for their weaker brethren would be 'counted to them as righteousness'. Carruthers remained silent on the issue but *Glad Tidings* was not prepared to stand the doctrine of salvation by faith on its head. It thought that mercy might be extended to those who would have been converted in the ordinary course of their lives had not battle intervened, though even that posed a theological problem, but their patriotic services would not save those who were merely godless and careless.[6]

The Church was involved in many important practical issues during the war years. Having spiritualised the struggle into a crusade against barbarism, materialism and paganism, and having determined that the war presented a great opportunity for the spiritual reformation of the nation, nothing could be permitted to detract from that end. The God who overruled man's destiny and who had allowed the war for divine purposes might delay victory until the nation had indeed undergone a moral reformation. For this reason, it objected that alcohol, whether in the local training camps or overseas, was likely to lead both to the moral degradation of the new crusaders and the reduction of their military efficiency. Both Conference and *The Methodist* opposed 'wet' canteens from the start and gave enthusiastic support to every sign of 'voluntary prohibition' from overseas, as when the King, Cabinet and Commander-in-Chief became abstainers for the duration. At home the best that could be hoped for was the early closing of hotels and Methodists supported that campaign eagerly and successfully, occasionally attacking the Holman Government along the way for its apparent subservience to liquor interests and its unwillingness to bear the responsibility for acting against them.

The Church had other responsibilities towards the soldiers. It had to provide chaplains to encourage them in right living, to convert them before they went to meet the foe and to comfort them when confronted by death. It had to pray for them and for the Empire's cause and Conference enjoined its people to stop where they were at twelve each day to do this. Special services had to be held to dedicate honour boards and to remember the dead. Worst of all, the ministers had the dread task of delivering the bad news of the loss of loved ones and of consoling their families. This was a heavy load to bear and one which made it difficult for ministers to carry out their normal pastoral role.

The Newcastle Central Mission gave its Seamen's Institute as a club room for soldiers, though it did retain a voice in the management of the room. The 1915 Conference sent Rev. E.M. Boyer, a probationer, as the first full-time chaplain of any denomination to the Liverpool camp. As men began to return, a Sydney committee was empowered to help them find employment and the Manly circuit became involved in voluntary work in the Frenchs Forest area in connection with the settlement of such men, including the provision of Methodist services.

Whatever extra duties it performed because of the war, the church still had to carry out its normal duties and had do so with reduced resources. The ministers, probationers and students who went as chaplains or ordinary soldiers reduced the ranks of the ministry and presidents found it difficult to meet pastoral needs and had to remind intending volunteers that there was important work to be done at home. Younger ministers were often under pressure to prove their support for the war in a practical way. While giving was generally well-maintained, there were limits to what people could provide at a time when heavy patriotic demands were being made.[7]

The hopes which had been held in 1914 for a war-led revival of religion were not realised. Before the armistice it was realised that war had 'disturbed and weakened religious life instead of helping it'. The faith of many had grown weaker and that of others had been destroyed altogether; church was less well attended, Sunday less honoured and the Bible less diligently read. War had brutalised the world. When peace finally came, the Methodist church offered to God its hymns of praise and prayers of thanksgiving though it was not clear that either nation or Church 'deserved' peace since no spiritual regeneration had occurred. Even the soldiers, who, it had been said, were attracted by the doctrine of the cross, were not coming to the churches which had been so loyal to the things for which they had suffered.

In August 1922 an unnamed contributor to *The Methodist* drew the conclusion that the war had been 'the greatest set-back Christianity ha[d] experienced since its inception'. It had handicapped missions and impeded the brotherhood of man. War was unchristian and unromantic and could be tolerated no longer. There must now be a Christian crusade for a warless world.[8] Instead, the church set about erecting an appropriate memorial. Under the guidance of its President, former Chaplain-Colonel (he loved the title and the uniform) James Green, the 1919 Conference decided on a hospital, though others would have preferred something less utilitarian. It was appropriate enough, more appropriate than much that the church had done during the war. The Vickery family, long among Methodism's chief benefactors in the State, gave their mansion 'Edina' at Waverley and a considerable area of land with it. Under Green's leadership, an appeal was launched for a further £25 000. Yet, despite his considerable authority, it was slow to achieve success. One section of the hospital was opened in 1921 and the whole project in November 1922, but in early 1924 the fund total was stalled at only £21 333. This was not a great achievement for a church which had waged war so enthusiastically.[9]

Evangelism

Evangelism had been the 'glowing heart' of Methodism in nineteenth century New South Wales, but the years 1914–45 provided a more difficult environment. A different approach resulted from the 1909 Chapman–Alexander mission which led the Methodist church to establish a League of Prayer and Service throughout the State to pray and work for the success of further evangelistic effort and to appoint a connexional committee charged with the promotion of evangelism. This Committee was empowered to appoint connexional evangelists and to engage other agents who might be available from time to time. In a sense the scheme was a revival and enlargement of one which had operated briefly during 1885—87 when Conference itself had appointed a connexional evangelist. In effect, this development marked a break in the church's approach to evangelism.

The original intention of the Evangelistic Committee, as it became known, was to engage the famous English evangelist,

Gypsy Smith, and to ask the central mission to release W.G. Taylor for a time. This made little sense as Smith was hardly likely to be available for a long-term appointment and Taylor was no longer young and would have found constant missioning 'on the road' a considerable strain. Nor could he be spared from the central mission, which was still consolidating its own position in its new Pitt Street location. A much younger man, Rev. A.E. Walker, already experienced through his two-year involvement in the Tent Mission, offered himself. Before his candidature for the ministry Walker had been a central mission evangelist and was well-known to Taylor who probably encouraged his young friend to volunteer.

Walker began in 1910 without even a guarantee of his expenses being met. His work was undoubtedly successful spiritually but struggled financially, depending heavily on the generosity of members of the Committee. According to Taylor it also suffered because circuits did not organise properly: there was little advertising and few preparatory meetings because the minister and circuit officials were indifferent to the work. This led Taylor to claim, exaggerating a little, that the Methodist church had ceased to be evangelistic in action though it still professed an evangelical theology. He thought that 'Our Church is gradually becoming highly "respectable" and self-satisfied, and conventional and cold'. In 1912, the Committee added a second evangelist, Sister Francis, who had gained wide experience at the central mission, in New York and in the Welsh Revival. In 1913, Walker returned to circuit duties as a consequence of the serious illness of his wife and was succeeded by Raymond Preston, a layman who had been a connexional evangelist in England for several years.

Preston continued Walker's work under difficult conditions and was later ordained by the New South Wales Conference. In the decade 1913–22, he conducted 183 missions around New South Wales. Often the work was made needlessly hard because circuits would not plan ahead and Preston could not group missions but had to waste time and energy in unnecessary travel. It was still difficult to persuade circuits to prepare thoroughly for the missions though experience taught that this was essential for success. The Committee considered it necessary to 'preach up' the mission and pray for it in services for at least a month beforehand. A week of special prayer meetings should also be held and there must be adequate local advertisement.

Preston was an outstanding missioner. The number of his converts was moderate rather than large, but his work lasted. By 1923, eighteen of his converts had entered the ministry and more would do so later thus providing the best possible assurance of the quality of his work. His successor from 1928, when he retired from the position, was Rev. R. O'D. Finigan, a more emotional preacher who exhibited a more shallow theology. Finigan won more converts but relatively few of them 'were added to the visible Church' and it was hard to assess the meaning of the experience to them.

The work of the church's Evangelistic Committee and the connexional evangelist may be seen as an attempt to bring to the work of evangelism the advantages of the connexional system: the combination of central policy direction and financial assistance with local initiative. But Taylor's criticism had substance and the setting apart of a Conference Evangelist did reflect the decreased likelihood that each circuit minister would see evangelism as his own proper work and that of his local preachers. Central planning may also have tended to stifle local initiative. The experience of the evangelists seemed to confirm the view that people saw the work of the evangelists as a substitute for their own local activity.

Sometimes, however, the church could still prove that it had a wonderful talent for winning people to its Lord. So it was in the tiny settlement of Lawrence on the Middle Clarence in 1914 when, after some influence from a Preston mission in neighbouring Brushgrove, the work of the lay evangelistic team of a Mr Downey and his daughter caused witnesses to claim exultantly that 'Public houses and billiard rooms have been deserted for the mission . . . The whole town has been religiously awakened'. As one amazed young man commented, 'Everybody speaks to everybody at Lawrence now, and everyone has a smile and a handshake for everyone there'. Newly converted people busily organised their own services and class and prayer meetings. Most of the converts came from right outside the church and even included 'a sly-grog manufacturer, a pugilist, several confirmed drunkards, and many blatant infidels'.[10]

In 1929 New South Wales was visited by a young English

evangelist, Rev. Norman Dunning, as part of an Australia-wide tour. Dunning conducted seven missions in New South Wales between mid-January and the end of April, the final Sydney mission being a Simultaneous Mission involving many of the suburbs, about eighty ministers and a substantial lunchtime witness in the city. While the Simultaneous Mission claimed 711 converts, most from within the church, the campaign generally was not regarded as successful. Ministers thought Dunning's message was directed too closely to church folk while the missioner was disappointed by a lack of support from the Conference hierarchy. But Dunning was important as the first prominent evangelist to make much use of the social Gospel in his work.[11]

Problems with the Conference evangelist system, and the fact that Methodism was not growing at a rate commensurate with the population, led the Evangelistic Committee to plan major state-wide campaigns, first in 1934 and, when that achieved only very limited success, a second in 1935. In general, these failed: less than half the circuits held missions in either year and preparation was often inadequate. It was as if the Methodist church no longer knew how to conduct a successful evangelistic campaign on a large scale. That problem in itself, as well as the church's tradition, led to a further decision to celebrate the bicentenary of Wesley's conversion (1938) with another State-wide crusade. To sharpen the focus and give greater coherence to the organisation, the Conference chose A.E. Walker, by far its most experienced evangelist, to lead the campaign. He was not expected to carry the whole burden but would conduct missions in strategic centres, whence, it was hoped, influence would radiate out to surrounding circuits. A panel of about twenty ministers was chosen to assist elsewhere.

Although central planning began six months in advance and circuits were given clear instructions about preparing for local missions, three weeks before the opening the President was alarmed because more than one hundred circuits had still to respond to a questionnaire sent seven weeks earlier to identify their need for campaign literature and other help. He had even met one suburban circuit steward who was 'utterly ignorant' about the whole crusade! The opening in the Sydney Town Hall, however, was crowded and regarded as an outstanding success.

Many of the missions around the State conducted by Walker himself were well-received. A non-Methodist from Kurri, Rev. C.M. Elliss, thought the message appropriate and well-presented, with a strong emphasis on essentials. Yet, at the end, while Walker felt that there was great cause for gratitude, he did not think that the mission had made vital contact with the outsider; conversions had come largely from those already within the church's influence. Despite the direction given, inadequate preparation had still been a problem in many circuits where people expected results without effort.[12]

The striking fact in this period is the apparent unwillingness or inability of many ministers to conduct their own missions, with or without the aid of their local preachers. In part this was due to a weakness in their training, for they were not trained to be evangelists, and the consequence was that, unlike his nineteenth century forebear, the Methodist minister was now more likely to see himself as pastor than evangelist. Yet, as *The Methodist* argued, if the local minister did not evangelise his own circuit, no one else could do it for him.[13]

Local preachers continued in their prominent role within the Methodist church and conducted the greater number of services in rural circuits, though they were used to a lesser extent in the cities. Their impact was reduced as they were no longer involved in the pioneering exploits of the nineteenth century and there was no opportunity for the development of a Tom Brown or a Silas Gill. Yet men like A.J. McCoy at both Orange and Wollongong, J. Stringfellow (Parramatta and a variety of other places for more than fifty years) served their church well. None did more than David Doust who served for seventy-seven years and who, when two days short of his century, assisted in a service in the Bellingen church. He had taken 2500 services in his time. As with the clergy, so with the locals, the fires of evangelism burned lower than in earlier years despite, or because of, their better organisation and education.[14]

In July 1920, a group of Methodist laymen (J.W. Kitto, W.A.F. Waitt, W. Arnott, E.R. Turner and A.L. Lonsdale) formed the Methodist Men's Federation (MMF) which met every Thursday night for a quarter century. Numbers varied from as high as sixty in the early days to about twelve during World War II. The

MMF was the last link in a capital city chain of identical organisations. The Federation brought together spiritually-minded men in a context very like the old Methodist class meeting for prayer, hymn singing, testimony and very rich fellowship. It also provided an opportunity for evangelistic service. Carefully selected and prepared bands were sent into suburban or near country circuits to conduct missions. During the first year of its existence, the Federation conducted sixteen such missions, about one every three weeks, but this work was given up in later years because the men were all so busy in their own churches. These Federation missions were always more successful at securing re-dedications than new commitments and most of the latter were among senior Sunday school scholars.[15]

The decline in evangelistic fervour was also reflected in the level of interest in overseas missions. It was true that there was expansion on the existing fields and that the missions were generally much better at making new Christians than was the home church, but there was no increase in the number of fields and the mission report for 1921 commented that mission work:

> . . . is usually considered a laudable object, but it is so far from the track of ordinary Church life that only the few realise the scale and sweep of its activity. There is no thought of urgency. The Church at Home, through her concentration on things near at hand, is in danger of losing her vision.

It might have made the same comment in any and every one of the following twenty-four years.

Income held up reasonably well though giving in New South Wales was probably a lower proportion of total Australian giving than might have been expected and that during a period of a steadily increasing accumulated deficit. The deficit of the 1920s was finally obliterated during the 1930s when heavy retrenchment was forced upon the church and, during the war, when activity was necessarily restricted, a reserve was built up to prepare for the expected demands of post-war reconstruction. These were expected to be very high, for the rapid advance of the Japanese forces in the Pacific area had devastated the mission stations, especially in Papua and New Guinea, the Solomons and New Britain. Whole staffs, European and native, were presumed captured, though no one really knew. The projected reconstruction would have to be carried through in greatly changed circumstances.[16]

The Women's Auxiliary to Overseas Missions contributed strongly to the establishment of the George Brown Memorial Home for training mission sisters (which opened in 1920) and undertook to support a number of sisters in the field. Branches corresponded with particular sisters with whom they had links and often engaged them as speakers when they were at home on furlough. Apart from that, it provided substantial prayer support and disseminated information broadly through the 122 branches and 160 affiliated Ladies' Church Aids which existed by 1942. During the Depression, its financial support may have been crucial. However, the Laymen's Missionary Movement, established by the 1917 Conference in imitation of the Victorian church where such an organisation had existed helpfully for several years, appears to have been an almost total failure.[17]

Although some Methodists were still practising the old evangelism, or something very like it, with decreasing success, many were content to leave it to the specialist. Others were concerned to improve this situation in the future. They knew that in Britain there was a growing sensitivity to the limitations of the older methods of evangelism and a recognition that salvation concerned the community as well as the individual. Evangelism could occur through the witness of the Christian community in its worship, family life and social activities, though they took little comfort from that fact in view of the relatively low state of spiritual life within the church.

From 1936 there was limited discussion about how best to revive the work of making Christians. Change was in the air. James Green, by then a supernumerary, thought that the traditional evangelism would no longer draw the outsider but that a message relevant to the needs of the day would. Rev. R.N. Grout was of the same mind. The young Alan Walker saw the point of this, lamenting the contradiction that while the church had talked of brotherhood the pitiless competition of modern capitalism had grown up, and the 'White Australia Policy' had remained untouched. During the war, Rev. P.L. Black urged the church to make good use of radio, especially with Christian drama. Films also had their place in the evangelistic process. A.E. Walker, from a lifetime's experience, argued for the creation of 'cells of evangelism' within congregations and circuits to educate their members and to pray together. The understanding and closeness to God that this would develop would lead eventually to soul-winning. Such thinking gave some ground for the optimism that Methodism might yet recover its old genius.[18]

Church extension

If the Methodists of New South Wales no longer dreamed, as W.B. Boyce once had, of 'carrying the colony', they still yearned to 'cover' it. In the period 1914–45 the most interesting and romantic aspect of this desire was the creation of the three inland missions. These involved the aggregation of several former circuits into one large mission area under the pastoral care of a team comprising an ordained Superintendent Minister and several probationers. These mission areas involved the young ministers in exploits which were sometimes dangerous and always exhausting as they rode unreliable, belt-driven motor cycles across country alternately drought-ridden and flood-bound on unmade roads, where the highway was often only distinguishable by the line of discarded petrol cans.

Not all members of Conference favoured the inland mission policy. Some asked what advantage there was in the projected change. It did not increase the manpower in any of the areas, at least in the early years, and there was no change in the capacity of the local people to give to the work of the church. The policy seemed to them to involve no more than a new style of administration, the consolidation of an enormous area likely to prove difficult to oversee and operate. In fact the advantages were real. The mission system brought to the outback experienced Superintendent Ministers. Previously the circuits making up the Far West and North-west missions had been worked by probationers of little experience and, often, little training. Far from the benevolent reach of the Chairman of the District, they had to rely entirely on their own judgement and had no senior brother to turn to for guidance or encouragement. Under the new system help was closer at hand and more regularly available and the sense of spiritual isolation was reduced. Equally important, an ordained superintendent remained in a circuit for from three to five years, a probationer only one or two. Consequently, the new system brought a greater continuity of policy, a greater chance that something, once started, would be finished.

The inland missions, operating under the aegis of the Home Mission Department, could and did appeal for financial assistance throughout the whole State. Had they remained a part of the circuit system, they would not have been permitted to appeal beyond their own boundaries. This was important in areas where the population was scattered and often poor because of the effects of drought on settlers just getting started on their properties. The extra finance meant that there was provision for motor vehicles— at first mainly motor cycles were used but later, when it was realised that bikes were too hard physically on young preachers in territory where roads were virtually non-existent, cars were made available. The vast distances, the summer heat, and the need to balance the requirements of the 'dispersion' against those of the base towns, all contributed to making motorised transport the *sine qua non* of effective outback work.

Of course, motor vehicles posed their own problems. Few men knew how to drive and when posted to the missions they needed a 'crash' course in both driving and mechanics. As time went by this was done more adequately and the problems abated considerably. The establishment of a sinking fund of several thousand dollars, the interest from which could be used for mechanical repairs and the replacement of vehicles as the harsh country destroyed them very quickly, was no less essential and was available only to the Home Mission Department.

Not all of the questioning and opposition in Conference reflected genuine doubt about the value of the mission system: some was the consequence of stubborn conservatism which thought the circuit system best in all circumstances and some sprang from envy of the right of the missions to seek financial help outside their own boundaries.[19]

All three missions were the lineal descendants of the ill-fated Gospel Car Mission of 1899–1902 which proved that a preacher with a roving commission and a supply of books and tracts was an asset in the back country. But it had also proved that, given the nature of the Australian climate, a horse was not an appropriate source of power.

Discussions held over more than a year led to a decision at the 1914 Conference to send out a probationer, Rev. H.S. Doust, to be a 'prospector', unhampered by circuit boundaries, looking for Methodist families and establishing preaching places wherever appropriate. The real centre for his work was the area bounded by Wagga, West Wyalong, Griffith and Corowa and on the outskirts of a number of Riverina circuits, but he also visited such distant places as Deniliquin, Hay and Hillston and held services among the men working on the Wyalong to Lake Cargelligo railway. This was his beat for two years, after which he handed over his Hudson motor cycle to Rev. A.T. Newton having covered over 32 000 km, all on unsealed roads.

Proof of the success of the work is to be found in the gradual absorption into regular circuits of the country first opened up, and the consequent movement of the main centre of mission further north and west until its base was at Lake Cargelligo and its area of coverage the territory bounded by Cargelligo, Hillston, Goolgowi and West Wyalong. As sheep stations were broken up for wheat farms and the railway line was pushed through, two, or sometimes three, men were there to look after the spiritual interests of those lonely people. It was a proud Methodist boast that there was no other 'ecclesiastical building' within 50 km of their church at Weethalle![20]

As a result of the success of the Riverina Mission, the 1916 Conference sent its active and imaginative Home Mission Secretary, Rev. W.H. Jones, through its Western District and he, with Rev. A. Graham, Chairman of the District, and Rev. C.P. Walkden-Brown of Orange, devised a scheme for a Far West Mission incorporating Cobar, Nyngan, Wilcannia, Bourke, Canbelego, Nymagee and Brewarrina, with Cobar as its headquarters. This began in 1917 with a married minister as superintendent, two probationers and two home missionaries. The superintendent, Rev. G.R. Holland, had a car and the others had motor cycles.

The Far West Mission began in the midst of the terrible drought which gripped the west for three years from 1917 and was justifiably proud that it had been able to maintain its incipient witness in the Wilcannia area while other churches felt compelled to withdraw their men until the return of better times. Together, the group patrolled a territory larger than England and Wales and covered almost 130 000 km in the first six months by which time Holland, himself a tireless traveller, thought that the difficulties of negotiating the almost trackless country had largely lost their terrors. After his term as superintendent, Holland was succeeded by Doust whose most important achievement was probably the establishment of the correspondence Sunday school to assist those settlers in far distant places who felt unable to give their children an adequate religious training. He also reported occasional acts of brotherly assistance between himself and Catholic settlers, refreshing after the sectarianism so evident in Sydney. A later Far West superintendent, Rev. S. Drummond, was responsible for starting the mission's Children's Seaside Health Scheme in which all churches eventually co-operated. In the later 1930s, Rev. Ralph Sutton pioneered the use of motion pictures in the mission's work, thereby vastly increasing the congregations to which he could preach. He also started a 'Saturday Sunday school' at Nyngan, since that was the day on which people from outlying properties came to town to do their shopping. This flourished and supplemented the work of the correspondence Sunday school. Late in the period, in 1942, a wireless patrol based on Wilcannia and linked into the Flying Doctor network was established.[21]

The obvious success of the Far West Mission led the 1923 Conference to appoint a commission to visit the circuits of the north-west and devise means to advance Methodism there. As a consequence the 1924 Conference incorporated the Moree, Narrabri, Boggabri, Coonabarabran and Collarenebri districts as the North-west Mission, though Coonabarabran was later reconstituted as a separate circuit. The total area of the mission was about 65 000 km^2, much smaller than the Far West Mission, but its population was considerably larger. There were three agents in the area, the superintendent with a car and the probationers with motor cycles.

Each of the men travelled 1600 km a month, working the area from Coonabarabran in the south to Mungindi and Boggabilla in the north and from Bingara in the east to Pilliga and Wee Waa in the west. Whereas in 1923, under the old circuit system, Methodism had occupied four churches and thirteen other preaching places, by 1930 it occupied the same four churches and forty-six other preaching places. In 1923, ministers had visited nine schools; in 1930 they visited seventy. That was a substantial gain for the church.

An attempt was made to confront what Methodists saw as the great curse of the outback, organised Sunday sport. In all three mission areas 'Organised Sunday sport [was] the accepted thing, and it [was] almost impossible to hold young people when they reach[ed] the age of 13'. Narrabri was no worse than other outback towns in 1925, but on winter Sunday afternoons people came in from as far away as 115 km to attend the football and a town of a little over 4000 inhabitants had regular Sunday football crowds of 3000–3500! The combined Sunday attendance at the three Protestant churches was no more than one hundred and there were only forty to fifty children in Sunday school. This was a battle which the church was unlikely to win, but one which it knew it had to join.[22]

The task of 'covering' the State concerned the city of Sydney and its ever-growing suburbs as well as the vast inland missions. It was there, in metropolitan Sydney, that Carruthers's 1916 statement that 'there is a general feeling that all is not well, and that the bulk of the community is largely untouched by the Gospel appeal and is rapidly drifting into secularism, materialism and irreligion' was particularly true. Sadly, twenty-one years later, F.W. Hynes, editor of *The Methodist* could still write truthfully of the church and the metropolis that 'Thousands of people hardly know we exist, and care less. And from our side it must be confessed that we only dimly visualise the unshepherded multitudes'.

From time to time *The Methodist* drew attention to the relentless suburban expansion and the indisputable fact that the church was not keeping pace with it. All suburbs were growing, but in the period 1891–1923 the population of Randwick had tripled, that of Canterbury had quadrupled, Waverley had doubled, Ashfield had risen by 75 per cent and Bankstown had multiplied more than six times. Only in the Bankstown area had Methodist development kept up with the region. In 1912, Lakemba had been separated from the Ashfield circuit and in 1921 Bankstown had been added to the former from Homebush to create the largest circuit in suburban Methodism. Between 1917 and 1923, the number of scholars in the Sunday schools had risen from 384 to 1100 and seven new buildings had been constructed, two had been enlarged and a further church site had been purchased. The circuit was spiritually progressive and had held a Sunday school convention, bringing together more than fifty teachers to study and pray. It had also held a weekend mission and had undertaken a campaign of personal evangelism, sending members out 'two-by-two' to make contact with newcomers.

An important point emerges from the Lakemba–Bankstown experience. It was declared a circuit in its own right at a crucial time and acquired a Quarterly Meeting attuned to the development of the area and prepared to work hard to keep pace with it. The Hornsby–Asquith experience was similar as was that in the near country area of Camden–Picton. Where no new circuit was constructed, the Quarterly Meeting usually drew its members from older established areas and was preoccupied with church maintenance in those places and lacked either the time or the inclination to take initiatives in the developing areas. Where the new developments fell between existing circuits, it was even less likely that they would receive due attention.

A good example of this Quarterly Meeting conservatism occurred in Randwick circuit, where the Quarterly Meeting was fully occupied with a well-established area and quite unable to cope with rapid growth in Kensington and Daceyville. The Randwick minister, Rev. T. Jenkin, rejected blame on behalf of himself and his laymen, arguing that the circuit had for some time been seeking division and was unworkable as it stood. Once the Home Mission Department's Church Extension and Sites Committee put a home missionary into the new suburbs to work them intensively, they began to make progress, a fact which illuminates both aspects of the point being made.

Some argued that the Church should have had the manpower available to create additional circuits since it had for years rejected qualified candidates for the ministry on the sole grounds that it lacked money to train them. This, it was argued, showed some lack of faith. If men were employed as 'faith workers' in the first instance the people would find the money to support them.

Not all suburban circuits were actual or potential trouble spots requiring the employment of special resources for their development. Manly, which combined the features of a well-established middle-class circuit with those of expansion by younger folk into new areas on the edges of the old circuit, was able to maintain a healthy spiritual life which peaked during the ministry of the gifted evangelist and pastor, Rev. Frank Rayward (1928–31)—he had to amplify his evening services to a large audience in cars and the nearby park. It was said that 'The overwhelming majority [had] lost the duty of church attendance in its joy'. Men's, women's and young people's organisations flourished and membership soared despite the removal of the suburbs of Dee Why, Mona Vale, Brookvale and Frenchs Forest to form the new Dee Why circuit in 1923.[23]

The inner city remained a special problem. Despite occasional successes, like the Men's Question Circle which began at Balmain during the Depression and continued into the war years, the Sunday school work at Rozelle, the open-air preaching at Bourke Street, and the Home for Aged Women (1924) at South Sydney, the old suburban missions were neither healthy nor successful at this time, except perhaps as centres for the distribution of aid during the Depression years. More successful was the most recent, Newtown, inaugurated in 1928, though it had been worked in the fashion of a mission for two or three years before that. The continuing emphasis of its founder, A.E. Walker, on the spiritual life, and the will to succeed of those who had undertaken to launch the project with him, ensured that it would indeed flourish in terms of evangelism (especially open-air preaching), pastoral care for children and adults and, inevitably, philanthropic aid for the unemployed through the long Depression years.

The inter-war years were not a high point even at the much better-endowed and better-known Sydney Central Mission. True, under Hoban it had perhaps the largest congregation it would ever have, and Charlie Woodward, the 'converted burglar', carried on the most efficient evangelism ever among men from the gutter. The Dalmar Children's Home grew in importance as did men's relief work, and the Pleasant Sunday Afternoon provided a link with those not attending church, but it was a time of great difficulty and the achievements of these years were muted compared with those of earlier or later times.

The Newcastle mission was as effective as any during this time and would have been more so had it not been seriously hindered by the old Newcastle problem of debt. For a time it continued its Girls' Rescue Home. The Seamen's Institute was strong while the well-known H.D. Gilbert was in charge of it. The Men's Brotherhood was for years 'the jewel in the crown' and its aid was invaluable during the Depression when the mission undertook much work among the unemployed. Street preaching remained effective longer in Newcastle than Sydney and was considered worthwhile throughout these years. Once Rayward came to Newcastle (1931–38), he sought to deepen the spiritual life, established an Evangelists' Institute which offered some help to the District churches as well as to the young men, and added his infectious enthusiasm and zeal to what was already being done. His long ministry, and the size and nature of the city of Newcastle compared with Sydney, probably explains the relative success of the Newcastle Central Mission in the period.[24]

The country towns and their immediate settled hinterlands were regarded as Methodist heartlands and ten of the State's fourteen Methodists Districts and 135 of its 210 circuits were located there and scarcely a country town was without its Methodist church or preaching place. About 70 per cent of the Methodist membership was country-based. Yet many areas had their difficulties in the inter-war years. Both Goulburn and Bathurst seem to have experienced a gradual decline in their spiritual life as a multitude of social activities and pressures took their toll of believers. Rev. R.H. Campbell, visiting the non-mission parts of the Riverina for the Home Mission Society in 1929, thought the Methodist church was in trouble there, partly from the prevalence of Sunday sport and partly from the shortage of church workers and the lack of pastoral visitation outside the towns. When he returned in 1933 he felt that the last of these problems had been overcome but that the first was worse than ever.[25]

Of all the areas outside Sydney none was more difficult or important than the South Maitland coalfield. The burgeoning population, estimated by a Methodist visitor as 45 000 in the mid-1920s, was out-running the capacity of the three ministers and one home missionary operating in the area, while the existing church buildings were generally unattractive and inadequate. Nor was the situation improved by the industrial antagonisms endemic to the field or the opposition of many of the more radical miners to the church. Some thought it would be better to use the available manpower on this populous field and not in the empty wastes, as they saw it, of the Far West Mission. The District Synod established a 'Coalfields Commission' in 1926 to determine the future shape of work in the fields and, in particular, whether a 'Coalfields Mission' should be set up. Little came of this initiative until much later.

Conditions deteriorated as industrial strife increased at the end of the 1920s culminating in the lockout and deaths at Rothbury. E.E. Hynes, Chairman of the Maitland District, appealed for assistance on behalf of the hundreds of innocent sufferers in the area, describing it as 'a direct challenge to the Christian Churches in this State, and [one] which they dare not ignore or evade'. By and large they could and did. The churches in the coalfields towns had no money of their own with which to help the people. Collections were very low—one congregation even asked that the offering plate be not circulated for a time—and debit balances were growing everywhere. Local preachers were leaving to seek work elsewhere and it was increasingly difficult to fill services.

The church, which had clearly not known how to handle the industrial situation, but which had been proud of the spirit of brotherliness which had continued to exist among its members, be they workers or bosses, was mightily relieved when the trouble did end and it could get on with the work it understood. A mission conducted by the Cessnock circuit minister, Rev. A.J. Skinner, early in 1932, and another by Leigh College students later that year, seem to have met with some success and it may be that the troubles and the Depression between them aided that work, making it appear the more positive and life-giving.

In the winter of 1943 the Methodist minister in Cessnock, Alan Walker, with his Anglican and Presbyterian colleagues, tried a new approach to the problem of relating the church to the miners in their social context. After a substantial period of preparation in which each minister carefully built up his contacts among the miners, they organised a series of discussions on neutral ground in a disused shop in the main street of the town on such subjects as 'What do we mean by God?', 'Is the Bible True?', and 'What price man?'. Each talk and discussion was in the hands of a prominent churchman suited to the task. The regular attendance at the series was about one hundred and included both workers and management. At the end the ministers felt that their efforts had helped to break down prejudice against the church, but the South Maitland coalfield remained an area where its achievements were limited.[26]

The New South Wales Conference bore responsibility for the Australian Capital Territory. Until a Quarterly Meeting was created within the Territory it was administered by the Home Mission Department, but this lasted only a short time as a probationer, Rev. R.J.F. Boyer, was appointed in 1915 and Canberra was then constituted a circuit. Two years later it became a part of the Queanbeyan circuit. In 1924 the Home Mission Department co-ordinated the selection of a central site for the so-called 'cathedral church' on the south-west slopes of Capital Hill. At much the same time a permanent congregation was formed in the Kingston-Forrest area, meeting in a galvanised iron building owned by the Church of England.

From 1926 there was a full-time ordained appointment, Rev. E.L. Vercoe from the Victoria and Tasmania Conference, and plans were drawn up for the central church building, for a suburban church at Reid, and for a parsonage. The parsonage was completed at Kingston-Forrest in 1927 but the central church was set aside for a time and that at Reid opened in October 1927. The real reason for the delay with the main church was that it had to be costly to be considered 'worthy' of Methodism and money was not subscribed rapidly enough to allow it to proceed. In any case, Reid was probably the better position at the time.

For a time there was great hope that the Congregationalists, Methodists and Presbyterians of the Australian Capital Territory would be able to lead the nation in co-operation, but these hopes faded in the face of Presbyterian intransigence. The Methodists of the capital had to go their own way, worshipping in the Central Hall which they had opened in 1930, until they were able to build their 'cathedral church' in the post-war era. The details of this story are better dealt with under the heading of church union.[27]

The Home Mission Department (formerly the Church Sustentation and Extension Society) had been formed in 1858 to 'spread scriptural holiness across the land' or, more specifically, to raise money for loans to assist circuits with the building of churches and to subsidise marginal circuits which needed, but could not fully support, a minister. By the Second World War its role had increased greatly. At first there had been the appointment of a home missionary here and there, and then its supervision of the Evangelistic Committee. Later came the establishment of the inland missions with their organisation and equipment. Still later it took over the work with immigrants, which will be discussed briefly later, and provided two full-time and an army of part-time visitors to hospitals. The Women's Home Mission League, formed in 1930 under the leadership of Mrs J. Woodhouse (President 1930–48) to raise money for, and educate women about, home missions, fully supported Sister Francis who spent her later years in hospital work.

During the Depression, the Department provided assistance to more than one-third of the circuits in the state. It supervised the work of the Men's Own Movement—which sought to link the church with industrial workers—and provided assistance to first-time offenders at court and to prisoners released from the State's gaols. It conducted open-air services in the Domain to reach the unchurched, supervised and supported the work of the Church Extension and Sites Committee in the developing suburbs and employed sisters in the central missions. Indirectly, it was also a means of bringing men into the ministry for, of the more than 300 laymen whom it had called from New South Wales or England to be Home Missionaries, 111 had taken the extra step into the Methodist or another ministry. The Department's grip on the church was strong, and its capacity to draw money considerable. Although it suffered during the Depression, as did all branches of the church, the trend of giving to it over the entire period 1914–45 was strongly upwards.

A few thought it too strong. In late 1939, Rev. E.W. Hyde contributed an article to *The Methodist* arguing that it had become 'the controlling agency in the activities of our Church in New

South Wales'. It was not merely carrying out the behests of Conference, to a great extent it was 'the creative institution out of which the programme and policy of our Church is generated and evolved'. Hyde believed that the Committee of the Home Mission Department largely elected itself and did not reflect the collective wisdom and aims of the whole church. So dominant was it that 'weak men may seek its friendship to achieve their personal advantage and others be silent lest the frown of the Department should, for them, be the way that leads to the wilderness'. The result had been 'a stereotyped policy and a single-sided outlook upon the Church's functions and objectives'. That policy had led to the steady regression of Methodism over the preceding thirty years and the church must make a dispassionate survey of its machinery and policy to overcome the problem.

That the Home Mission Department had become a powerful body within the Methodist Church of New South Wales is beyond question, but many of Hyde's points smacked more than a little of envy. If there was a problem, it had probably grown in part because the Department had attracted to its service some exceptionally able and energetic men, of whom Rev. W.H. Jones, its long-time secretary, was the best example. These were men who would, and presumably should, have exercised influence, and even power, whatever role they filled. The real problem lay more in the tendency within the church to centralise power, in the decline of the old balance between circuit and connexion, than with any particular department. The reasons for that changing balance were doubtless complex but, as was argued in the particular case of evangelism, they included a loss of purpose at the periphery. Nevertheless, Hyde's case should have been fully debated and the truth determined. That did not happen.[28]

Church union: the 'tortuous trail' begins

The movement for union between the Congregational, Methodist and Presbyterian churches extended over more than seventy-five years before it was partially fulfilled by the creation of the Uniting church in 1977. The story has been told substantially elsewhere and all that is appropriate here is a brief discussion of the events in New South Wales and their significance for the life of the Methodist church there.[29]

Occasional statements, official and unofficial, during the nineteenth century meant little, despite the obvious practical advantages of either co-operation or union in a situation where none of the three churches named ever had the human or financial resources to minister effectively to the whole colony and wherein all three together never accounted for more than 25 per cent of the population. The co-operation of individuals and groups in such interdenominational bodies as church councils, Sunday school unions and the Australian Student Christian Movement may have been an indication of genuine interest in the possibility of Christian union but nothing significant could be achieved until each of the three churches had consolidated its own internal affairs, as the Methodists did with their union in 1902.

The first tentative step was taken with the grandiose and unrealistic proposal, put forward by Rev. T.E. Clouston in the Sydney Presbytery of the Presbyterian church in March 1901, and endorsed by the General Assembly of Australia the following year, for 'one grand Church of Australia' or 'a United Evangelical Church of Australia'. Originally the Anglicans, Baptists and Churches of Christ were invited to participate in the discussions, but they quickly dropped out leaving only the three previously named denominations. Both the New South Wales Methodist Conference (1903) and the General Conference (1904) responded with interest, as did the Congregational Union, and a committee was established to undertake discussions.[30]

Social and political factors, such as the federation of the Australian colonies, doubtless helped to draw the denominations towards union, but the Presbyterian Assembly of New South Wales had isolated the central issue at the very beginning when it argued that the Protestant churches were preaching almost identical versions of the Gospel and that the theological differences which once had separated them were no longer live issues. They differed from each other only in matters of church government and forms of worship, which none of them regarded as essentials and which certainly did not counterbalance the advantage of presenting a united front 'to the forces of sin and unbelief'.

Over the next few years a variety of practical advantages were adduced by those who favoured union. It was believed that union would impress the community with the 'reality and effectiveness of true religion'. Considerable emphasis was put on the perceived advantages of combining the financial, manpower and physical resources of the churches: overlapping and competition would be eliminated, social and philanthropic enterprise would be strengthened, missions could be promoted more vigorously whether in the inner city, remote areas or overseas in non-Christian countries. In a more philosophical vein it was noted, though without great emphasis until much later, that union would give 'practical and visible effect to the Saviour's prayer, "That they may all be one . . . that the world may believe that Thou hast sent me" '.

In 1910, the Methodist General Conference and the Congregational Assembly each approved a scheme of church government and a doctrinal basis, but the Presbyterian General Assembly gave only a general approval because the majority of its presbyteries had already indicated that they were against the continuation of the negotiations. Presbyterian unionists were beginning to learn the difficulty of carrying their co-religionists with them. So great was the frustration of the Methodists that their 1913 General Conference discharged its Committee on the Union of Churches.[31]

Interest was rekindled by the experience of co-operation between the churches during the First World War and because the war had compelled the churches to realise that 'the world is too strong for a divided Church'. The knowledge that progress was being made in the movement towards union in Canada may also have had a positive effect. The 1917 General Conference reappointed a committee to prepare a basis of union and take all steps necessary to achieve 'a Federation or organic union of kindred churches'. This led to the production of a basis of union document in 1918 and to a decision that a vote would be taken in the September Quarterly Meetings of 1919 to determine whether or not they were in favour of union.

This was the first point at which the Methodist people of New South Wales had any real involvement in the movement and, indeed, the opportunity to learn what union would mean for them. James Carruthers, himself an advocate of union, was undoubtedly correct when he argued that the Methodists were not prepared for union at that time. Indeed, their lack of direct prior involvement made it impossible for them to have any real understanding of the subject. However, *The Methodist* did its best to remedy the problem by publishing a large number of articles and letters on the subject after a preliminary presentation from the New South Wales Joint Committee on Union which, in a curiously negative approach, argued that 'there was no difference of doctrine on vital points, and no difference in polity in which conscience was involved, to bar the way to union'.[32] Thus it would be fair to say that no new arguments in support of union were introduced at this stage and that when the case was put more positively the favoured view was simply a less precise restatement of earlier arguments: that union would allow the church to fulfil its God-given mission more effectively.

The vote showed that eighty-three Quarterly Meetings were in favour of union and seventy-seven were against it—there were eight meetings where the vote was equal and two did not vote. Several features of the vote warrant mention. There was a unanimous vote, one way or another, in seventy-five circuits, which might lead to the conclusion that voting was influenced by either the minister or some other powerful figure. That view could be reinforced by the fact that in thirty-nine of those circuits there were ten or less persons attending. Yet too little is known about individual views and, where they are known, there are too many doubtful cases to draw any firm conclusions. Where larger numbers attended, say twenty-five or more, there seemed to be a greater likelihood of a divided vote and also one against union. Most interesting of all, Rev. James Green, President of the New South Wales Conference, claimed that about 10 000 persons were entitled to vote in the Quarterly Meetings, yet only about 2200 did so. It seems certain that no one tried to 'stack' meetings and that Green was correct when he drew the conclusion that these results revealed 'a decided hesitancy and uncertainty' and that Methodists still had to be persuaded that union was desirable. Furthermore, it was clear that much of the opposition was to that section of the basis of union document which preserved the rights of those ministers already in a parish or church and thus seemed to advantage the Congregational and Presbyterian ministers over their Methodist colleagues because of the permanence of their appointments.[33]

The basis of union document was submitted to the membership of the three churches in 1920. Material favourable to union was produced by the Methodist Committee on Union while opponents set up a Methodist Defence Committee which also produced its own literature. During July–August 1920, the editor of *The Methodist* provided generous space for both sides to present their cases to readers. In September, Methodist members were asked to vote on two questions: whether or not they approved the organic union of the churches and whether or not they approved the proposed basis of union. On the best figures available, which are probably slightly incomplete, of the 24 903 members entitled to vote, 73 per cent of Methodists voted on the first question and 71 per cent on the second. Of those who voted, 78.5 per cent were for union while 74 per cent supported the proposed basis, though there seems to have been some misunderstanding about whether everyone should vote on the second question or only those who answered 'yes' to the first. In New South Wales, Methodist opposition to union was stronger (or support for it lower) than in any other State. Throughout Australia, the vote for union was 88 per cent, almost ten per cent above that in New South Wales.

The Presbyterian vote in New South Wales for union was 65 per cent, which was higher than the national vote of 57 per cent. The Congregational vote was 85 per cent, slightly better than the Commonwealth vote of 84 per cent. As only 51 per cent of Congregational members and 46 per cent of Presbyterian members exercised their franchise this vote could not be interpreted as offering strong support for union.[34]

Union could not proceed on that basis for, as J.E. Carruthers had said earlier:

> . . . a nominal union, on whatever basis it may be affected, will be valueless and inoperative unless accompanied by those conditions which will ensure the spiritual solidarity of the united Church, and give assurance of increased zeal in the promotion of the interests of the Kingdom of the Lord Jesus Christ . . .

In any case it had been suggested that legal barriers would prevent the Presbyterian church, under its existing constitution, from joining any union. Negotiations collapsed and the Methodist General Conference of 1926 discharged its committee on union while *The Methodist* commented that 'we imagine there will be a sense of relief for the present . . . [that] these expensive and fruitless negotiations are come to an end'.[35]

The opportunity for a practical expression of unity by the three churches occurred with the establishment of Canberra as the federal capital. The Canberra Methodist Quarterly Meeting held in March 1928 resolved to plan for co-operation in the development of the three churches in the city area and a Canberra Co-operative Council was formed in 1928. This encouraged interchange between ministers and congregations and a committee was appointed to arrange combined Sunday school services at Eastlake. Each of the denominations had been granted a city site, but the council agreed that the Presbyterians alone should build on their site on the understanding that the building would be available to the other two churches for services. The Methodists would erect a hall for Sunday school and community purposes.

In December 1932 representatives of the three churches gathered at Braddon, with high hopes, to discuss the formation of 'The United Church of Canberra'. Yet, within a few years, these hopes were shattered. Several months before the opening of St Andrew's church on 22 September 1934 the Presbyterian members of the Co-operative Council informed the council that it would be for the exclusive use of Presbyterians and would not be available for use by the other two churches.[36] The failure of practical co-operation in the new city of Canberra had a depressing effect on relations between the three churches and symbolised their total inability to overcome what many others saw as minimal differences. Some negotiations continued between Methodists and Congregationalists and a door was left ajar for the Presbyterians but there was really nothing to be done except for each denomination to go about its business with little reference to the others. Clearly, Carruthers's minimum requirements for a satisfactory union had not yet been fulfilled.

Caring for the church family

Maintaining the church family was a major preoccupation throughout the years under discussion and was probably the area of the church's greatest success. Youth work expanded, though that among children continued to run into problems, adult organisations were often strong, and the church struggled, with only partial success, to build the strong ministry necessary if it were to regain the influence it had lost in the community.

The Young People's Department (Sunday School Department to 1918—the name change reflected a major development of function) was a significant force within Methodism over the years 1914—45 and another example of the centralisation to which earlier reference was made, though its directors were less powerful men than those in the Home Mission Department.

Much of the Department's general and Sunday school work can be discussed best in relation to the report of the Youth Work Commission (1933–36). Established by Conference at the Department's request, this was chaired by a Methodist member of the Legislative Council of New South Wales, Hon. E.C. Sommerlad, and included Harold Wyndham, later Director General of Education in New South Wales.[37]

The number of children in Methodist Sunday schools had reached a low in 1923, had not risen greatly through the 1920s but had spurted in the years 1930–32—only to fall back to something like the 1920 figure by 1934. In the age group nine to twelve years, the Commission thought that schools were reaching more than 90 per cent of their constituency, though only about two-thirds of that number were present on any given Sunday. Among older children, the proportion reached was much lower. It argued further that the mood of scepticism following the Great War, the indifference of many parents, the encouragement of social evils by the State and the increase in weekend motoring and rail travel all played their part in decreasing attendance. In the Commission's view, the churches and Sunday schools themselves were not without blame: teaching methods were often inadequate, equipment was obsolete, the tendency to regard the school as separate from the church and the relegation by synod and Conference of Sunday school and youth work to 'a minor and insignificant place' in their deliberations had been important. Teachers must be both dedicated and trained, homes must be visited and the school must be seen to be a real part of the total work of the church.

Of the youth groups, it was suggested that Christian Endeavour seemed to be losing its grip, the Order of Knights and Girls' Comradeship displayed considerable power to hold, though there were doubts about their spiritual depth, and the Crusader camping movement was highly praised for its achievements. The need to present Christian discipleship to young people as something costly and involving commitment to the world as well as to Christ was raised and, in keeping with the times, the Commission seemed anxious to create links between church youth groups and the League of Nations Union in the interests of peace. Many specific recommendations for changes in Methodist law relating to junior members, or for action by the New South Wales Conference or the Young People's Department, were included.

The main immediate outcome of this report was a greatly increased emphasis by the Department on the training of teachers. Over the next few years, much of the time of the Associate Directors of the Department was devoted to this activity. Rev. Alan Walker undertook a series of weekend (and occasionally longer) visits to suburban and country circuits to undertake mixed teacher training and evangelistic work. Typical of these was one to Wollongong in August 1937. It began with a tea table conference on the Saturday evening with Walker speaking to about one hundred Sunday school teachers and youth leaders from the surrounding area about child psychology and teaching problems. After tea there was an evangelistic youth rally and on Sunday morning Walker spoke to the Christian Endeavour group and preached at a service at which there was a parade of all the local youth organisations. That evening there was a further 'tea table' conference with renewed discussion of youth work problems followed by an evangelistic service. Such visits kindled Christian enthusiasm and aroused interest in teaching techniques. Walker later published a book, *Concerning Teaching*, to provide guidance for those not reached through his visits.

His successor, Rev. G.A. Wheen, concerned himself particularly with the use of drama with older students and the need for appropriate surroundings. He also stressed that the Department's provision of occasional special training sessions, and of training camps during the summer vacation, could not replace regular local discussion groups to prepare weekly lessons and deal with particular problems.[38] It would be interesting to know whether either the report or the influence of these two young men had any bearing on the overdue post-war decline of the old Sunday school examinations.

Difficult though the Sunday school problem might be, that relating to public schools was far more intractable. There was some co-operation between the Methodist, Congregational and Presbyterian churches over the preparation of lessons and the staffing of classes, but the Methodists still found themselves overwhelmed by the magnitude of the task. They serviced a higher proportion of their constituency than any other major denomination and continued to worry that this was the only way in which probably half the Protestant children in State schools would ever be reached. In 1937 Conference appointed the Rev. S.M. Barrett to head a subdepartment on school religious education, to help organise Methodist resources for the task in the Sydney and Newcastle areas and to provide training for ministers or lay people who needed it, but the problems could not be solved in this period.[39]

Until the outbreak of World War I, Methodism had relied very heavily on Christian Endeavour for youth work. In the first half of 1915, Rev. Harold Wheen, the General Secretary (Director) of the Young People's Department, introduced the Methodist Making of Manhood Movement in an attempt to meet the special, but very old, problem of boys dropping out of the senior years of Sunday school and being lost to the church, often for ever. This involved the men of the church keeping a friendly oversight of the boys to encourage their continued adherence. The organisation had no machinery and need hold no meetings unless they were felt necessary in a particular locality. It was too amorphous and ill-defined to succeed and soon gave way to the Order of Knights.[40]

Knights, the characteristic Methodist youth organisation of the period, began almost accidentally. Alec Bray, an 18-year old, was asked at very short notice to take over a small class of boys at the Hurstville Sunday school. Having nothing prepared, he talked to them about King Arthur and the Knights of the Round Table and suggested they form a 'secret society', the Order of Knights. With his superintendent's permission, he expanded his work to include a week-night meeting and an occasional Saturday picnic. He developed rules, a pledge and a brief ritual for his organisation and his minister, Rev. G.W. Payne, assisted with an impressive 'installation' ceremony for the officers of the new organisation. Other churches began to enquire about the group and branches were formed at Kogarah and Wollongong. There was an Easter camp in 1916 and a Round Table Conference involving the three branches in February 1917. Two months later, Bray offered his organisation and services to the Young People's Department which decided to make it an official church organisation and employed Bray part-time to develop it. There were further developments of the ritual by Revs F.R. Swynny and Harold Wheen, the characteristic shield and badge of the organisation were adopted, and the Order was ready to spread widely among Methodist young men for the next forty years or so. The development of District and High Courts and of the various 'degrees' through which members might progress came later.

The Order of Knights made rapid progress and, by 1935, there were 226 active courts in New South Wales with 5421 members. Yet not everyone approved of the movement. Rev. C.J. Prescott thought its 'high sounding titles' unnecessary and in bad taste and preferred the simpler designations of the Methodist Girls' Comradeship, the parallel organisation set up for girls in imitation of the Knights. The point was valid, but overlooked the fact that these over-grand titles were an important part of the Order's appeal to young lads. More important was the criticism, referred to earlier, that the organisation, whilst able to grip and hold boys, was lacking in spiritual depth.[41]

The real wonder was how an organisation based on a romantic, dubiously Christian, legend, and depending heavily on an anachronistic ritual and symbolism, ever managed to be accepted and grow to such an extent in the cynical years following the Great War. Yet the mention of the Order of Knights still brings light to the faces of many now elderly men who once gave the organisation great loyalty and found it a valuable medium through which to express their Christian faith. Probably there is a parallel between the appeal of the Order of Knights for boys and that of the Freemasons for older men.

The Crusader Movement also attracted considerable devotion in the 1930s and 1940s. It sprang from a group of young Methodists, led by Don Wilcox, who attended a Presbyterian Fellowship Camp at Nowra at Easter 1929 and who thereafter worked with the then Director of the Young People's Department, Rev. S. Varcoe Cocks, to develop a camping programme for the Methodist church. The first Methodist camp was at Camden on the 1929 Labor Day weekend and thereafter the programme expanded rapidly. Soon multiple 'regional' camps had to be held to cope with the numbers seeking the healthy mixture of fun, worship, fellowship and study which was provided.

Crusaders found some opponents among the conservatives in the church because, while it emphasised the importance of a personal commitment to Christ, it also stressed the role of the Christian in the world. Rev. Dr J.W. Burton was a major intellectual influence, while Ralph Sutton, Eben Newman, Robert and Jim Staines and Brian Mowbray each played a significant role. Not that the conservatives had much reason to complain since Methodist Christian Endeavour camps and the interdenominational Christian Endeavour rallies throughout the State generally provided adequately from their perspective. Crusaders also played their part in post-war evangelism through the work of the large, popular and capable Crusader Choir under the dynamic leadership of Roy Scotter. With the assistance of Sir Frederick Stewart, Crusaders acquired its own property, Otford, in 1937, though it was not really developed until after the war. That gave the movement an ideal base for its activities.[42]

The Conference of 1918 appointed an Educational Policy and Sites Committee to consider the educational policy of the church and acquire suitable sites on the Milsons Point–Hornsby Line, and elsewhere in the State, with a view to erecting Girls' and Boys' Colleges. This presupposed a substantial extension of the church's involvement in education. Nothing further need be said here of the 'old' colleges, Newington and Methodist Ladies' College, Burwood, except that they continued to grow despite periodic financial difficulties. But it was the existence of this Committee which led in 1924 to the purchase of Miss Mabel Fidler's 'Ravenswood' school at Gordon and its incorporation under the MLC banner until it began to move towards independence in 1932 which it achieved in 1947. Enrolments at the school dropped for some years after the change of control and the school's future was not secure until a boarding section was established in 1935.

Other new colleges grew without the intervention of the Committee. The first, the North Coast Methodist Girls' College, was at Ballina. The real motive for this school was sectarianism, as there were several Catholic girls' schools in the area covered by the North Coast District of the Methodist church and it was known that there were Protestant girls attending each of them. Broached first in 1919, this college never received the support hoped for and, when it finally opened in 1926, it bore a heavy debt burden. Despite an apparently good staff and appointments it did not attract the clientele expected and, in the year of its demise, 1929, had only eighteen boarders and seventeen day girls instead of the thirty boarders and twenty-five day girls who had been expected.

Annesley College, Bowral, opened its doors in 1925 and, like its sister school in Ballina, was deeply in debt. It survived beyond World War II through the generosity of one of its founders, E. Boardman, the hard work of the Ladies' Advance committee and of one of its treasurers, R.J. Lukey, but it was always on the verge of trouble. It was able to maintain enrolments only because it was less expensive than Sydney boarding schools, was situated in an area with a healthy climate and kept country girls away from 'the perils of the city'. Yet a doubt remained whether a 'finishing school' was really the most appropriate institution for Methodist girls.

Wolaroi, the boarding school for boys at Orange, began operations in 1926 after the purchase of an existing institution. The object was to service the educational needs of the entire western region, as well as Orange itself, by providing a school which was both cheaper and closer than those in Sydney. The school was attractive to country people because it taught book-keeping, typing, wool classing, stud management and horticulture. Numbers dwindled through the Depression and there were further financial difficulties in the early war years, but in 1945 Wolaroi was still the only 'specialist' Methodist school.

In 1940, Conference tried to centralise aspects of its education work under the auspices of a new Colleges Investigation and Advisory Board. The object was not to interfere in the internal affairs of the colleges, but to link them together financially into a Methodist 'system' under the Board. The advantages for the schools related mainly to assistance with their capital debt problems and to some extent with recruiting and the provision of bursaries. On the other hand, the Board was trying to tighten the bonds between schools and Conference and to relate them more closely to the Methodist constituency by offering more bursaries and thus opening them to a larger number of Methodist families. It did not get far beyond the provision of some help with capital debts before the loss of its founding chairman and moving spirit, the dynamic R.H. Nesbitt, led to a decline of vigour and purpose.[43]

The years immediately after the Great War also saw a significant outburst of Methodist interest in the opening of hostels in both Sydney and some country towns. These were intended to provide safe, supervised board for children attending regional high schools or for girls going to Sydney for teacher training. The move was initiated from within the Young People's Department executive but little came of it. A hostel for girls was established at Hay and one for boys at Orange and each lasted for several years before declining. The only hostel which was genuinely successful over an extended period was the one in Sydney for female teacher trainees. Opened in March 1922 in St Peters, it worked effectively for many years, having to move in 1931 to Annandale which was closer to the University of Sydney and which offered better recreational facilities.[44]

Between the wars the Methodist church in New South Wales made a determined effort to meet the needs of its young people. It gave more care than ever before to its Sunday schools, though it continued to be dissatisfied with their performance. Its youth organisations were more extensive than they had been before the Great War. As far as numbers were concerned, Knights and Comrades were more effective than earlier organisations had been, though they could not match Christian Endeavour in spiritual depth. Crusaders provided a new and immensely valuable dimension to youthful Christian thinking. The church knew that few of these organisations were fully effective and it tried through its impressive Youth Work Commission to determine the problem more precisely and to find answers. Within its limits of manpower and money it sought to implement those solutions, though the process was far from complete by 1945. The church's decision in 1945 that its memorial to the fallen of the 1939–45 war would be a Youth Leadership Training Centre marked another step in this process. It was a commitment that the effort of the inter-war years would continue and intensify.[45]

A church exists for mature adults as well as for children and young people. The regular Sunday services were a major part of the provision for them but, beyond this, a range of adult organisations was maintained. The chief fellowship group of earlier years, the class meeting, was now largely, though not entirely, defunct. Prayer meetings, once a normal weekly part of church life, were either held less often or were less well attended. For some men in Sydney the Methodist Men's Federation provided a substitute for both class and prayer meeting. But the characteristic groups of this period were those with directly practical, money raising and social purposes. They always had a spiritual purpose as well, and they continued to provide fellowship, but these aspects were less to the fore than they had been in earlier days.

For women there existed the Women's Auxiliary for Overseas Missions (WAOM), founded in an earlier time (1893) but working strongly through the inter-war years and into the post-Second World War period. Both central body and branches were of the greatest assistance to mission work and provided an essential missionary education for Australian Methodist women. That function was performed by affiliated Ladies' Church Aids where the WAOM itself did not exist. The Women's Home Mission League performed the same function for the relatively small group who belonged in Sydney and Newcastle (and probably a few other places). Elsewhere, it too relied on an affiliation with the Ladies' Church Aids which continued to provide intra-circuit fund raising services and social and spiritual activities for its members but, as they followed the same course as in earlier years, there is no need to discuss them further. A Young Women's Missionary Movement, a Sisters' Fellowship, and a Primary and Junior Sunday School Teachers' Association were groups with specialised functions. The Girls' Comradeship served young women. The Dalmar Ladies' Committee worked hard and effectively as did the Methodist Women's War Service League during World War II. The Methodist Ministers' Wives and Widows' Association served a small but important group. Some of these groups were vital to the functioning of a particular part of the church.

July 1931 saw the formation of another women's organisation, the Methodist Women's Federation, which was intended to be a peak group co-ordinating the work of all other women's organisations where that was desirable. It was to become a very significant body after 1945, but it did not achieve great prominence in the years now under discussion.

Even more important than these organisations was the growing role of women in the church at large. More women were beginning to find a place at the circuit Quarterly Meeting. A very few became circuit representatives to the annual New South Wales Conference. The number of female local preachers began to grow, though it still remained small. One woman, Mrs James Puck, averaged nine or ten services a quarter and occasionally took two on the same Sunday, perhaps driving more than 50 km to do so. Some even suggested that women should enter the ordained ministry, though when the Secretary of Conference wrote to Quarterly Meetings seeking their views on this, they tended to find the time 'inopportune'. These were but straws in the wind, but they did indicate that some minds were daring to turn into new paths.[46]

Men had less separate organisations, partly because they were in paid employment during the day, but also because they continued to dominate the major committees of the church as well as providing by far the greater number of church stewards and local preachers. Young men had the Order of Knights while the work of the Men's Federation and the rather limited Laymen's Missionary Movement have already been mentioned. The characteristic men's organisation of these years was the brotherhood which operated in many circuits and was usually a monthly meeting held on Sunday over either an evening meal or, less often but very successfully for several years at Newcastle, a breakfast. Apart from fellowship, there was normally a speaker, often a prominent individual, to introduce some significant social or religious issue for discussion. The strength of these brotherhoods varied greatly from time to time and even one of the most successful of them, that at the Newcastle Central Mission, had to be restarted every few years though, at its peak, it had over 200 members and an average attendance of 160–70. Others which were highly successful for at least a reasonable time were based in Leichhardt, Bathurst and Goulburn. Brotherhoods often provided strong support for the church during this period and undertook considerable relief work during the Depression, a fact which is discussed further below. The local brotherhoods were linked through a central committee.[47]

The church could not be strong without an adequate ministry. The opening of Leigh College during the Great War has already been mentioned and thereafter Methodism had its long-awaited theological training institution. Yet, for some time after the end of the war, there was a shortage of candidates. That was not surprising. A number of probationers and home missionaries, as well as ordained men, had volunteered for the AIF and not all had returned. Many of those who did return no longer wanted to enter the ministry—the war, with all its horror, had destroyed the faith of some while others were simply no longer able to serve in that way. Men who had been too young to go to the war felt its impact and they too were lost to the ministry. It was some years before numbers increased (there were only four or five candidates in 1921) and men were again sought from England. Twelve arrived in 1928 and a similar number in 1929. When the number of candidates did increase the facilities at Leigh College were inadequate to take them comfortably and had to be expanded.

The problem of a shortage of tutors was overcome by the formation of the Joint Theological Faculty with the Presbyterians and Congregationalists, though not all Methodists approved of their young men passing through the hands of the modernistic Professors Angus (see below) and McIntyre. On the other hand, *The Methodist*, taking a liberal line, expressed disappointment that so few theological students were undertaking university degrees. It argued the need for a knowledge of psychology, anthropology and economics, adding that 'One has only to name these matters to be thrown back into the heart of our Bible, which through great prophets of their times, through Christ and His Apostles, speaks to us of the spacious religion of redemption for men and society'. In 1930 a record twenty-nine candidates were accepted and facilities were strained to the uttermost, but it did mean that as they came out into the circuits the shortages there were eased for a time. That group included several who were to leave their mark on the church in future years. Thereafter numbers fluctuated again, with only six accepted in 1933, largely because of fears that depressed finances would prevent circuits from meeting their stipends, eleven in 1937 and sixteeen in 1938. Just after the end of World War II, Rev. A.G. Manefield produced figures which showed that, from the early 1920s until his time of writing, on average, only seven young men entered ordained ranks each year, a figure which barely covered the number of those retiring and provided no margin to cope with the population increase. He believed that the number of candidates accepted had to be increased to at least fifteen a year over the long term if the church was to become seriously involved in the extension work so necessary in the post-war era. Among Methodists, the stewardship of talents had not been good in this special area.

But the ministry was more than its young men and trainees. The 1930s saw the maturity of a small group of very able senior men, some of them with new and interesting approaches to their work. Dr J.W. Burton has already been mentioned, but Dr E.E.V. Collocott, with his passion for social justice, his interest in economic and international issues and his high intellectual qualities was a treasure for any church. Rev. C.M. Churchward shared many of these qualities. If these were men to be savoured, that does not mean that the Methodist church always appreciated them or even listened to them, for many were able to cope with neither the depth nor the breadth of their minds. C.J. Prescott was another rare spirit, though cast in a different and more conservative mould, but he was in the twilight of his day and his main impact had occurred at an earlier time.[48]

After the Great War the old debate about science and religion revived to some extent though it was probably less widespread and less fierce within Methodism than it had been earlier. The conservative *Glad Tidings* attacked Professor S. Elliott Smith of Sydney University for a lecture he had given in London on evolution and conservative laymen occasionally wrote to *The Methodist* condemning clergy who accepted this concept. But by the 1920s, the connexional paper itself knew that 'There can be no opposition between the works of God and the Word of God' and was pleased that the old arrogance of science and intolerance of religion had largely passed away. The elderly C.J. Prescott noted that the church should accept with gratitude what science discovered in its own realm while insisting that the kingdom of values was at least as real as the kingdom of facts and that the universe had a personal author.

At much the same time, the publication of Peake's commentary on the Bible roused conservative hackles. The older clergy, like J.E. Carruthers, J.A. Waddell and W.G. Taylor, could not accept the probing and questioning which had to be a part of serious biblical scholarship after the higher criticism had done its work. Laymen of similar outlook wondered at the wisdom of requiring, or even permitting, theological students to pollute their minds with such material. Peake found his most ardent defender in the former Primitive Methodist minister, James Green, curiously a thorough-going conservative on almost everything else.

The sharpest debates over modernism were raised by the teaching of Samuel Angus in the Joint Faculty. The Conferences of 1921–22 saw theologically conservative ministers question the wisdom of exposing Methodist theological students to his 'heretical' teaching. The 1923 Conference rejected a motion by Revs J.W. Harrison and J.E. Carruthers that Methodist students be withdrawn from his classes, but set up a committee to explore with the Congregationalists and Presbyterians the problems raised by the Joint Faculty. In 1933, when his orthodoxy was under question, Conference actually instructed Methodist students to cease attending Angus's lectures, though it revoked the decision in 1938 when Angus promised to keep his teaching consistent with orthodox Presbyterian views.

Writing in the early 1940s, the gentle and scholarly E.E.V. Collocott drew the threads of both debates together. The church must relate its message clearly to contemporary thought and not only accept, but actively declare, that God spoke through the patient labours of those who devoted their lives to scientific discovery. Science was a part of the divine revelation and the church must never ask man to believe what, on other grounds, was incredible. Modern biblical interpretation had also enriched our faith greatly and the church should welcome and use it. To remain faithful to old forms, once the breath of life to those who had coined them, simply because they were old was spiritual cowardice, it was faith in someone else's faith: 'What we need . . . [are] "faiths that can be woven into the pattern of practical life and determine the daily conduct of ordinary men; and can do this because they are believed by any enlightened mind as true" '.[49]

Community witness

During the inter-war years, in response to the demands of the times, the Methodist understanding of the social responsibility of the church began to change and become more complex. The traditional moral issues of Sabbath desecration, alcohol, gambling and sex still caused great concern, but its Social (later, Public) Questions Committee began to take an interest in economic and international questions, realising dimly that 'So much of our work is stultified or undone by adverse social and economic conditions that are definitely un-Christian'. Yet when the committee arranged a meeting to discuss economic questions, the attendance of both ministers and laity was so small that it was clear that this realisation had spread neither very far nor very fast and that the bulk of the church remained apathetic about these matters of great importance.[50]

Before the Great War, Methodism, through the central mission, had made some provision for the reception of British migrants coming to New South Wales. Afterwards, *The Methodist* urged the church to encourage immigration for sectarian reasons. It believed that the Catholic church was 'organising astutely' to increase its proportion of adherents and thought it necessary to counter this. Nothing significant was achieved until 1926. At

Conference that year it was decided to support a scheme of group nomination instituted by the YMCA which sent two agents into the country to seek nominations for suitable families from Britain. At the other end the British Wesleyan Methodist Brotherhood had established a migration office to assist with the selection of suitable migrants. The first of these arrived on the *SS Berrima* on 20 April 1926 and over the next two years sixty Methodist families (328 persons) were placed on the land and ten teachers found employment with the Education Department. This certainly did not justify the claim made in *The Methodist* much later that in the years 1918–28 the Methodist church had 'left nothing undone' with respect to migration. There were few migrants during the Depression and just as the church was about to resume its efforts a new war intervened.[51]

Many writers, Donald Hansen and Michael McKernan among them, have noted an outburst of sectarianism in Australia towards the end of and after the Great War. Methodism in New South Wales took its full part in this unfortunate occurrence. For *Glad Tidings*, the Catholics had added a new crime to the old ones of false doctrine, moral inadequacy and authoritarianism: disloyalty. 'Loyalty to the Pope is inconsistent with loyalty to the King', it proclaimed, thereby demonstrating its inadequate understanding of the behaviour of the Catholic community during the war. *The Methodist*, not to be outdone, trumpeted its disgust with the Lord Mayor of Sydney, Alderman Fitzgerald, and with the State Attorney-General (a Catholic) for honouring that 'prince of seditious priests', Archbishop (later Cardinal) Mannix. It also published a serial in eleven instalments, *Ne Temere in Esse*, demonstrating the peril and pain likely to result from a mixed marriage carelessly contracted. It was passionately anti-Catholic and a stern warning to any and every young woman. The role of sectarianism in relation to immigration and the Ballina college has already been discussed. Later, the State aid issue re-emerged before an election and at Cootamundra the Methodist minister, Rev. W.C. Francis, organised a unique joint meeting of the Church of England Parochial Council, the Board of Management of the Presbyterian Church and the Methodist Quarterly Meeting to try to stave off the evil.

Yet it is undoubtedly correct that this sectarian activity, as well as being a provocation, was a response to incidents like the Ligouri case and the attempted formation of the Democratic Party in the Catholic interest. The *Ne Temere* serial makes the point well as Catholic insistence on the invalidity of any marriage involving a Catholic but not performed in the presence of a priest had understandably incensed Protestants.[52]

From Conference to local circuit Methodism continued to fight the good fight against Sunday desecration which, at this time, mainly related to the growing desire of the community to play organised sport in public parks on Sunday and the growing willingness of District councils to allow this. Battle was joined in such diverse places as Manly, Balmain, Annandale, Hamilton, Cessnock, Bathurst, Goulburn and Ballina. That at Ballina raged particularly fiercely and cost a number of retiring councillors their seats as good alternative candidates, backed by a well-conducted church campaign, triumphed. At Bathurst, Rev. A.J. Bingley (1939), using an old English law, sued the local Football League and a gatekeeper at a match in the attempt to end Sunday football there. He lost the case because of his inability to swear to the identity of the gatekeeper and had to pay heavy costs which forced him into bankruptcy.

The Church's motivation was not mere wowserism, but a sincere desire to keep Sunday holy and to prevent interference with those activities which it considered proper to the day, worship and Sunday school. What the church failed to realise was that this could not be achieved either permanently or properly through legislation. Persuasion and example were the only valid avenues of approach to the problem.[53]

The early closing of hotels during the Great War was more the result of the community's desire to maximise the war effort than a result of the church's enthusiastic campaigning. This was one of the last victories against the liquor trade that temperance forces were to achieve. The Methodist church, through its connexional paper, clergy and membership, played a significant part in the 1928 prohibition referendum campaign. *The Methodist* of 25 August was declared a special 'prohibition number' and almost the entire issue was devoted to the question. The paper interpreted the failure of the referendum as a vote against prohibition with compensation and not one against prohibition itself, which it seemed to think might have passed if unhandicapped by compensation. That was self-delusion of the highest order. Thereafter it became increasingly difficult for temperance forces to hold the line on club licences and to ensure that existing drinking laws were policed effectively.[54]

Two heavy defeats were suffered in the area of gambling. The first was the legalisation of the totalisator, and the second the introduction during the Depression of the State lottery. Methodists objected to the lottery above other forms of gambling because it set the State's imprimatur on gambling. The most disappointing aspect was the failure of Stevens' government to repeal this hated Act, despite the fact that Premier B.S.B. Stevens was a Methodist local preacher and a prominent figure in the church.[55]

By themselves the central missions had never provided an adequate response to the alienation of the working classes from the church. No one recognised this more clearly than Rev. F.T. Walker, who had spent the early years of his ministry in industrial centres such as Cobar and Lithgow and who had gone to considerable lengths to understand the aspirations of working men and to strike up a meaningful dialogue with them. Walker became convinced that he should devote his whole time to this work and asked the 1916 Conference to release him from circuit work for this purpose. Walker and his committee were to bear full responsibility, including financial, in return for complete freedom of action.

Walker called his organisation the Men's Own Movement (MOM) and launched it on the grand scale in the Sydney Town Hall on Easter Sunday 1916. His declared aim was to apply 'the teaching of Christ and the principles of Christianity' to the life and problems of the workers. Contact was made through a series of public meetings, private meetings with employers and union secretaries, regular lunch–time visits to most of the major 'works' in Sydney and the distribution of the movement's paper, at first called *Men's Own* but later bearing a variety of other titles. The paper was regarded as the heart of the work and had a circulation of 50 000 over the first year, though actual paid subscriptions were only a little over 700.

From 1917 the Men's Own Movement was again linked with the church, first through the Sydney Central Methodist Mission and later as a part of the work of the Home Mission Department. Conference probably did more in this area than any other Protestant church at this time, guaranteeing the movement's existence and providing Walker's salary as well as a small grant. Yet neither Conference nor the Methodist church really accepted the work. Circuits were willing to allow Walker to use their pulpits to spread his message, but they were much less willing to offer financial assistance, despite the importance of the work.

Some Methodists were actively antagonistic to the movement. Walker did not merely want to help workers who had fallen by the wayside under the capitalist system; he wanted to change the system itself. He was prepared to debate with communists and to consider the necessity of introducing some form of socialism as well as fighting sweating and exploitation. He readily admitted that the church had been slow to speak out against the evils of the existing economic system because it had, to some extent, fallen under the patronage of the wealthy; it could not question the source of their wealth when it needed a share of it.

In the aftermath of the Bolshevik Revolution, Walker's support for churchmen involved in the 1917 strike caused some, unjustifiably, to accuse him of taking the pennies of the children (given to the Home Mission Department) to spread a vicious, unchristian and un-British doctrine. There was at least one attempt to have him returned to a circuit to do the 'real' work of Methodism and his successor, William Coleman, was largely deflected from the main objective by having thrust upon him the added burden of court work with first offenders. Walker realised that dangerous divisions were growing within Australian society and that they would become worse after the peace. He expounded a theology that was not common in Australian Methodism at the time, though it had been partly accepted in the United States for some time: not only was Christ the personal Saviour of individual men and women, he was also the Great Reconciler, the one who could break down barriers and remove class hatreds, for the Incarnation made prejudice and class hatred unacceptable.

The Men's Own Movement made contact with the official labour movement and brought about an exchange of delegations between the Trades Hall and the Conference on occasion. This contact was neither deep nor broad, but it was better than nothing. Industry was not immediately christianised, but church folk were made more conscious of the legitimate aspirations and grievances of the labour movement and more aware that capitalism was not a divinely ordained socio-economic system which might never be altered. The movement, under Walker and Coleman, did much to interest the Methodist church in industrial issues and to prepare the way for the major industrial and social pronouncements which would come later, though others would also be involved in that work.[56]

The question of social and economic order was raised from other perspectives from time to time. Early in 1919, *The Sentinel*, the Mayfield circuit paper, warned in lurid language that 'Bolshevism' threatened the heart of Australia through the union movement. In *The Methodist* an unnamed minister (probably C.M. Churchward) was accused of preaching Bolshevism because he argued that a limit should be put on individual wealth (though he also found several defenders). Much later *The Methodist* complained that the New South Wales Labor Conference wanted Marxist doctrines taught in State and even Catholic schools, and the Weston (Coalfields) Quarterly Meeting refused to contemplate appointing delegates to a Christian Socialist Committee meeting at the Anglican Rectory!

There was nothing wrong with a desire to support a conservative economic and social theory, and it was particularly understandable that church people should be fearful of movements which appeared to challenge the religious as well as the social and economic status quo, but the conservative reactions were largely Pavlovian, unthinking and certainly lacking in rational argument. None of the conservatives was able to challenge Collocott's call for a dispassionate consideration of the 'Russian experiment' which he thought to be 'Incomparably the most important experiment being made today'. The essence of Christian economic relations was that they should be non-exploitive and based on love and the common good, not the pursuit of power. In that context socialism could not be cast aside without a second glance. Collocott, Churchward and some of the younger men, must have found encouraging the General Conference

Pronouncements 'Christianising Industrial Relations' and 'A Christian Social Order'.[57]

The limited nature of this debate indicates that the Methodist church was unlikely to have any real answers to the Depression when it struck in 1929, although there were ample warnings in the shape of unemployment and labour troubles throughout the 1920s. Like all the Protestant churches, it tried to spiritualise the problem. The statement issued by the heads of those churches (and signed by J.W. Burton for the Methodists) took as its starting point the view that 'While [the Depression] is an economic, it is even more a moral crisis'. Relief works were necessary, but the moral and spiritual issues must also be faced for '[The Depression] is the outcome of a way of life which has exalted material interests above moral and spiritual ideals'. A humble and contrite turning to God was necessary, along with a sharing of sacrifices: 'If we calmly, unitedly, and in brotherly love face our difficulties, then through the blessing of God a brighter day will soon dawn'.

Among those who made their views known, few had anything worthwhile to say. Collocott, showing courage and understanding, pressed the view that, while the relief of present want was urgently needed and must be given immediately, any solution which did not also seek the radical reform of human institutions was inadequate. Rev. Rupert Williams, Superintendent of the Sydney Central Mission, also knew that it was too simple merely to blame either the 'apostles of revolution' or those who were suffering. It was the church's responsibility to stir men to action in order to reform the social system. There were few others who shared the insights of Collocott and Williams.[58]

Moved by love and compassion, the church did seek to provide an ambulance at the bottom of the cliff. It is neither necessary nor possible to document all the relief work attempted. Sometimes there was a conscious decision that church members should help through general community mechanisms, as in the Manly circuit. Elsewhere, help was given on a circuit basis, as at Lambton, Mayfield and Wollongong, areas where the suffering was particularly bad.

The Methodist Unemployment and Relief Fund, commonly known as the Brotherhood (Relief) Committee and convened by

A.B. Lalchere from the Five Dock church, began work in November 1929 and continued to give help to those in need beyond World War II. The method of operation was to seek money from those who had it to give and jobs from those who could offer them. Men were then offered a period of casual work and paid for it. This fitted in with the philosophy generally espoused by Methodists that the dole demoralised men and that the offering of work was the best way to help. The system worked well at first but was dependent on the charity of New South Wales, and especially Sydney, Methodists. Within eighteen months of the beginning of the movement, the flow of both funds and jobs was slowing and no amount of advertising in *The Methodist*, or of support by the President, could increase it again. The continued depressed economic conditions were drying up either or both the ability and will of Methodists to assist. It is impossible not to wonder whether there was any connection between this reduction in the level of help offered and the indication from the 1933 census that only one in seven Methodists was unemployed, a figure not only substantially below the community average but less than that for any other denomination.[59]

The major sources of aid from Methodists during the period were the Central Missions. Of these, three (Sydney, Newtown and Newcastle) were particularly important in this respect. At Newtown in 1929–30, which included only the early months of the Depression, 533 persons or families in need were helped, but that figure rose to 1373 in 1930–31 and reached 2070 in 1932–33. Thereafter, it declined but relief work remained an important activity. The Sydney Central Mission had opened its 'people's hostel' in Princes Street in 1916 and had taken over the Sydney Night Refuge in 1922. By mid-1930 it was assisting one hundred and fifty men a day in some way. This was the major channel of Methodist relief in Sydney.

The Newcastle Central Mission initially provided free daily breakfasts for between seventy and eighty men, as well as other relief for families. Later, the Brotherhood, aided by men from Toc H, daily provided an evening meal for an even larger number, though it is not clear whether this was a substitute for the breakfasts or in addition to them. As late as 1937, the Newcastle Central Mission was serving over 50 000 meals a year.

In September 1931 it opened a hostel for men in an area beneath its social hall—seven years later it was moved to Wickham and continued to serve men throughout the war years. Apart from this, non-residents in need were provided with meals or clothing as the opportunity arose.[60]

War—again!

By 1928, *The Methodist* had changed its attitude towards the issues of war and peace and its editor, Rev. F.W. Hynes, was urging the use of the anniversaries of the outbreak and end of the Great War to preach and pray for peace rather than to commemorate war. In a 1930 note on the outbreak of the war, he commented that '. . . it is a mind entirely out of the time which would look towards preparing for peace by preparing for war'. The churches must beware of the spirit of nationalism which was 'very much alive' in all nations and was a peril to peace. In 1932, he deplored the fact that the last Conference had given the impression that 'our church will need considerable education before it is ready to lead the moral revolution which the Peace Campaign is'.

Surprisingly, that very year, the New South Wales Conference, influenced by a General Conference resolution on the promotion of peace, and in response to a motion by its President, J.W. Burton, requested the Council of Newington College to disband the school's cadet corps and substitute general physical education in its place. It also resolved to explore the legality of chaplains to the armed forces not wearing military uniform. The Newington council rejected the Conference resolution, but what really mattered was that it sparked a significant debate in the connexional journal. Burton himself had been provocative in his address to Conference stating that 'War is, without question, the negation of all that Christ taught and meant, and yet, as in bitter irony, there are professedly Christian men who defend it, as their forefathers defended slavery'. While Burton found enthusiastic support from an Arnhem Land missionary, Rev. T.T. Webb, he was strongly attacked by ex-chaplain James Green and others who saw pacifism as cowardice and likely to provoke attack.[61]

Support for the peace movement grew strongly in the church in the congenial environment of the 1930s. The proposed establishment of the Methodist Peace Fellowship in 1935, and the designation about the same time of a 'Peace Sunday', gave the movement impetus and ensured that the subject would be kept open to the readers of *The Methodist*. E.E.V. Collocott provided intellectual stimulus, arguing that the search for peace in the international arena must be firmly based on its pursuit in our personal, commercial and national life. He advised his readers against adherence to such obsolete concepts as national sovereignty, since it prevented the proper working of international machinery. The gentle B.L. Webb, pleased to find that the atmosphere of his beloved church had changed over twenty years, rejoined the discussion, while Revs William Coleman and Brian Heawood also lent support as did layman A.O. Robson. Of course, this was a subject where logical argument, on either side, did not necessarily prevail.

A United Christian Peace Movement was formed in early 1937. Collocott was its foundation President and the Anglican, Rev. W.G. Coughlan of Kingswood, its Secretary. This provided a broader focus for those many Christians, both lay and clerical, in all churches, who were beginning to find war incompatible with their conscience and who believed that peace was not the mere absence of war but 'a positive condition of society, deliberately and universally based on the essential Christian principles of Truth, Justice, Mercy, and Love . . .'[62]

Spurred by such events as the invasion of Abyssinia and the bombing of China, the debate continued, sometimes rational and sometimes not, but always vigorous and usually gentlemanly in tone, though occasionally an impatient note was sounded. Yet when war came in September 1939, there was an immediate change of tone, especially, but not only, on the part of *The Methodist* itself. It was not a rallying to the colours as in the Great War, nor was there the same certainty that God would overrule and bring good from evil, and especially there was not the same sense that the war would provide the church with a great opportunity to win and hold the people. The editor simply argued the need to join with fellow citizens in saving the nation and the world from a great evil. The means was not liked and had not been sought, but the cause was just and there appeared to be no other way. F.W. Hynes believed in the British cause, but he was no 'jingo', neither would he censor his own paper.

There were more to dispute this point of view in 1939 than had been the case twenty-five years before. The most dramatic disputation was that offered by the 'Coalfields Manifesto', a document published widely by Anglican, Congregational, Methodist and Presbyterian ministers on the South Maitland coalfield. In measured terms, it condemned the idea that war could ever be just or righteous, urged the people to avoid the vindictive attitudes of the Great War and saved its most provocative sentence for last: 'We believe that prayer for the victory for arms for any one side is unchristian, but do join our prayers for a just and enduring peace'.

Conference 1940 steered a careful course and probably pleased no one completely. It deplored the war, urged prayer for early peace, and reminded the church that it must make its well-informed contribution to the achievement of a stable peace. Governments should not inhibit debate and should not use the war as an excuse for allowing social conditions to deteriorate unduly. But, if Conference was cautious, its President for 1940–41, Rev. P.L. Black, was not. In an emotional address, he told 'the extreme pacifists' that if they thought themselves 'fools for Christ's sake' they were deluding themselves; rather, they were 'just plain fools'. By pushing their principles too far, they were doing great harm. Christians could not remain neutral. It was true that war was unchristian, but they had to choose between resistance and extinction. Yet when Black later became editor of *The Methodist* (April 1942), he appeared to follow the example of Hynes rather than Carruthers and gave free access to all in its columns.[63]

As the church, like the community, settled down for the long haul, it did the things that were expected of it, regardless of whether or not it supported the war. Some ministers became chaplains, others ministered to those who sorrowed at home for loved ones absent or lost. Entertainment was provided for the young men in camp. Congregations blessed their lads when they left, tried to keep in touch with them while they were away, honoured them if they were killed or wounded and welcomed them when they returned. The church castigated the government over the provision of 'wet' canteens and the continuance of racing and other forms of gambling during the war, and it objected to the opening of picture shows on Sunday for troops, believing it would not be possible to close them again later. Whether on the local or the State level, the Methodist Women's War Service League, under the aegis of the Home Mission Department, worked hard to provide comforts for the troops and to ensure that chaplains were fully equipped with everything they needed for their work.[64]

A few leaders realised that if the church were not to be left hopelessly behind in a greatly changed post-war world it must begin planning immediately so that leadership could be offered to the community. In particular, the economic and education systems and the world of entertainment had to be redeemed if the changed world were to be a better one. The Social Service Department began work on principles of economic justice which Conference could adopt, while a Christian Commonwealth Conference was held at Cessnock to bring church leaders like C.M. Churchward, R.F. Sutton, E.V. Newman, Alan Walker and R.G. Staines together with leaders of labour and industry to discuss such issues. This conference may have given rise to the Christian Distributors Association (see the following chapter) since it included many of the people involved. Certainly the aims of the conference and the Association were closely related.[65]

World War II was an altogether different war for the Methodist church from its predecessor. There was genuine, if limited, debate about the relationship between Christianity and war and, if numbers were still in favour of going to war, debating ability was in favour of pacifism. The old jingoism had largely, though not quite completely, gone and there was more maturity and sensitivity than had existed twenty-five years before.

The years 1914–45 were difficult for the Methodist church, yet they brought some significant achievements. If Methodism had allowed its evangelic passion to cool a little, the record also shows that it continued to work hard at church maintenance and at 'covering' the state, having more success in the former than the latter. The church's own statistics reinforce the point. The number of circuits in the State increased from 172 to 219, though most of that occurred before 1930, and the number of ministers rose from 218 to 253. The number of local preachers and the total number of preaching places declined absolutely. The number of members (including those on trial) rose by 71 per cent over the thirty years, while the number of regular attendants at worship fell by almost 34 per cent and the percentage of Methodists in the total State population declined very slightly between the censuses of 1911 and 1947. Methodist allegiance remained approximately three times stronger in middle-class suburbs than in those occupied mainly by the working class. Numbers in all youth groups had more than doubled, but Sunday school enrolments had fallen by 14.6 per cent and attendance had become markedly less regular (61 per cent instead of 67 per cent).

The church had tried some new approaches. There had been theatre services at Manly, making use of neutral ground, and radio and film had provided a new means to project the church's message. By 1945 the Waverley 'Forum of the Air' provided a different quality of contact between church and people. The biggest and most worthwhile experiment of all, though only partially effective, had been F.T. Walker's Men's Own Movement.

But two wars, the 'gay twenties' and a Depression had each in their way shaken the people's faith in God and their belief in the church as an organisation relevant to their lives. One prominent clergyman commented ruefully early in 1934 that the Christian faith was being challenged as never before. The problem was not open antagonism, but apathy and 'practical atheism' springing from the pursuit of pleasure and material possessions. Such things led to uncertainty and lack of conviction in the church and it needed to offer an aggressive spiritual leadership if it were to reconquer the paganised areas of community life.

Early in the war years F.W. Hynes used the editorial columns of *The Methodist* to express his view that the churches needed 'prophets' in the mould of Isaiah, men of vision who would proclaim God's word not in abstract terms but in a manner that demanded a response from listeners. Probably Hynes was thinking of men who would speak to the community at large and some such would begin to make their impact soon. But first the church itself needed to listen to a prophet of many years standing who had a message which it needed to heed.

In September 1941, J.W. Burton, speaking to the Sydney Methodist Ministers' Meeting on the subject 'Two Beatitudes', told them that piety was not enough; the church must be active. The only activity Jesus mentioned in the Beatitudes was peace-making, but true peace involved the entire reconstruction of human society on broad and abiding bases. It was only possible when men were impelled by motives of sacrifice and self-denial rather than gain and self-interest. Inequalities of wealth, the use of brute force, pride of race and nation all militated against peace and stability. In future, the economic implications of the Gospel would affect its mission in the world far more than would theological discussions. Hitherto the church had condemned liquor and gambling interests because they affected few of its people; now it needed the courage to deal with economic exploiters even though that might involve the loss of some members.[66]

6

Ministering to a secular society

Some years later, in an address given on his retirement from the office of President-General of the Methodist church, Burton urged his younger colleagues to meet the challenges of the deeply changed world. The church must become a truly national body and its General Conference must have the right to speak for the whole church and to affect the nation at large. It must take the lead in spreading goodwill and understanding so that the world might be freed from prejudice and the fear of war and it must also persuade the nation to unfaltering support for the United Nations until nations were prepared to resign at least some part of their national sovereignty for the sovereignty of humanity. Methodism must recognise the alienation of the common man from the church and try to understand his point of view. It must preach a gospel which really was 'good news' to the toiling man. It must also try to win back the intellectuals who had often rejected the church and put it to shame with their effort and self-sacrifice. There was an urgent need for a higher quality of living if the world were to escape disaster, but before the church could successfully call others to that, it must deepen its own fellowship.[1] This vision, born of the faith of one of Australian Methodism's noblest sons, provided at least a starting point for the church in the last phase of its independent history, 1945–77.

An enlarged social conscience

Methodism's social conscience, which had already begun to broaden during the inter-war period, continued to enlarge as the church realised that no part of the life of the host community should be beyond its influence and as it came to a fuller and clearer understanding of the concept of the 'prophetic ministry'. Through its Social Service Department (later, Department of Christian Citizenship), its central missions, and through the work of a significant and active minority of ministers, Methodism took an active interest in a broad range of political and economic matters and in national and international affairs. It was also deeply concerned to assist the troubled, the handicapped, the delinquent, the aged, the sick, migrants, children and social outcasts. As always, it remained concerned about the traditional moral evils.

In the decade immediately following the end of World War II there was a deep concern about the role of communism in Australian society. The Cold War situation, which divided the world into competing and potentially hostile camps based on the USA and USSR, was in itself enough to ensure that this was so. But the situation was made worse by the deep involvement of Australian communists in the disruptive industrial disputes of the day and by the efforts of conservative forces to exploit these problems to their own political advantage. The many socially conservative Methodists shared this concern to the full. P.L. Black, still editor of *The Methodist*, saw the problems basically in simplistic terms as a confrontation between the (Christian) forces of law and order and the (communist inspired) forces of anarchy. In his view, Australia at the end of 1946 was well along the road to communist authoritarianism and the real question was whether it could be brought back. To the economically conservative layman, Ray Gillam, a senior civil servant and prominent Manly Methodist, the capitalist system was 'the' Christian social system; any criticism of it by a minister or any praise of socialism played into the hands of the communists and betrayed the trust of those who paid his salary to preach the Gospel. That the comments by such ministers were usually carefully restricted to the support of resolutions passed by the General Conference was no defence;

rather, it was the Conference which was at fault for carrying resolutions for which it had no mandate from the membership.

Yet the church could hardly shy away from the difficult industrial situation which existed in New South Wales, the industrial heartland of Australia. Of all those problems, none was worse, nor more worthy of the church's attention, than the near disastrous position on the northern coalfields. Even Black believed that the church had legitimate concerns in this area. In August 1949, a meeting of more than eighty ministers, including all those from the city and suburbs, unanimously sent a deputation comprising the President, R.B. Lew, W.J. Hobbin (Social Service Department), Alan Walker and Brian Heawood to Canberra to explore the possibility of church assistance in the resolution of the strike on the Maitland coalfield. There were few to complain, especially when it became evident that the Deputy Prime Minister and the Coal Tribunal had greatly appreciated the effort. Ultimately, the church representatives were not able to be of real assistance, but the point had been made that the church had something to contribute to the industrial world through its ministry of reconciliation. Properly, the collateral point was also made that Christian laymen must play an appropriate and active role in their unions and employer associations. One of the outcomes of this concern was the notion of an industrial chaplaincy, a concept which provided a valuable contact with the workers and employers and which also helped to bring to the church an understanding of the problems of industry which it must otherwise have lacked.

It would take some time for the point to be accepted, and it would never be accepted by all, but several of the ministers coming to maturity at that time argued that ultimately, if a minister was going to preach the Gospel of Jesus, he must sometimes talk politics because 'The Christian message is social as well as personal . . . The fashioning of Christian personality must include the creation of Christian judgements and a Christian conscience . . . To do this involves the Church at some stages in talking politics'.[2]

This important difference of approach between brother Methodists was not really about the propriety of raising political issues, which the conservatives had always done in their own fashion, it lay much deeper. Indeed, it was not even the radical, pro-change, viewpoint often adopted by the new men which aroused conservative ire; after all, Churchward and Collocott had been equally radical. The fundamental problem lay in the determination of some preachers to descend from general principles to concrete examples. To talk about the brotherhood of man was acceptable to all; to refer to its practice in the world of industry or international affairs could cause dissension.

Of vital importance was the Methodist concern with the questions of peace and war. A 'Christian Peace Conference' was held at the Waverley Church on 4–5 November 1944 to 'think hard about the nature of peace' and to ensure that Christian viewpoints were heard early and had their effect. Other similar conferences, often of an ecumenical nature, followed. Individual Christians, Bill and Phyllis Latona of Manly circuit were good examples, participated fully and consistently in general peace conventions even though this sometimes earned them the disap-proval of those who thought them duped and used by commu-nists. The advent of the atomic and hydrogen bombs sharpened the concern for peace because of the realisation that such weap-ons, for the first time, gave the human race the power to annihilate itself. The 1949 New South Wales Conference declared that 'War today has become a supreme sin against God and a degradation of man'. It asserted its belief in the possibility of peace and called on all men to support every effort at reconcil-iation because 'By the seeking of social and economic justice for all men, by generosity of judgements, by casting from personal and national life the evil which makes for war, we believe peace can be secured'. In 1950 Conference specifically empowered its Social Service Department to extend its activities into the field of international affairs and to organise a Methodist Peace Fellow-ship. As time went by Methodism joined with other churches in the attempt to prevent further nuclear testing and to encourage disarmament as alternatives to the total renunciation of war, if the latter was thought too radical a step. Over the years, the General Conference gave a consistently strong lead in favour of peace without ever taking a totally pacifist position.[3]

Throughout the debate it was clear that the leadership of the peace cause came primarily from a section of the ministry. With notable exceptions, the laity was less involved. This debate was qualitatively different from that before World War II in that it was cast almost entirely in practical terms and had only limited theological content. No one ever challenged the depth of theological argument that Linden Webb had produced at Hay in 1915.

The second phase of the peace debate began in the mid-1960s with the decision to commit Australian troops to Vietnam. The general question of peace and war was thereafter almost entirely subsumed in the specific issues raised by that particular conflict: whether or not it was right for Australia to join in a war of prevention in someone else's country to save a possible later war on its own soil; whether or not that particular war was just; whether or not the so-called 'domino theory' was right; whether or not it was moral for the government to conscript young men for the war in question, especially by the means then employed; whether or not the provisions for conscientious objection were adequate; and, especially, whether or not objection to a particular war should be allowed.

Methodists were divided on all these questions and a substantial, and sometimes intelligent, debate ensued in Conference, in *The Methodist* and elsewhere. The most consistent anti-war stand was taken at the central mission's Lyceum Platform, where Alan Walker had been superintendent since 1958 and was determined to present a strong case against the war. The Lyceum was the regular venue for protest meetings and Walker himself participated fully in the protest movement. There were those, like the conservative lawyer R.H. Grove, who thought that Walker had turned the Lyceum into a political platform entirely unrepresentative of Methodist opinion and that the case he presented was seriously distorted.

The 1966 New South Wales Conference itself began badly with a debate which was less than well-informed, but it appears to have lifted its game sharply in 1967 when the debate was led by Ray Watson, QC, for the Department of Christian Citizenship. According to *The Methodist*, it was held 'In an atmosphere of genuine emotion and unparalleled concern'. Ultimately it was resolved to call for an immediate ceasefire, to ask the Australian government to do all within its power to implement this without delay, and to pledge itself to stand with Christians the world over until peace was restored. Conference had moved a long way from its position regarding the Great War.

The bravest stand by any individual Methodist against the war was the decision by Rev. D.A. Trathen, Headmaster of Newington College and a former serviceman, to urge publicly that young men should defy the National Service Act and refuse to be conscripted. His dismissal by the council, and his subsequent reinstatement when its action was found to lack authority, provided high drama, but the mass of correspondence and petitions on either side illustrated the deep divisions within the church (and, indeed, the whole community) over his action and the issues which led to it.

Despite the intensity of the debate there is no evidence that the Methodist church was ever in danger of tearing itself to pieces over the Vietnam issue. The General Conference offered strong pro-peace leadership and the New South Wales Conference followed more tardily. The ministry was certainly not unanimous: Revs F. Trafford Walker and L.G. Williams were as vigorous in support of Australian involvement as Revs Alan Walker, D.A. Trathen and B.R. Wyllie were against it. Among laymen, the lawyers R.H. Grove and R. Watson were on opposing sides, while no one wrote as effectively against involvement as Sydney University lecturer and Liberal Party activist, I.V. Newman. Despite this, all remained conscious of their oneness in Christ.[4]

Racism was another area of significant Methodist concern. This involved a number of separate matters, the 'White Australia Policy', apartheid in South Africa, racial issues in the United States and policy relating to Aboriginals in Australia. Even before the Second World War, clergy like J.W. Burton and Alan Walker had been openly concerned about the white Australia issue. Very soon after the war, Walker took it up in a booklet produced by the Christian Distributors' Association and the 1948 General Conference began to show unease about deportations of coloured persons from Australia under Arthur Calwell's administration of the national immigration policy. The early 1950s saw Rev. Gordon Dicker pleading with Methodists to do what they could to help Asian students who, in spite of having been invited here to study, often suffered severely from racist attitudes. Not later than the mid-1950s *The Methodist* itself began to support modification of the policy to remove all semblance of colour prejudice and by 1958 the notion of a quota of Asian immigrants had found favour in the church.

The late-1950s and early-1960s saw concern with apartheid in South Africa and with the racially discriminatory policies of Rhodesia and the United States but, ultimately, all Australian views of racism had to be judged by the attitude taken to the Aboriginals, since criticism of racism abroad could be an easy means of salving the conscience for wrongs committed at home. Some, at least, were aware of this trap and sought successfully to avoid it. In 1958 *The Methodist* editorialised strongly on the need for the church to support and aid Aboriginals as they sought to shape their own lives. Alan Walker and Rev. R.G. Pearson of Nambucca Heads used the Lyceum Platform to expose the racist attitudes of a minority of whites in that town. Revs C.F. Gribble and T.D. Noffs were also frequent contributors to this debate. Noffs not only provided the Foundation for Aboriginal Affairs with its first home at the Wayside Chapel in 1964, but himself practised a genuinely multiracial ministry. Methodist leaders, like those of other churches, supported strongly the 1967 referendum to recognise the Aboriginal population by including them in the census. In 1971, the church opened a hostel in Redfern for young Aboriginal men working on apprenticeships or other training courses. It was little more than a token gesture in terms of numbers, but at least it was a sign of goodwill. Later, in 1973, the old Epworth Printery building was leased to the Aboriginal community as a Black Theatre. Again, during the early 1970s, the Department of Christian Citizenship took up the question of land rights, advising the federal government on the issue and urging it to pass legislation immediately to grant freehold rights over original tribal lands.[5]

On each of these religio-political issues, the church was much more concerned with the education of its own people and the general community than with the direct pursuit of change. The Christian Distributors' Association, a small group of ministers and laymen, mostly Methodist, and led by Rev. Ralph Sutton of Glebe, circulated a large number of able pamphlets on politics, racism, war, economics and kindred subjects in the late and immediate post-war period. These sold well and doubtless provided material for many a circuit study circle. The Forum of the Air, from the Waverley church, provided discussion of a wide range of topics by capable speakers from a variety of viewpoints. It reached beyond the church itself, as did the later and more important Lyceum Platform. *The Methodist*, by publishing sermons and articles by prominent clergy, by reviewing books, and by providing a substantial opportunity for debate through its letters column, assisted with this process within the church. Conference debate probably only influenced those who actually took part in it. It is impossible to make any attempt to estimate the effect of these various media, though it is evident that a kaleidoscope of views continued to exist within the church on all issues. That was true among both clergy and laity and was, in itself, significant, since before World War II, the church generally had taken a conservative position on all such matters.

Methodist concern with the traditional social evils continued. Sabbatarianism had lost much of its strength, but the church was still anxious to defend Sunday against the inroads of professional sport. Rugby League was the pacesetter. Late in 1953 the League announced that it was programming some matches for Sunday afternoon during its 1954 season. *The Methodist* pointed out that if enough Christians protested about this the courts would have to support them. That nothing was done presumably indicated that not enough lay people, and perhaps even ministers, were sufficiently concerned any longer. In 1958, the League regularly set its 'match of the week' for Sunday. Even *The Methodist* made a concession that would have been unthinkable a few years before: 'The trend of modern-day social activity allows some laxity in the previous rigid attitude of the Church to Sunday sport. If youth attends church on Sunday morning there cannot be any harm in healthy sporting activity in the afternoon'. But it still opposed organised sport on the ground that it was the enemy of the peace and quiet which people needed on Sunday if they were to be able to face up to the problems of the working week.[6]

The paper had missed the important point: society attitudes to work had changed. Even in the middle classes the weekend was no longer seen purely as a time of quiet to gather one's strength for the real business of life. It was becoming more of an end in itself, a time for gaining the enjoyment of the world which was denied during the week by the need to earn a living.

The temperance issue was an almost unmitigated disaster for Methodists. In 1954 the six o'clock closing referendum was lost by a narrow margin notwithstanding a strong campaign by the temperance forces. Despite a temperance victory over the first attempt to introduce Sunday trading, that too slipped away later and there was an ever continuing extension of liquor licences through the club system. Even within the church itself it was becoming harder to hold the line and as early as mid-1962 a group within the Narromine Ladies' Church Aid, upset that it was not permitted to cater for functions at which alcohol was served, formed themselves into an 'outside' charitable group so that they could raise money in their own way for the church while refusing to abide by its laws. Ultimately Methodism agreed to sacrifice its longstanding anti-liquor position to the supposedly greater good of church union.

Poker machines were introduced through the clubs in the 1950s despite Church opposition based on the belief that they were 'morally vicious' and would confront many people with an almost irresistible temptation to spend money which they could ill afford. Revenue-hungry governments ensured that gambling facilities of all kinds continued to grow at a rapid rate until, from a Methodist point of view, it seemed as if the whole State had been turned into one vast casino.[7]

The 1950s saw the Methodist church change its position on one longstanding social issue. Ballroom dancing had long been prohibited on church property or at functions organised in the name of the church because of the supposed sexual nature of the activity. Methodists were not prohibited from attending other dances, though it was strongly discouraged and those who did so were often regarded as lacking in spiritual depth. There had been signs of a change in attitude on the part of some of the clergy in the 1930s when a short, sharp debate had occurred. The issue blew up again in 1946 and a public debate of lamentable quality ensued. The General Conference of 1954 decided to allow dancing on church property as part of a social programme subject to the permission of the local Leaders' Meeting. Thereafter the issue died.[8]

Methodism's social conscience included more than high policy issues like those discussed so far. Above all else, it was concerned with the ordinary people of the community in which the church worked: the aged, children, the sick, migrants, the troubled, the handicapped, social outcasts and the delinquent. It is to its work for these that we must now turn.

The provision of care for the aged began at South Sydney in 1924, but for many years the church most intimately concerned with it was the Sydney Central Mission which opened two homes, one for women and one for men, late in 1929. Under Rev. Frank Rayward, these were further extended and a new mixed facility opened at Sylvania in 1948. The Lottie Stewart Hospital at Dundas opened the same year, Hoban House opened at Pagewood in 1961 and, after the offer of Commonwealth assistance in 1972, six more homes opened in a dramatic expansion of the work made necessary by the realisation that the Australian population was aging rapidly and that only swift action would avert a major crisis in accommodation for the elderly. The Leichhardt mission, under the leadership of Dr Harold Hawkins, had also built a full range of facilities for the aged.

Other Methodist facilities also existed. A Department of Christian Citizenship list produced in October 1975 indicated that twenty-seven facilities were operational in Sydney and suburbs with another five being planned; there were sixteen in country areas with four more being planned. Such institutions ranged from those for independent living to those which offered full nursing facilities and were to be found in most areas of Sydney except the outer west. In the country districts, they were lacking only in the Riverina District and the Far West and North-west mission areas. As well as the provision for homes, a number of 'schools for seniors' had grown up in Sydney and Newcastle on the model of the Sydney Central Mission.[9] The interesting factor common to all of these facilities is that each was the creation and responsibility of a circuit, or combination of circuits, and never of a church department. The importance of that in terms of the sense of belonging and the provision of care and concern was considerable.

The Newtown mission, under Rev. S.W. McKibbin, made a different kind of contribution to the well-being of the aged late in 1949 when it inaugurated its Blue Nursing Service. Initially, this comprised one nursing sister, Marjorie Wilkinson, the former pioneer of the Far West Nursing Service (see later), who travelled in a Morris Minor to nurse the elderly and other needy sick persons in their homes. Within eighteen months there was a staff of three, with two cars, and by the end of the second year the service was seeing thirty cases a day. By 1954, the staff had grown to a matron and eight sisters and the work had been extended to cover new areas. Late that year, something soured the relationship of the then superintendent (Rev. J.W. Spencer) with his officers and, in particular, with the nursing service. The matron and seven of the nurses resigned. The service contined to operate and the Quarterly Meeting reorganised the management to reduce the role of the superintendent. About a year later (mid-1955), the Newtown Nursing Service was copied with the creation of the Newcastle District Methodist Home Nursing Service.[10]

Rising costs and changing social conditions subjected Dalmar, Methodism's only children's home, to new and intense pressures. The need to turn away large numbers of children in urgent need of care led to the first expansion of facilities for many years with the opening of the Bernard-Smith home at Pymble and the Gateway home for emergency help at Lewisham in the early 1960s. The type of care began to change and a considerable emphasis was put on the role of the social worker in trying to keep the family home together and to keep the children out of institutional care if possible. This was enormously time-consuming and expensive and it was a constant struggle to keep the work operative with only limited assistance coming from successive state governments.[11]

Of the many important steps to assist the troubled, including extensive work in pre- and post-marital guidance, the most significant was the establishment of the Life Line 24-hour telephone counselling service in 1963. The aim of this service was to meet the psychological needs being generated by the intense pressures associated with life in a great modern city. Preliminary steps were taken in 1961 when Alan Walker called a large group together to discuss the project. The need for careful planning, and for equally careful training of the host of volunteer telephone counsellors required, meant that Life Line did not commence operations until 16 March 1963. Even in the first year there were over 11 000 first contact calls and by the last year of the independent existence of the Methodist church that number had grown to more than 25 000.

This successful experiment was quickly copied elsewhere. In mid–1964, after his dramatic midnight rescue of a lost and nearly frozen telephone caller, the Rev. John Chegwidden of the Newcastle Central Mission suggested that his church consider copying the Sydney example. Again a substantial interval ensued as they first carefully investigated the need and the commitment in financial and personal terms and then trained personnel. Newcastle Life Line, with Denis Milliken as Director, opened on 7 May 1966. This was very much an act of faith for the local community had not responded well to the financial appeal, there being less than one hundred replies to 1400 appeal letters. The shortfall was $15 000 out of $36 000. Yet the need was there. From twenty calls in the first week the number grew to more than fifty after three months. Other early Life Line centres were established at Wollongong, Manly (operating out of Balgowlah church), Central Hunter (Maitland) and the Parramatta Regional Mission.[12]

The handicapped have always had a legitimate claim on Christian aid, yet organised help on any scale was rare until relatively recent times. The church was too much in step with a community which preferred to neglect such people whenever it could. Three initiatives will be discussed here as examples of what New South Wales Methodism undertook in its final period.

In the early part of 1961, a Christian technical college teacher in Newcastle, Hilton Hayes, found himself looking for an avenue of service on Sunday afternoons. His attention was drawn to the physically handicapped who were frequently denied fellowship because of the difficulty they experienced in moving from place to place. Hayes discussed the need with Rev. John Chegwidden of the Newcastle Central Mission and then called together a small group of friends to plan the introduction of the group which was to become the Crossroads Christian Fellowship for the Handicapped. Initially, this group met at the central mission and sought to meet social, intellectual and religious needs, though, as time went by, the attempt to meet intellectual needs was largely abandoned. Ultimately the group also included people with intellectual handicaps and it provided a weekly social occasion, with a variety of local church groups providing the programme. Occasional Saturday outings were offered and, later, a New Year holiday of a week to ten days at a suitable church youth facility in New South Wales or interstate. The group quickly became interdenominational and eventually spread to Sydney and other centres.

When Annesley College closed its doors as a girls' school in 1964, Rev. W.J. Hobbin of the Department of Christian Citizenship sought to use it as a home for mildly retarded girls. Under the name 'Westwood', it took its first residents in May 1965 with the intention that they should be trained socially and in essential skills to the point where they could take their place in the community and find simple employment. By mid-1968 a few of the first admissions were beginning to work in the community on an experimental basis. Costs were partly covered by government grants and by the girls' invalid pensions, but church support was also needed. Late in the Methodist period it was decided to extend the training facilities by building, with a Commonwealth Government subsidy, a workshop worth $240 000.

The first Methodist sheltered workshop for the handicapped was Leichhardt's Goodwill Industries which opened in 1959 after Dr Hawkins had spent some time in the United States investigating the work there. The workshop employed twenty-five intellectually handicapped young people and sought to train them in a range of skills for which they were paid. The intention was to increase their sense of independence as much as possible. The Sydney Central Mission also entered work for the handicapped in the early 1970s when it opened its David Morgan Centre as a sheltered workshop for people with both physical and intellectual handicaps. In 1975 it also opened the Pinnaroo Lodge for the intellectually handicapped.[13]

Provision for social outcasts continued through the various inner-city missions. The Sydney Central Mission had long been involved in caring for homeless men in some way, but its work expanded greatly from 1966 when Deaconess (later Rev.) Noreen Towers was appointed to build up the 'church for homeless men'. Not only did she do that but she also established a day centre for the men and a 'half-way house' at Galston for alcoholics. From 1974 planning and work went ahead to completely renovate the old Bourke Street Methodist church with the purpose of centralising its services—the day centre, church services, the medical and other facilities and the necessary office accommodation. A six-storey accommodation block, the Edward Eagar Lodge, was built behind the church to give some privacy to the men and to encourage the development of self-respect. This was not opened until beyond the Methodist period (1979) but, when it was, it provided an excellent base for this expanding work. Parramatta also entered this form of work from 1975 with its Hope Hostel.[14]

As child delinquency grew steadily in the post-war years, the Department of Christian Citizenship became more heavily involved in children's court work. This led to the desire for a home away from the city where boys could be retrained and could learn to take a useful role in society. The Iandra property, in the Young district, was purchased in 1955. It was far from the temptations of Sydney and it was hoped that the healthy life on the farm would contribute to the physical and spiritual good of the boys. The surrounding circuits of Cowra, Grenfell, Young, Forbes and Canowindra all became involved in this work. When the 'Iandra Methodist Rural Centre' was opened on 27 October 1956 before an audience of 5000 people, they heard the Hon. F.J. Cahill, State member for Young, commend the Methodist church strongly for doing something to arrest the problem of delinquency.

But problems soon arose in the form of constant troubles with the staff—the work was demanding and it was difficult to find suitable people prepared to live so far from Sydney. This distance also prevented the provision of adequate support for the staff. There were also conflicting claims about the home's success in rehabilitating boys and, in 1974, a report indicated that the number of boys either running away or in need of removal 'in haste' was 'uncomfortably high'. Staff attitudes and management were not good and the welfare of the individual boy was given a low priority. In September 1974 it was decided to close Iandra, sell the property, and use the money to create hostel accommodation at Burwood in the hope that it would provide a more useful facility.[15]

In mid-1955 the Department also decided to set up a home for delinquent girls, to be called Heighway House in memory of Deaconess Dorothy Heighway who had spent many years working among girls brought before the courts. This home, at 30 Alexandra Road, Drummoyne, was not opened until 15 October 1960 because it had to wait until the financial burdens at Iandra had eased. Heighway House was initially filled with twelve girls, aged from fifteen to eighteen years, from the Parramatta Training School. Six of them ran away in the first fortnight and some immediately set about earning a living on the streets. It was going to be a long hard road to rehabilitate them. W.J. Hobbin believed that Heighway was being given 'exceptionally difficult and uncooperative' girls from the courts and, in mid-1963, he refused to take any more of the toughest types, some of whom the house mother described bluntly as 'prostitutes'.

The following year the home moved to Thornleigh which was believed to be a more appropriate neighbourhood. A second property was opened at Coogee for a time, but declining government financial support closed that and the operation centred on Thornleigh thereafter. The same report in 1974 which led to the closure of Iandra declared Heighway to be 'effective' and suitable for expansion, while pointing out the need for improved performance in the area of parent contact.[16]

There was no better work done among delinquent youth, and those in danger of becoming delinquent, than that started at the Hamilton Wesley church by Rev. John Mallison in November 1965. The Newcastle Youth Service put a detached youth worker with psychological training on the streets to make contact with young people on street corners, in pubs, dances, games parlours and anywhere else that they could be contacted. His objective was to gain their confidence and to try, in a completely non-directive fashion, to assist them in whatever way was necessary. He himself was provided with strong support in the church and a panel of experts was also available to assist young people referred to them. The work was dangerous but had its successes. These depended on many factors: the care with which Mallison entered the work; the skill and dedication of the youth worker, T.C.

Waring, and many of his successors over the years; and the strength of the support provided for him. It continues to the present day.[17]

Ministering to New South Wales

One of the most important ideas introduced in the city and inner suburbs was the community church concept. There was nothing new about it since it had been investigated by Rev. James Green when he was in England at the end of the Great War. On his return to Sydney Green had tried to establish the concept at Paddington and gave it a particular orientation towards young men and, especially, returned soldiers. It failed at that time, probably because of this orientation, since returned men took little interest in the church.

In the midst of World War II Conference sent Rev. Ralph Sutton to Glebe in the hope that a young man might be able to revive the failing inner suburban mission. Sutton chose to pursue the community church path. Beginning with a club for adolescent boys, he made such rapid progress that he quickly ran out of room and the boys had to dig out 100 cubic metres of earth from the basement to allow an extension to be built. In time, clubs for younger boys and for girls were added and the total membership reached 300. Members had to attend a devotional period associated with the clubs, though they were not compelled to come to church. Many did, however, and ten decisions for Christ were made during 1945. Sutton's major problems were a shortage of accommodation and of funds. He needed £5000 for the first stage of an ambitious building project. But nobody in Glebe was going to give him that. The State government gave him £100 a year to indicate its interest in the work.

A little later (1944), Conference sent R.N. Gledhill to Paddington and Alan Walker to Waverley and each followed Sutton into the community church movement. Waverley, in particular, had great potential because of its location in an important business area and the relative wealth of the region on which it drew. Walker began with a day kindergarten and a boys' club in early 1945 and soon had a waiting list for each. A Social Action Group followed quickly and, later, as the new Centenary Hall was built, community centre facilities for women, a men's union and Forum of the Air. Walker had the inestimable advantage of active officers who gave him strong support and a community which saw the benefit of helping to provide the kind of facilities that were needed.

Ultimately the concept of the church as community centre spread widely to such places as Leichhardt, Lithgow, Newcastle Central Mission, Merewether, Hamilton, Wallsend, Annandale and elsewhere. The development of Wesley Centre at the Sydney Central Mission after the fire involved the same concept. In some of the smaller places the 'seven-day-a-week church' aspect of the concept was not viable and the centre could only operate on one night a week or fortnight.

The men who led the movement, principally Ralph Sutton, Alan Walker and Ron Gledhill, were absolutely certain that the concept was both valuable and viable, though each recognised the difficulties to be met in its application. Each of them stressed the social nature of Christianity and hence the entire propriety of the church becoming a social centre. Many of the problems of the city were caused by the intense loneliness which was so much a part of its life. Yet the community church had to remain evangelistic or its likely fate was to be secularised by the very society it sought to save. The ultimate aim had to be to make Christians and not merely to provide pleasant social occasions when people might add to their skills or their understanding of the world.

The method and problems of this approach were made abundantly clear in its most dramatic representation, the Sydney Central Mission's Teenage Cabaret. Designed to attract the city and inner suburban youth who did not go to church, it was essentially a modern dance entertainment with modern rock music. Added to this were some Christian songs, a Christian message from Alan Walker and contact with one or more of the Christian young people who were present for this purpose. There was also an invitation to the Lyceum services for any who were interested and the opportunity to use the services provided by the church. Converts were made. Not many, but some. It was a risky business but the alternative was to let the young people 'go to the devil because there was nowhere else to go'.

The initiative did not meet with universal approval. That the church should be a meeting place and a place of fellowship all agreed, but it was to be a spiritual fellowship. Some of them argued that the class meeting and Christian Endeavour were the kind of fellowship needed. They thought that the clubs which played so large a part in the community centre concept were a substitute for spirituality. Yet in the centres where the community church was being tried—Glebe was the perfect example—the old approach had not only failed but had done so over a very long period. The church had missed out on a whole generation or more of the population and the young people had little knowledge of Christianity. Traditional church groups had no meaning for them. Community churches had their problems and did not provide a panacea, but the number of conversions at the three main centres of experiment, and the number of young people going on to membership of the church, suggest that the concept was well worth trying.[18]

The other great, related, inner city experiment in the post-war years was the establishment of the Wayside Chapel at Kings Cross by Rev. Ted Noffs. Officially opened on 12 April 1964, the Chapel set out to be 'the Church out in the World', meeting people where they were and setting up a dialogue with them on their own terms. Workers went out in old clothes to all the beatnik pads in Woolloomooloo and the Cross to interest them in the coffee shop to be held above the Chapel. Soon there was no shortage of visitors to that or to come and talk. The Chapel witnessed through traditional religious services, through listening, through the coffee shop, art, poetry and drama. Its busiest hours were often late at night when good church people were usually tucked up in bed. Contact with drug addicts and potential suicides was an every day occurrence, demanding very special skills from the dedicated team that Noffs and his wife, Margaret, had gathered together. A Drug Referral Centre was set up in 1967 and a Drug Addiction Research Foundation established. Much important community knowledge and action in this area flowed from Noffs's pioneering work.

Noffs found many detractors among the traditional members of the church who were largely unable to understand either what he was trying to achieve or the value of his work. Yet Noffs wrote enough about the work, in *The Methodist* and his book *The Wayside Chapel*, and they should have been able to grasp the message. Many simply did not want to understand either the growing menace of drug addiction or the many problems experienced by minority groups at the hands of the majority community. His theological position sometimes seemed radical and perhaps it was—as radical as Jesus had seemed to the Jewish authorities. The Chapel was a daring Christian enterprise in an unpromising environment.[19]

After her appointment, Deaconess Kay Edwards undertook a rich ministry among the lonely and the migrant, through an extended Sunday school, through tapes and through philanthropy in the densely populated Woolloomooloo area. The overall ministry brought contact with many races and people of all religions. The Foundation for Aboriginal Affairs was one outcome of this.

The rapid growth and spread of population in New South Wales after World War II posed a difficult problem for the church. The major movements were in the dominant coastal cities of Sydney, Newcastle and Wollongong as a flood of migrants from Britain and Europe poured into the State. Many of these people went to inner urban areas in the first instance. After that they tended to flow to the outer suburbs and this brought many people into new living conditions and new problems as they faced long trips to work and lonely times, especially for the women, in areas where they, at least initially, had neither relatives nor friends. Short-staffed and lacking funds, the church again found itself ill-placed to meet the challenge or to grasp the opportunity presented.

The Home Mission Department was a major force in Methodism's attempt to come to grips with this problem. Its energetic post-war Director, Rev. A.G. Manefield, a man widely experienced in the outback missions and that most difficult of all areas, the South Maitland coalfield, knew that he lacked the resources to place men and erect buildings everywhere that they were needed in the new suburbs. His strategy was to use a young minister as a mobile worker in these areas. The first man chosen for the task was Rev. John Chegwidden—young, warm, capable and prepared to spend and be spent in a work as demanding as ever Methodism had laid upon one of its men. Chegwidden was provided with 'an up-to-date mobile unit' and sent to East Bankstown to begin. His unit was equipped with a movie projector, a gramophone, facilities for open-air preaching, Sunday school requisites and religious literature for sale. In a word, it was a mobile church and Chegwidden's task was to use it in the new housing areas to contact new people and attach them to the church. After a time, a temporary church would be established and the 'mobile minister' would move on, leaving the people under the oversight of the nearest circuit. The Home Mission Department, through its Woolnough Sites and Church Extension Fund, provided for the purchase of strategic sites and the erection of buildings. The project was a part of the Department's contribution to the Crusade for Christ.

It is impossible to assess the success of such work. Causes were created where they would not otherwise have been: some of them flourished, but not all. While he admired the zeal with which the Home Mission Department and its agents worked, Rev. R.J. Coleman expressed the doubts of many when he queried the wisdom of Manefield's strategy at several points. He wondered whether the resources, and especially the manpower resources, of the church were not being stretched too thinly and how well the work of the mobile agents would be consolidated after they had moved on. There was no point in opening up an area if it could not be consolidated. The policy of attaching new causes to neighbouring circuits, often already unwieldy and over-burdened, was 'short-sighted and unwise'.[20]

Some circuits were involved in their own extension work. Under the leadership of Rev. N.G. Pardey, the Manly circuit made an area survey which led to the establishment of a cause in the Allambie Road locality. Home Mission support was sought and given, but the work was primarily in the hands of the circuit. The Charlestown circuit sent out eight people in pairs to canvass the new Windale housing estate and commence work there, though it lamented that so few of its people were prepared to be involved and wondered how long it would take to complete the work throughout the circuit.

The major area for church development was the Illawarra. In September 1947, representatives of circuits from Helensburgh to Kiama met at Wollongong to develop strategies for future growth.

The primary need was thought to be additional ministers or other agents in the Bulli, Corrimal and Wollongong circuits and for help from the Home Mission Department to acquire portable buildings for use throughout the area. The problems sprang from the fact that the population of the area between Stanwell and Shellharbour had grown from 61 000 in 1948 to 91 000 by 1954. Corrimal circuit in 1950 included three schools but by 1955 had eight with two more planned. There was also a high school and the situation was further complicated by a large migrant hostel. The local church worked hard and some successes were achieved. An ordained minister was appointed to West Wollongong in 1955 and a church hall was opened at Unanderra in the same year. A Sunday school of 160–70 sprang up almost overnight at Unanderra but there were only four experienced teachers available to work there. The real problem remained manpower and Rev. C.J. Wells pointed out in 1957 that the Church had only thirteen full-time workers on the South Coast, the same number as there had been in 1927. Belatedly, in 1966, Rev. Heinz Eiermann went to the South Coast part-time to assist with work among migrants, but this did not work and, by August, he was back in Sydney full-time.[21]

The church was obviously on the horns of a dilemma over extension work. It lacked manpower and financial resources to do the job properly and yet it knew that it had to be done. To fail to undertake such work was to become a 'maintenance' church entirely and to abandon permanently large and growing 'pockets of paganism'. The work done by the Home Mission Department was limited and sometimes superficial, but if it had left it to the existing circuits it would not have been done at all in most cases. The limited effort at Windale makes the point. Even the effort organised on a district scale on the South Coast, where there was an acute awareness of the problem, did not lead to any great and enduring victories.

Out in the Far West mission the church was still making its mark. In 1946, largely through the efforts of Rev. L.M.K. Mills and Sister Ethel Helyer, a Methodist Nursing Service was established with its base at Brewarrina and with a charter to extend its services through such far-flung towns as Angledool, Goodooga, Lightning Ridge, Hebel, Enngonia, Barringun and Hungerford.

Staffed initially by Helyer and Marjorie Wilkinson (each of whom was a double-certificated nursing sister, a deaconess and a local preacher) the service brought medical, dental and religious aid to settlers who, in many cases, had no other contact with any church. They held Sunday school meetings, including one in a riverbank camp near Brewarrina for fifty to sixty half-caste children who had never before had any interest taken in them by white people. They held services in their cottage, introduced junior and senior Christian Endeavour and held fellowship teas on the verandah of their home. Over the next year or two the staff at Brewarrina was increased and a second base was established at Menindee on the Darling. In 1965, after almost twenty years, the existence of a fully equipped and staffed hospital at Brewarrina allowed the church to move its base 320 km to Hungerford where it was re-established in even more difficult circumstances.

The other interesting development in the Far West in this period was the introduction of the 'flying patrol' based in Cobar. This began operation in May 1966, with Rev. Neil Gough as the 'flying padre' and greatly strengthened the links with some of the more distant towns. Services could be held where none had existed before and with increased frequency in other places. It also allowed the Superintendent to exercise a more effective administrative control.[22]

A further major advance for Methodist organisation came with the development of the regional mission concept in the last decade of the Church's independent history. The Central Sydney Synod for 1967 sent forward resolutions seeking the creation of regional missions to provide a new strategy for the metropolitan areas of Sydney, Wollongong and Newcastle. It was argued that the greater mobility of the population allowed the abandonment of many small suburban churches and the consolidation of the church into larger units for worship and that these would have greater appeal than small 'butter-box' churches with limited resources and facilities. It would also be more efficient for service work of all kinds. A team ministry would allow ministers to concentrate their efforts on those aspects of the work to which they were best suited rather than being 'all-rounders' in the long-standing Methodist tradition.

Some were justifiably puzzled by the notion that larger congregations automatically provided a more desirable atmosphere for worship and helped to overcome the loneliness caused by life in the city, but the experiment was undertaken, though on a smaller scale than the enthusiasts desired. The first and most important of these missions was Parramatta which underwent its metamorphosis in 1971. Despite enormous difficulties, and largely through the untiring work of Rev. Gloster Udy, Parramatta was a success. With its Life Line, St Albans Centre, Epworth Press, Hope Hostel and Lay Academy it did the work of a mission and raised the level of religious provision in the region. But Parramatta was a very special area and an ideal one into which to transport a concept originally designed for the inner city. It might not work equally well elsewhere.[23]

The church reaches out: evangelism

In its final three decades, Methodism in New South Wales undertook two major evangelistic campaigns and assisted in the Billy Graham Crusades as well as continuing its more localised activities. One of the methods favoured for local work was the 'teaching mission'. This attempted to give greater depth to the work of evangelism than was possible in, say, a ten-day evangelistic campaign of the traditional kind. Solid biblical and theological teaching was given over a period of time, possibly some weeks, and the mission as a whole was geared to lead the participants to either first or renewed commitment. It was an answer to those who condemned evangelism as being superficial and it was very suitable for use over Lent and Easter, or in the lead up to Pentecost. Other circuits undertook lay evangelism in one of its many possible forms.

In Sydney, from the late 1950s, the Central Mission held its annual Easter mission. Designed initially to counter the growing secularisation of the Easter period, this developed specialised sections for community leaders and young people as well as undertaking a vigorous outreach into the general community using novel methods. It was a moderately successful and wonderfully positive approach to a problem which had often trapped the church into purely negative responses.

The emergence of a 'new' Department of Home Mission and

Evangelism, based at Chatswood where it was supposed to experiment with the methods which it recommended to others, reinforced the church's continuing commitment to evangelism, though it is not clear that the altered arrangements had achieved much before union.

The Methodist church fully supported the Billy Graham Crusades. Yet with the evangelist's constant, hammer-like use of the formula, 'The Bible says . . .', these were old-style evangelism at its most basic and, despite the general euphoria of the church, some worried that it would lead to a long-term loss of credibility among the intelligent, educated sections of the community.[24]

The long campaign known as the Crusade for Christ, of which the Mission to the Nation was the final phase, was born in the mind of J.W. Burton, President-General of Australian Methodism, in the immediate aftermath of the war. Burton had been moved by the eager involvement of the American Methodist Episcopal church in evangelism and had seen a vision of his own church reviving itself and reforming the nation under the slogan 'Australia for Christ'. Burton found support in the General Conference Committee on Evangelism which began to plan for a nation-wide Crusade for Christ, of at least three years duration, to be authorised by the General Conference of 1948 and to begin in 1949 after the State Conferences.

The first year (1949–50) was to involve work within the church itself. An emphasis on the active teaching of Christian doctrine was to lead to a 15 per cent increase in membership, while a community survey was to pave the way for a 'visitation evangelism' campaign which was expected to win back to active participation a number of Methodists no longer involved in their local church. (This particular aspect of the work was well-judged since a public opinion poll taken in September 1950 suggested that perhaps as few as 19 per cent of Methodists attended church every week while 54 per cent went 'rarely or never'.) The second year would concentrate on the stewardship of time, ability and money as well as winning 20 000 new Sunday school scholars, a 15 per cent increase in all local church groups and a 50 per cent increase in regular church attendance. There would be a challenge to full-time service for the young and to witness in daily work for all. An effort would be made to raise giving to all church causes by 25 per cent. In the final year, 1951-52, the Crusade was to be taken to the nation at large.[25]

The local church was to be the backbone of the Crusade. Some circuits, Manly, Goulburn, Waverley and Waratah among them, moved quickly to develop and implement the overall Crusade strategy in their area. At Waratah, by the end of August 1949, more than 500 homes had been contacted and over sixty Methodist families had been 'brought into direct association with the church'. The movement led to the building of the new Waratah South church, gave a considerable boost to the Broadmeadow church and developed a new sense of involvement among the young people of the circuit. But too many circuits were not willing to do the hard work. The New South Wales State Director, Rev. Norman Pardey, lamented the slowness of congregations to act to recapture the half-million lapsed Methodists (nationwide) revealed by the 1947 census. The customary circuit reports appearing in *The Methodist* bore all too few references to special activity for the Crusade. Some did not even undertake the community survey which was supposed to precede all other 'outside' activity and enable the local church to assess its situation.

By the end of the second year of the Crusade, the church was not ready to move out into the community in the planned evangelistic campaign of the third year. Consequently, General Conference extended the life of the Crusade from three to five years to allow the laggard circuits to catch up. Pardey wrote bitterly of the general disappointment that so many circuits were not fully committed to the Crusade and of the 'spiritual illiteracy and apathy' in many churches which had necessitated the change of plan.[26]

In 1952 planning began for the final year of crusading, intended to take the form of a six-month Mission to the Nation. Once again every local church was urged to be involved and to plan its own local campaign to its own people where they worked, lived and played. The most visible aspect of the mission was to be a series of ten-day missions, led by the national missioner, in each State capital with shorter campaigns in a number of major provincial centres. There was to be a weekly radio feature to present the Christian challenge to those who would not come out of their homes to hear. The unanimous choice of the General

Conference Crusade Committee as missioner was Rev. Alan Walker, superintendent of the Waverley mission in the eastern suburbs of Sydney. Rev. Rex Mathias of Melbourne was secretary with the duty of providing organisational and personal support.

The mission opened in Melbourne Town Hall on the evening of 8 April 1953 before a packed audience and the service was broadcast nationwide. Walker's message was essentially a simple one: that the Christian religion held the answer to the needs and problems of the day and that Australians must give God His rightful place in their national, community and personal life; the Christian religion held the answer to a world adrift because it offered each person the transforming power of Christ. This message was both personal and social and flowed from the missioner's personal conviction that, to have an impact on people outside the church, preaching must be 'prophetic', or relevant to the issues of the day, and not pietistic. In the course of a major campaign Walker related his message to problems of poverty, unemployment, corruption, exploitation, racism, sexual immorality and war, thus giving it a breadth and striking power lacked by more narrowly-based missions.

The campaigns were designed to meet people on neutral ground and were held in town halls or similar places. Traditional religious language was avoided. Lunchtime meetings in town squares or in industry were common and some campaigns included discussions with local civic leaders or well-known local non-Christians.[27]

One of the most successful aspects of the mission was the radio programme, 'Drama with a Challenge'. Centred around some significant issue of the day, and with the script written by a professional writer, these programmes were broadcast by over sixty stations and heard by an estimated one million people weekly. The heavy mail in response to this programme suggested that many people were being stirred by the dramas. Some local churches formed listening groups and then discussed the issues raised over a cup of tea. This method of presenting the Gospel was more costly than anything the church had ever done before, and that cost had to be met by commercial and other sponsorships.

Radio evangelism continued in 1954 with a programme entitled 'Life has a Purpose' and in 1955 a new drama series was produced which was claimed to be the most successful of all. Certainly several remarkable conversions were recorded and, on at least two occasions, interest groups were attacked with such vigour on a programme that they protested to the Macquarie Network which was on the verge of cancelling the contract until the Methodists agreed that equal time be granted for reply to any group which felt itself aggrieved by one of the programmes. This final series drew between 2000 and 3000 letters over its time on air.[28]

In the country centres of New South Wales much necessarily depended on the preparation and follow-up by the local church and those circuits and towns which had done more in the early stages of the Crusade were generally prominent again. At Goulburn the local Ministers' Fraternal, chaired by Dr Burgman, Bishop of Canberra and Goulburn, began planning early for a joint effort and Walker's visit in September 1953 became the climax of six weeks of local campaigning and was an outstanding success. Similarly at Orange, Revs Wesley Douglass and Guy Walker canvassed the local press and radio thoroughly beforehand so that they were keen to get interviews, provide editorials and record addresses for rebroadcasting. Their reward was that 'The Mission to the Nation became a very live subject in Orange'.

The highlights of the Sydney mission in September were a Procession of Witness by an estimated 25 000 people with another 50 000 lining the streets, an extraordinary opening meeting, and an unusual Youth Rally which brought 10 000 to the open-air Stadium at Rushcutters Bay on a wet Saturday evening.[29]

The decision to continue the mission into 1954 and 1955 was almost inevitable considering the substantial successes of 1953. Less emphasis was placed on the major capital city campaigns while more country centres were visited and two new elements were introduced: 'schools of evangelism' for ministers and laymen and, in New South Wales, a mission to secondary schools.

One of the major successes was in Newcastle, which had not had a successful mission since the great tent missions at the beginning of the century. A combined camp meeting at Maitland followed by a Procession of Witness in Newcastle by 4000 people and led by Alan Walker and the Methodist Lord Mayor, Alderman F.J. Purdue, gave the mission a good start. Major daily meetings had crowded audiences and there was a series of worthwhile lunchtime visits to various industrial establishments. The concluding rally on 17 October was held in a packed Town Hall and was widely heard in the churches and homes of the district through radio station 2HD. A total of 16 500 attendances during the week was something of a marvel for Newcastle.

Elsewhere the usual pattern was to hold an eight-day mission with the national missioner conducting the services during the final weekend after someone else had broken the ground through the preceding week. This was considered to be a very effective way of missioning in regional centres and was the recommended approach for the future. The schools of evangelism were successful but the lack of comment about the missions in secondary school suggests that they may not have been.[30]

Mathias later described the First National Christian Youth Convention, held at the Sydney Showground in January 1955, as 'the single greatest happening in the whole program of the Mission to the Nation'. More than 3000 young people were present from all States of Australia and the Pacific. As well as a March of Witness, the customary Bible study sessions and inspirational speakers, there was a Parliament of Youth which published a declaration to the people of Australia on various issues confronting the nation at the time and this caused some concern in conservative political circles. The Convention ended with an open-air Festival of Faith, held in the pouring rain, as a major act of witness and dedication. An unforgettable feature of this festival was the performance of Rev. Arthur Oliver's specially written and powerful drama, *Truth in the Arena*.[31]

Throughout the 1955 campaign certain local missions continued to be successful with those at Manly, Willoughby and the development area at Revesby being notable among them. But the major and bitterly disappointing failure of the final year was the mission's inability to draw a sufficient proportion of the local churches into active participation through visitation evangelism. The church seemed incapable of sustaining the effort of mission once the excitement of the great campaign was over, or would do so only if an active and enthusiastic minister gave a strong lead. In New South Wales, at least, that may have been partly due to those changes in the Methodist machinery, already noted, which led to the decline of the old balance between centre and periphery.[32] After the completion of the Mission to the Nation it had been intended to follow the American church by establishing a permanent Federal Board of Evangelism to continue the work. That intention was defeated, though that was the fault of States other than New South Wales, and the mission formally ended on 17 March 1957.

There is no adequate means to measure the success or failure of the Mission to the Nation. The missioner was careful never to claim too much. Despite unprecedented audiences for rallies and radio dramas, he admitted frankly that there had not been a religious revival, though scores of people previously unconnected with the church had been won to it. A spotlight had been directed onto some 'sore spots' in Australian life and religion had become both 'news' and 'a talking point' as the mission had attempted to answer the questions that people were really asking and had faced up to the issues that troubled men and women at that time.

From 1953 to 1957 the number of members of the Methodist church in New South Wales increased by 3055 (6.5 per cent) and the number of regular attenders at services by 4989 (9 per cent) at a time when the percentage of self-proclaimed Methodists in the population was actually falling. The number of local preachers rose by 24 per cent over the same period and of paid agents of all kinds by 18.8 per cent by 1963. (In the latter case, some time must be allowed before those who felt themselves 'called' during the mission affected the numbers in active service.) Ministers of other churches sometimes claimed increases in their congregations as an outcome of the mission.

The real areas of the mission's failure lay elsewhere. Its impact on the church had been less than that on the community. As might have been expected, conservatives rejected the liberal 'total Gospel' approach which Walker had taken and thought he should have spoken more about Christian principles and less about what they referred to as 'his own political beliefs'. But much of the church also remained tied to its old, failed, ways and unwillingness to try new methods. The strongest possible evidence for this view lay in the fact that perhaps 90 per cent of Methodist circuits (nationwide) failed to join actively and vigorously in the visitation evangelism programme which had been intended to cap the mission and to ensure the vast increases in membership which had been sought. Even after six years of continuous crusading, their apathy was unbreached. Likewise, in 1954, in New South Wales alone, thirty-four circuits failed to respond even to a Conference direction to take up a retiring offering for the mission and in 1955 the number of circuits which had not responded by mid-September was one hundred. It was an important failure that no continuing national Board of Evangelism was established to carry on the work.

On the other hand, Methodism in New South Wales and elsewhere had made a greater effort than ever before to bridge the gap between the church and the ordinary person in the street. Its evangelism had been socially responsible and intellectually and emotionally respectable and did, as Walker suggested, mark the first great break with the nineteenth century evangelistic style. People listened and, forty years later, it is still possible to meet non-Christians who admit that the one time in their lives that they were 'almost persuaded' was during the mission. In almost every case, it was the prophetic nature of the preaching which influenced them.[33]

The final great evangelistic crusade of the Methodist church in New South Wales was the 'Newness New South Wales' campaign authorised by Conference for 1970–71 and led by Alan Walker as his main contribution in his presidential year. Planning began in February 1970, and in May a special committee was appointed to carry it forward. The campaign opened in the Sydney Town Hall in October 1970, during Conference, then the missioner moved around major centres in the State through a series of eight-day missions. A panel of ministers conducted other local missions in less strategic towns. This campaign featured the same socially responsible evangelism which Walker had employed in the Mission to the Nation. Special attention was paid to youth evangelism, the use of mass media and the mobilisation of the laity. The public relations firm of Hansen–Rubensohn was engaged to advise on advertising in the electronic and other media as they had during the Mission to the Nation.

The launch, during Conference 1970, took many by surprise.

The account by the *Sydney Morning Herald* indicates why: 'Strobe lights, a pop group, jazz ballet dancers and a giant panda with balloons joined with a Methodist choir last night at the Town Hall to bring "Newness" to New South Wales'. There were more shocks for the traditionalists at the first of the eight-day missions in Parramatta as the church employed 'the surfie parson', John Hirst of the Churches of Christ, to lead youth activities and coffee shops. Much of the adult-related mission activity was held in a car park. The great achievement of Parramatta was the commitment of several bikies from the gang 'Satan's Slaves' and their participation in some of the later missions.[34]

The most unusual mission of all was on the Central Coast in January 1971. Well over one hundred young people joined Walker to take the Gospel both to the locals and to the hundreds of holiday-makers who crowded the region at that time. These young people called themselves 'Jesus people' and were a part of the 'Jesus revolution' which broke out in the United States and New South Wales at much the same time. In the morning they taught children on the beaches; at lunchtime, at The Entrance, Gosford or Wyong, Walker held one of his 'crossfire' (question and answer) sessions and, in the afternoon, the young people were back on the beach mingling with teenagers and seeking to interest them in Christ. In the evenings there were open-air meetings, a 'major' meeting at a neutral venue, and two coffee shops for the young people. If the Central Coast missions had no other impact, and they almost certainly did, the effect on the lives of the young people helping there was profound. Walker felt that a youth 'movement' was taking shape.[35]

The major youth event of the year was the 'pop' festival at Vision Valley over the Anzac weekend. With an audience of 3000 for two-and-a-half days of almost continuous music—pop, Christian, folk, and even light classical—the potential was obviously there for either triumph or disaster, and many traditional church members were uneasy at the level of risk involved. The *Sydney Morning Herald* reported that the festival had been 'uninterrupted by violence or drug "freakouts" ' and that police, church members and young people had all agreed that it had been the best-organised pop festival held in Australia. Mission sources claimed that more than half of the 3000 who attended were from beyond the confines of the church and many were from outside the groups that it was normally able to contact. They believed that such festivals 'might yet be able to redeem the pop festival scene' and claimed that a major breakthrough had occurred.

Not all churchmen were equally confident, however. John Edwards, who had been at Vision Valley and who wrote to *The Methodist* thought that very few contacts had been made right outside the church and that most of those attending were 'on the fringe'. The Christian stage presentations had been low in quality compared with those of the pop groups while few of the 'Newness Youth' movement had taken much interest in meeting and talking to non-Christian young people, preferring their own 'holy huddles'. It 'was not so much a breakthrough into the pop culture as a breaking free from traditional church patterns by the use of pop media'. It was a worthwhile beginning and worth doing again, but it needed a lot more work. The church should also train elite groups to go to ordinary pop festivals and work there to reach real outsiders.[36]

At Armidale, Walker ran into substantial opposition at the University of New England while some within the church thought his selection of social issues on which to base his addresses was unwise. Later, at the University of Sydney, the Student Christian Movement refused to support the mission because the Methodist church had admonished Rev. Norman Webb for actions he had taken as Master of Wesley College, and the Evangelical Union likewise refused support because of Walker's 'whole Gospel' approach. His support there came from the Roman Catholic chaplain and the Arts Society. There was nothing surprising about the Catholic support, since Cardinal Gilroy had urged it and it had been given most generously in many other places as well.[37]

Looking back Walker thought that 'Newness' had achieved a deeper penetration of the lives of the people in both church and community than any other campaign in which he had participated. He himself had led twenty-six missions and had spoken to 230 000 people. There had been sixty other missions throughout the State with a total of 2000 commitments. Ninety-seven young people had 'enquired' regarding full-time service, though possibly only twenty-four actually carried through with this. 'Newness' had made evangelism the first priority of the church, as it should be. Walker was especially gratified by the development of 'Newness Youth'. The experience of witnessing which had been gained that year, and new forms of worship which had been devised, would remain with the church and enrich it in future years.[38] This view, however, proved to be over-optimistic. Where change occurred, it seems to have been on the fringes rather than at the heart of the church. Yet the way to further change was probably more open than it had ever been. Most importantly there was no great spiritual awakening. Secularism continued to flourish, and while the number of confirmed members rose briefly but significantly in 1972, it plunged again thereafter. Even a well-planned and imaginatively executed campaign could, by this time, create only a very temporary and limited success.

7

Ministering to the church family

As well as reaching out to the community at large, the Methodist church continued to care for its own faithful members. Problems relating to work among both youth and adults increased greatly as did those associated with finance and the church had to struggle with these issues hard and long. Always the situation was complicated by the involved and seemingly endless negotiation over union, but this issue also raised hope of a stronger and more faithful church.

Caring for young people

The task of caring for the young people within the church became enormous in the years after World War II. In 1966, the Department of Christian Education (as the once Sunday School Department was then called) covered the following areas of activity: Sunday schools; a mailbag Sunday school for remote areas; religious instruction in day schools; the Harold Wheen Free Kindergarten at Redfern; a variety of youth groups, including Knights, Comrades, Endeavour, Methodist Youth Fellowship, Crusaders and others; camping at eight regional conference centres; the Bible College offering a variety of courses to both internal and external students; adult education in the circuits; university chaplaincies; in-service training for existing leaders; and the Order of St Stephen.

In 1945 it had 55 000 children enrolled in its Sunday schools and youth groups and this number peaked in 1961 at 85 000 only to drop away to about 41 000 at the 1976 Conference. The Sunday schools had experienced fifteen years of rapid growth followed by fifteen years of even more rapid decline, ending the period with many less scholars than they had at the start when the population was much smaller (31 000 in 1976 against 36 000 in 1945). The picture with the youth groups was more complex. Christian Endeavour continued its long-term steady decline. Senior OK courts had a similar pattern from the time when figures were first given for them, but the junior courts had increased until the mid-1950s and then declined. By ·he end, Knights had a total membership only 20 per cent of that in 1934. From the mid-1930s, Comrades followed a similar path but more slowly and Rays, the junior branch, managed to continue growth until the beginning of the 1960s. No separate numbers were given for the Methodist Youth Fellowship (MYF) until the 1960s, but from there on it lost members consistently and at the end it retained only 29 per cent of its 1961 membership.[1]

Sunday schools continued to experience their long-standing staffing problems. The editor of *The Methodist* argued in 1951 that, in the past, untold harm had been done by the appointment of teachers who had no personal experience of Christ's transforming power. Such people gave the impression that while the Christian religion was 'quite a good thing' it was not really a matter of great urgency or importance whether one committed oneself to Christ or not. Only fully committed leaders could advance the cause of the Kingdom of Christ.

That remained true and the church found no answer to the problem. All it could do was to attack the parallel problem of teacher training and hope that as it improved the skills and Bible knowledge of its teachers that they might also come to a personal experience of Christ. Training was never better organised and never undertaken with more enthusiasm and determination. In the mid-1960s a series of superintendents' conferences were held in the various districts and 'Operation Outreach' sent a team of skilled people around the State to gather large numbers of teachers together for weekend and other conferences. These were hard-working occasions and, in the country districts particularly, drew excellent attendances from people anxious to improve their skills.

In the suburbs the pattern used for a group of young people from the Denistone East, Dundas–Carlingford and Eastwood Sunday schools during 1963 was sometimes a better proposition. There, staff from the Department were able to offer training on a weekly basis over six months with observation and practice teaching sessions being offered as well as lectures and discussion. Not only did that train a group of new teachers, but it led to the establishment of a continuing training meeting thereafter.[2]

Despite all this effort and the fact that the church now had the best-trained teachers using the best-prepared lesson material and best-equipped schools it had ever had, Sunday schools demonstrably failed to achieve their aims and lost scholars at a rapid rate. Of course they would never be as well-equipped and staffed as the day schools which the young people attended. Those young people who came were more questioning than earlier generations and had more distractions, including Sunday football and the ubiquitous motor car with the almost endless possibilities it had opened up for spending a day which had once offered no other form of relief than Sunday school. Most importantly, the percentage of their parents attending church had declined considerably and parental pressure was more likely to be against, rather than in favour of involvement.

The variety of youth work has already been noted, along with the pattern of its decline. Again, this occurred against a background of improved training of group leaders. The Country Youth Leader Camps, initiated in January 1947, set a pattern, first at Otford and, much later, at Elanora, the Victory Thanksgiving Youth Training Centre eventually built on land donated by Sir Frederick Stewart. Long before this, the virtual gift by Mrs William Arnott of the family home, Gowanlea, at Gordon provided an important centre for such work in the metropolitan area. At the beginning of the 1960s the Bible College situated in Walker Street, North Sydney, offered yet another opportunity for young people to train for leadership, lay or ministerial, in the church.[3]

Apart from the usual centrally administered youth groups, some circuits offered youth work specifically designed to suit local needs. Manly tried after-church discussion groups dealing with a wide range of issues. Initially successful, these seem to have failed later for at least two reasons. No attempt was made to focus the discussions from a specifically Christian point of view and hence they lost purpose and relevance as church groups. In some cases non-church youth outnumbered church youth and an inadequate leadership was unable to control the situation. The role of Teenage Cabaret at the Sydney CMM has already been discussed, but both before and after that a large range of organisations sprang up in the attempt to provide a bridge into the church for the non-Christian youth of the city. These ranged from the relatively sedate Couriers for Christ and sporting and social clubs in the days of Revs R.J. Noble and R.C. Coleman to the more exotic 'J.C. Coffee Shop' and 'Jesus Family Gathering' during the 'Jesus Revolution' of the early 1970s.

Far away from the city, Mullumbimby, a town with its own problems, experimented with its own version of Teenage Cabaret and a Coffee Shop. Under the leadership of Rev. Ron Elliot, and with considerable community assistance, this attracted many though it was never really able to advance to the next stage of getting a significant number of the young people so contacted to attend the special youth services held in the local church.[4]

Rarely before had the church tried to do more than provide for its own youth, but now it also sought to use its own young people to reach out to non-Christian youth. In this work it was bold, imaginative and well-intentioned, but its success was limited. This was not surprising since the task was difficult. The tragedy, from the church's point of view, was that its work with its own youth fell into a hole from which it could not be extricated. Nor did any one of its major standard youth groups for church kids do better or worse than the others. Christian Endeavour, Knights and Comrades, and Methodist Youth Fellowship all failed together. Many of the factors which caused Sunday schools to fail also affected the older youth groups.

The church worked energetically to improve the standard of religious instruction given in State schools. From 1949 seminars were presented for ministers and home missionaries on this aspect of their work. Expert teams were involved in the programme. As well as theoretical training, there were sessions in lesson planning, demonstration lessons and some practical work. Similar sessions were also held for lay helpers. One such course in the Parramatta–Rockdale area involved six half-day sessions and was led by Mrs Jean Staines, a former infants' demonstration teacher. From 1960, co-operation between the New South Wales and Victorian Councils for Christian Education in Schools led to the provision of a published syllabus for use in both States.

The major problem was always to find enough people, with or without training, to put in front of the classes week by week. As attendances at Sunday schools declined, the day school work became more urgent. It was only there that many children ever received any religious teaching at all. If the church failed them at that point, they were condemned to a life entirely ignorant of the Christian Gospel. The problem was never solved simply because it was insoluble. Nor did the church's own schools help much with this problem, since increasing fees put them out of the reach of many Methodist families and their interest in what had once been the basis for their existence often seemed limited.[5]

Caring for adults

Worship naturally remained the church's primary provision for its mature members. The realisation that the average church service was no longer attractive to the majority of the population came to many in the early post-war years. What to do about the problem was another matter entirely.

There had always been a 'high church' movement within Methodism. In the early days it had manifested itself in the desire to introduce a more liturgical order of service and had successfully struggled to describe Methodist buildings as 'churches' rather than 'chapels'. At that time it had strong links with the pursuit of 'respectability', discussed earlier. In the twentieth century it revived and took a new turn, putting increased emphasis on clerical dress as well as on ritualism. Architecturally, the removal of the pulpit from the centre-front of the church to the side-front, with the communion table taking its former place was another manifestation of this 'sacerdotalism' and suggested some change in the balance between preaching and the sacraments. It is possible that there was a connection between these developments and the decline in evangelistic activity in the circuits.

Elsewhere, attempts were made either to enliven, or give added dignity to, the traditional Methodist service. At Waverley, the choir was gowned in maroon and white and processed into the service American style. It left during the last hymn and sang the Gloria from the vestibule. There and elsewhere written orders of service were introduced to allow the congregation a larger participation through the repetition together of responses. At Wallsend Rev. Errol Towner held a special service for youth and the whole act of worship, which included the use of popular religious tunes and instruments and short addresses, was conducted in 'the language of teenagers'. Less adventurous clergy simply added a fellowship hour after the evening service once a month. Morning services were moved to an earlier and more congenial hour.

Manly circuit was bold and innovative: in 1966 a question time was introduced in the evening service at Seaforth and an open discussion followed immediately after. In 1972, at Seaforth again, they tried a 'barbeque communion', an unrecognised modernisation of the old Methodist 'love-feast'. Though it was regarded as a success at the time, it seems not to have been repeated. Balgowlah's monthly 'Happiness Happenings' (1973) were an attempt to get people to 'deepen [their] understanding of a Christian perspective of happiness' but failed because they seem to have been confused and chaotic and unrecognisable as an act of worship. At Paddington, Rev. Peter Holden's 'village church' was a valiant, if only partially successful, attempt to break into an extremely difficult constituency which had largely lost contact with the church.[6]

The significant fact about each of these experiments, and others elsewhere, is not whether they succeeded or failed, but that they occurred at all. Such approaches were indicative of a church searching for new avenues of worship which would be meaningful to its adherents in their particular environment. In part, this search was forced on the church as the introduction of television adversely affected evening worship and caused a move to the morning but, in any case, it deserves sympathy and commendation. That the church failed to find ways which proved attractive in the long term to a wide range of members was damaging.

Another aspect of this change was the development of a charismatic movement within Methodism, as happened within every other mainstream branch of the Christian church in the late 1960s and 1970s. This movement was sufficiently significant for Alan Walker to call a convention on 'Rediscovering the Holy Spirit' at Wesley Centre in June 1968 to attempt to keep the two sides in the debate together. Almost four hundred delegates attended. By 1971, Conference thought it desirable to issue an authoritative statement on 'Pentecostal Experiences and Charismatic Ministries'. This document accepted the validity of pentecostal experience but stressed the variety, and equality, of the Spirit's gifts to individuals. It recognised the authenticity of the gifts of tongues and of healing but insisted that gifts were only genuine if they deepened a person's concern for, and relationship with, the whole church. The main work of the Spirit was to witness to the Lordship of Christ. A 1973 questionnaire revealed that possibly 600 people in eighty-one circuits were influenced to some degree by the Charismatic Renewal Movement. Some problems had occurred in congregations where people on either side took an unduly rigid stand.[7]

While the two movements were not identical, it is difficult not to see a parallel between the Charismatic Revival Movement and the Holiness Movement of the late nineteenth century. This parallel extends both to the nature of the movement and the problem of relationships within the church. In time, it may also extend to the outcome of the charismatic movement.

Adult education for church members became a major activity. This took a variety of forms and only a few can be mentioned. The College for Christians begun in the social hall of the Newcastle Central Mission in mid-1953 was one of the earliest of such institutions. Intended as a Mission to the Nation project, its purpose was 'to equip Christian people for more effective service'. The idea was copied at the Sydney Central Mission in 1959 where it not only served well but was able to survive longer than it had in Newcastle where the pool of able people who could run such a thing was much smaller.

All-age Sunday (or church) schools were tried in many places in the 1960s to encourage members to see religious education as a continuing process regardless of age. As a secondary purpose it was hoped that the mingling of the generations in these schools would reduce the leakage of teenage scholars which was so regrettable a feature of Sunday schools of the old style.

The earlier Bible College in North Sydney and the later Evening College in the city both had the same purpose as the institutions already mentioned: to help lay people to know and understand what they believed for their own sake, to equip them better for service in their local church and to enable them to deal on equal terms with well-educated non-Christians in the community. The work was necessary in the kind of community which had developed in post-war Australia, but it faced considerable difficulties: how to make it broadly available when there were only a limited number of workers; how to overcome the apathy of some members; and how others who were heavily involved in the life of their circuit would find the time to participate whatever their will to do so.[8]

Ministers also needed the opportunity to update their training and 1962 saw the Western District Synod initiate a move for continuing theological education. It took some time for the proposal to bear fruit, but the first refresher course was held in May 1964 and attended by eighty-five ministers. District Schools in theology and guided reading courses were also to be arranged wherever possible.[9]

Among the adult fellowship groups, the Men's Brotherhood spread even more vigorously in the post-war era than it had in pre-war days. It was reported that by 1955 it had 105 branches, fifty-nine in the country and forty-six in the city, and a total membership of 3000–4000. It was declared (by its sponsors) to be 'the most effective State-wide organisation in the Church', democratic in its constitution, providing for cultural, moral and spiritual development and having considerable impact on both church and community. The 1960 Conference Brotherhood Dinner was attended by 600 people.

That the Brotherhood flourished in a wide variety of locations is beyond doubt and it is equally certain that it provided yet another means of self-education for many churchmen and a way into the church for some whose interest had never been more than marginal. No branch was stronger than Manly where it was ideally suited to the mix of professional and business men who lived and worshipped there. Richard Thompson, a leading layman and a member of the Legislative Council, had all the skills that were needed for dynamic leadership and an endless string of interesting contacts who could be invited as speakers. This branch served the church at large by offering a scholarship for a local person undertaking theological studies at Leigh College. Its members at times invited African and Asian students in Sydney under the Colombo Plan into their homes and to their meetings. Later most such groups tended to decline.

The Women's Auxiliary to Overseas Missions, the Women's Home Mission League and the various Ladies' Church Aids continued to provide women with fellowship and with important opportunities for service which they generally seized eagerly. They were, in many respects, the backbone of the church and continued with little change from earlier times. The New South Wales Methodist Women's Federation continued its work of representing the interests of women as it had done since 1931 but with greater vigour than in its early days. It had a particular concern with the closing of hotel bars on Anzac Day and backed its efforts in that direction by joining the Women's Inter-Church Council in serving cups of tea to ex-servicemen after the march. In 1959, after a major naturalisation ceremony at the Sydney Town Hall, it entertained over one hundred new citizens.[10]

Members, preachers and clergy

The number of members (including those on trial) had increased steadily in the inter-war period and continued to do so until 1963, though membership was decreasing as a percentage of population. Thereafter the decline became absolute and by 1975 the church had only 906 more members than it had in 1955. Attendance at public worship declined steadily in absolute numbers from 1914 to 1945, increased slightly to 1950, fell away disastrously to 1955 and then climbed again to 1960 when it began a further decline. By 1965, Methodist attendance was only about three-quarters of its 1945 level or half of its 1914 level.

Methodism alone does not bear all the ignominy of this decline since it affected all denominations across many countries. Education and prosperity led many to dispense with God. The upward social mobility and the new certainties of life which they brought seemed to make faith unnecessary. The central message of Christianity, with its emphasis on humanity's dependence on the grace of God rather than its own cleverness, and its concern with the moral demands of citizenship in the Kingdom of God rather than self-interest, had little appeal to people constantly encouraged to seek fulfilment in material things.[11]

Despite the Church's desire to enlarge the ranks of the ministry, the number of candidates remained variable in the early post-war years and was always less than was needed. The high rate of loss from among those who had offered was a further contributing factor to the shortage of ministers. The problem was sometimes attributed to the low spiritual state of the church, and that view was supported by the difficulties encountered in the early years of the Crusade for Christ (see above). The Mission to the Nation stimulated spiritual life and improved the rate of candidature and was at least one cause of the sharp increase in the number of clergy from 247 (ministers and probationers) in 1953 (only twelve more than there had been twenty years earlier) to 302 in 1965. There was an alarming decline during the next ten years and the gains were almost totally lost. This was a time of great uncertainty over the whole question of ordained ministry.

Variations in the presentation of figures makes it hard to be sure what happened to the number of home missionaries and deaconesses (Australian Methodism had, in any case, been slow to develop the latter order), but the number of local preachers followed a pattern similar to the ministry, increasing from 896 in 1950 to 1217 in 1964 and falling back to 933 by 1975. The number of known Methodist agents of all kinds preaching the Gospel in New South Wales reached an all-time high of 1568 in 1964 but, by the time of church union, it had fallen back to earlier levels before the Mission to the Nation initiative. No one believed that the number of paid agents was adequate. Such shortages made it harder to introduce specialised ministries, as was being done increasingly overseas, and helped to explain the decline in full members which set in at the same time. The increasing complexity of the minister's task served only to accentuate the deficiency in numbers even further. Yet, even if the men and women needed had been immediately available, few of the circuits had the money to employ them.

In the circumstances it is surprising that sheer pragmatism did not lead Conference to consider early the question of the ordination of women, but it did not. Despite the fact that several Methodist churches overseas ordained women it was 1966 before the issue was debated by the General Conference. Until then the only avenue of full-time service open to women was the Deaconess Order where small numbers continued to find satisfaction despite the fact that the church never granted it a particularly high status. Although it decided to allow the ordination of women, it was 1968 before the General Conference Standing Committee took the final action necessary to make their candidature legal.

At the General Conference of 1972, Jean Skuse, a New South Wales representative, launched a wide-ranging resolution seeking to improve the status of women in the church and the community at large. Yet the New South Wales Conference continued to evade the spirit of such resolutions. An Australian Council of Churches Commission on the Status of Women which attended the 1973 State Conference noted that female representation on committees was still low, especially on the powerful committees like the Board of Finance and the Standing Committee. It commented that 'the NSW Methodist Conference did little in 1973 to dispel the belief that, in practice, it has a very long way to go before it offers justice to the majority membership of women in the Methodist Church'. The faithful women of Methodism had to wait until the inauguration of the Uniting church to gain a larger and fuller role.[12]

Church finances and the 'new saviour'

Methodist finances were rarely secure and attempts by James Woolnough in the 1880s to encourage the widespread use of the envelope system so that giving would be more systematic have been discussed. Such initiatives depended on the enthusiasm of individual ministers and were never widespread and rarely long-lasting and the basic problem remained unsolved. The serious inflationary trend in the years after 1945 forced the issue. General costs climbed rapidly and ministerial stipends became a heavy burden for circuits without ever placing the ministers in a secure or comfortable position.

The first response of most circuits, with the encouragement of Conference, was to implement the envelope system with greater vigour than before. In a very few places, Weston was one, this seemed to solve the problem for a time. Elsewhere it effected a considerable improvement but left the problem unsolved because an insufficient number joined the scheme. Wollongong was a case in point: only one-fifth of the congregation took envelopes and although they contributed one-third of the offering the improvement still left a deficit. Many circuits tried to keep a firmer control over their expenditure, Goulburn showing the way with its establishment of a Finance Committee.[13] There was little likelihood that such means would prove adequate on a permanent basis when inflation was both long-standing and severe.

From 1954 the Wells organisation offered its services in Australia to conduct financial canvasses with the aim of putting church giving on a fully pledged and systematic basis and so relieving churches of their seemingly endless special efforts to overcome deficits. Eventually, both the Home Mission Department and the Young People's Department (Department of Christian Education) offered the same service to Methodist circuits. The latter dropped out after a time but the former continued for many years and conducted the majority of Methodist canvasses in New South Wales, though other private organisations were also operative in the field.

In 1968 a Church Commission reported to Conference on the fourteen years experience of planned giving in the Methodist church. In the first two years of the Wells scheme more than fifty Methodist churches or circuits had adopted it. There had been 'spectacular' increases in income in a number of cases, but, within a few years, antipathy developed towards commercially conducted campaigns and this led to the situation noted above. By 1968, half of the circuits had experienced 'several' campaigns, one-seventh had held two campaigns, another one-seventh one campaign, while the remaining one-fifth had not used the service and did not intend to do so. The Commission considered that many circuits which did plan campaigns in the future were likely to rely on local resources to save the cost of using experts.

Canvassers and canvassed circuits frequently maintained that the primary purpose of the work was the renewal of spiritual life and that any financial returns came as a consequence of that. One enthusiast declared that 'A new kind of revival is sweeping through Australia today. It can be described in the phrase: Spiritual Renewal Through Giving . . . What we failed to do in the Mission to the Nation campaign is now being done through this canvas [sic]'. The 1968 Commission was unconvinced, holding that the time allocated for most canvasses was too short to achieve major spiritual results and that the emphasis was squarely on fundraising.

This considered view was probably correct, but the available evidence does not allow firm conclusions to be drawn with confidence. Some circuits, Cessnock is the best known example, tried very hard to achieve and conserve spiritual results. While the figures already given show an increase in both membership and attendance across the early Wells years, there were other factors more likely to have been responsible for this. Some claimed that the Wells movement actually detracted from the spiritual benefits of the later years of the Mission to the Nation. That too remains unproven since the secularising tendencies of the late 1960s and 1970s could account for the observed losses.

In a purely financial sense, second and later canvasses were rarely as successful as the first. No one should have expected a repetition of the quantum leap forward that some first canvasses achieved, but sometimes pledges showed an actual dropping off even in nominal terms, as in the circuit of the enthusiast quoted above. More often there was a small nominal increase which did not compensate fully for the effects of inflation over the intervening years. As new methods were introduced to finance church departments, resulting in a central budget being established which was shared among the circuits in proportion to membership (instead of the old haphazard method of relying on each circuit to determine its own giving for the central work), many circuits found themselves in some difficulty meeting the new and annually increasing demand from the centre. Even a strong circuit like Manly worried about this and had to revert to special efforts to keep its head above water. It is also noteworthy that, while budgets increased for connexional work, there was also loss of a different kind in areas like Home and Overseas Missions as the teaching formerly given by the deputations, which had once travelled the circuits to raise money, was no longer readily available.

The Wells approach to church financing provided a breathing space rather than a final solution. What it did do, especially in rapidly expanding areas provided their financial management skills were good enough, was to give the circuits a chance to clear old debts and to erect buildings to cope with the increased population without incurring heavy new debts. It taught members the need to be more thoughtful about their financial stewardship and many, regardless of future canvassing, never allowed their giving to fall back to its old inadequate, some would have said 'unchristian', levels. Without this work the extraordinary levels of inflation might have left many circuits floundering.[14]

Church union: the 'tortuous trail' completed

Like the Great War, the Second World War put pressure on Protestant Christians to co-operate. In New South Wales the churches were drawn closer together as they shared in united intercessory services and, in some places, one minister served both Presbyterian and Methodist congregations. After the war, the meeting of the First Assembly of the World Council of Churches in Amsterdam, and the later activities of the worldwide ecumenical movement, constrained constituent churches to consider either union or co-operation in their own societies.

In 1942, a conference of the three federal committees on Christian unity was held in Sydney and proposed, on a Presbyterian initiative, a federal union. There would be co-operation in each State in areas where new churches were needed, in the training of the ministry, in youth work, over public questions, in home missions and evangelism. Regrettably this proposal also foundered on the rock of Presbyterian opposition as only the New South Wales Assembly gave approval, and that only in a general fashion.

Methodists resumed negotiations with the Congregationalists

for a bipartite organic union 'recognising especially that a divided world will not heed the preaching of the reconciling gospel of the One Lord and Saviour by a church which is itself divided'. Yet, after an able debate at the 1954 General Conference, it was decided at the last minute to defer arrangements for a vote on the proposed bipartite union until a last approach had been made to the Presbyterians. This was largely the work of R.H. Grove, a long time Sydney advocate of union, and W.J. Campbell, a disappointed Canberra unionist. The Congregationalists readily agreed to support this initiative and the Presbyterian Assembly of Australia, meeting in September 1954, responded positively and, more surprisingly, the State Assemblies, Presbyteries, Sessions and members also voted strongly in favour of resuming negotiations.[15]

In their desire to win over the Presbyterians and to ensure their entry into the united body, many Congregationalists and Methodists, despite misgivings, felt that they should concede some things which were precious in their spiritual heritage and church polity. This they did believing that union was important as an expression of their loyalty to the Gospel and to the God–given mission of the church. Regardless of their efforts and the concessions they made, the union finally achieved was not as comprehensive as they had hoped as some Congregationalists and a large section of the Presbyterian church chose not to participate.

A Joint Commission of twenty-one members, seven from each denomination, was established, including R.H. Grove and Rev. B.R. Wyllie from New South Wales Methodism. Convening in November 1957 it published a first report in September 1959 and a second in 1963 which incorporated a *Proposed Basis of Union*. This second report and the *Proposed Basis* were sent to all local churches in Australia for comment. Numerous submissions were forwarded to the Commission by Methodist Quarterly Meetings as well as by the respective courts of the other churches.[16]

The President of the New South Wales Conference designated 26 July 1964 as Church Union Sunday, hoping that it would be used to introduce the proposed basis of union to Methodists and to initiate group studies. Most churches responded and the New South Wales Committee on Church Union and the Board of Christian Education prepared six studies which were published in *The Methodist* during August and September. In the months following Church Union Sunday many articles and letters both for and against union were published. The most controversial proposals included one to have Bishops in the Uniting church and another to enter into a concordat with the Church of South India—in time, both were eliminated. Other strong Methodist criticisms, which were not accepted, concerned the reduced role and status of local preachers and the support given by the *Proposed Basis* to the doctrine of baptismal regeneration. Several of these criticisms had originated with the usually influential General Superintendent of Home Missions, Rev. Walter Whitbread.[17]

During these years co-operation between the three churches was unstable and unreliable. In 1962, Rev. K.L. Doust reported co-operation in the building of Lugarno church but, in the same year, Methodists resented the (new) appointment of a Presbyterian home missionary to Nyngan without prior consultation. Lack of co-operation led to the establishment of three 'pathetically small causes' at Lalor Park. There had long been a Committee on Church Co-operation but, with the exception of the war years, its achievement had been slight. To this point at least, it is legitimate to question whether the essential precondition for union stated by Carruthers in 1920 had been fulfilled as there was no evidence of either spiritual or any other kind of solidarity between the denominations.

A Joint Advisory Council was formed in New South Wales in 1965 to provide guidelines for the formation of joint parishes and to give some oversight to them. Methodists were involved in every joint parish and at the end of 1976 there were forty-four joint parishes in New South Wales with the Methodists contributing thirty-nine ministers and home missionaries. Such ventures prepared members of the three denominations to enter corporate union, although in at least one joint parish the Presbyterians voted not to enter.[18]

From 1965 the Joint Constitution Commission studied the vast range of submissions which it had received and published a new draft basis in 1970. At the request of the General Assembly of Australia there were some further revisions and the Joint Commission published a *Revised Basis of Union* in 1971, on which members of the three Churches voted. Again *The Methodist* published several articles in favour of union and provided generous space for correspondents to express their views both for or against. The main reasons advanced against union related to the proposed presbyterial form of government and to a claimed lack of information on what stance the Uniting church would take to the question of drinking alcoholic beverages.

In 1972 Australian Methodists voted 85 per cent in favour of union and Congregationalists 83 per cent in favour. Presbyterians voted on two badly constructed questions and the Christian Unity Commission was unable to interpret the meaning of the Presbyterian vote. A second ballot was ordered in 1973 and in this almost 69 per cent registered a desire to join the Uniting church. In New South Wales just under 70 per cent of those Methodists eligible to vote cast formal votes. Of those who did, 79 per cent voted in favour of union compared with 85 per cent for Australia as a whole. The necessary 75 per cent in favour was obtained in eleven out of the sixteen Districts. One hundred and forty-one circuits returned a majority of 75 per cent or more in favour and eleven circuits returned a majority vote against union. The remaining fifty-one circuits registered votes for union in the range 51–75 per cent. Unfortunately, after the votes were collated the papers were not retained and it is not possible to identify which Districts or circuits voted for or against union. In Conference, almost 83 per cent of the votes cast were in favour of union. It is not easy to explain why New South Wales Methodists favoured union less than their co-religionists in other States, although it is possible that it was a consequence of the perceived difficulties of both working and negotiating with the Presbyterians in that State.

The 1972 Methodist Conferences in the various States took an 'in principle' vote only on the question because of the difficulty over the meaning of the Presbyterian communicants' vote. Only the Queensland Conference produced a lower vote in favour of the principle of union than did New South Wales. In 1973, the Methodist Conferences voted again, this time on the specific question of entering into union with the other two churches. In each State except Queensland and South Australia the vote for union dropped below the 1972 figure. New South Wales showed a substantial decline to 76 per cent. It is not known why there should have been this drop in Conference support for union as the 1973 vote was taken and recorded in the minutes without comment. Nor was there any comment on the matter in the 1973 Pastoral Resolution.

The national courts of the three churches met in May 1974, and registered what were to be the determining votes. Congregationalists voted almost 98 per cent for union, Methodists 94 per cent and the Presbyterians 64 per cent. This unfortunately meant that many Presbyterians would not enter the union and in New South Wales the number of continuing Presbyterians was much higher than the national average as only 156 parishes there had voted to join the Uniting church while 186 had voted to remain Presbyterians. sixty-four Congregational churches, twenty-seven of them in New South Wales, also remained outside the union.[19]

The end of the 'tortuous pilgrimage' was delayed a little longer by the action of a number of Presbyterians. The Joint Commission had planned the inauguration of the Uniting church for 1976, but this was delayed for a further twelve months. About forty members of the General Assembly of Australia staged a walk-out from the May 1974 Assembly and constituted a continuing Presbyterian church. Having failed in their persistent battle to prevent at least a part of the Presbyterian church from entering Union, they embarked upon protracted and costly legal battles to delay the inauguration of the Uniting church.[20]

It seems strange that this momentous decision was taken at last almost without comment. No one stopped to explain why the vote for union was successful on this occasion when earlier votes were unsuccessful. Perhaps everyone—or at least all highly placed Methodists—had been living with the possibility, or necessity, for so long that it seemed inevitable and natural. Such a conclusion could readily be drawn from the words of the President-General, Rev. Rex Mathias, following the release of the 1972 voting figures:

> We Methodists have made unmistakably clear our serious intention and desire to go into union with the Congregationalists and Presbyterians in Australia . . . Let's stop wasting time. Let's take Methodism, nearer to its best, into the new church whenever it comes.[21]

A later statement by Rev. Dr A. Harold Wood, doyen of Methodist union advocates, pointed in the same direction:

The three Churches have felt that they are so close to each other in tradition and practice that it would be an offence against truth to remain apart. More than this, they have been impelled to obey the prayer of the Lord of the Church for his followers, 'that all may be one that the world may believe that thou hast sent me' (John xvii.21). Only when reconciled among themselves can members of the Uniting Church call upon nations to be reconciled to God and to each other. The Uniting Church also believes that its union is the first step in a growing together of more and more Christians in Australia, in obedience to the will of Christ who is Lord of us all.[22]

In 1975, a Joint Planning Committee was formed in New South Wales in preparation for union. The Methodist members were H.W. Tebbutt (chairman), Revs E.G. Clancy, R.E. Glover and J.S. Woodhouse. Heather Stevens was added a little later. The secretaries of the respective Churches were responsible for preparing regulations, combining funds, planning committees to arrange provisional presbyteries and parishes, co-ordinating denominational activities and setting up procedures to ensure a smooth transition into the Uniting church. The substantial human contribution of Methodism to the new Church has already been indicated. In terms of churches and institutions it was equally significant.[23]

The Uniting church in Australia was constituted in a session held in the Lyceum Theatre, Sydney, on 22 June 1977. On the same evening the inauguration of the Uniting church took place at a great celebratory gathering in Sydney Town Hall. The New South Wales celebration was held on the following Saturday night, 26 June, in the Horden Pavilion, Sydney, and on the next day congregations throughout the State (and, indeed, the Commonwealth) had special celebratory acts of worship in which they recognised that they were now part of the Uniting church. In some places there was a physical coming together of congregations; in others, where only the Methodist congregations were becoming congregations of the Uniting church, celebrations were still held.[24]

For some, those most involved in the movement, it did indeed mean the completion of a 'tortuous trail' and the ending of 'the scandal of disunity' in obedience to the prayer which Christ had offered for his followers. In its place, they had now found 'that unity which is both Christ's gift and His will for His Church'.[25] Others were more conscious of the practical advantages which union could bring. A third group probably accepted with little understanding or excitement the changes going on around them. A few, both ministers and members, stayed outside of union and found a place in other denominations but most Methodists loyally accepted the connexional decision and became members of the Uniting church even if they had some doubts about or had voted against union. Most of the more concerned would have continued to endorse the feeling expressed by the 1948 General Conference that:

> . . . while we cherish our Methodist heritage, we believe its essential features will not be lost, but, together with the heritage of other communions, will form a valuable contribution to the common treasury of a reunited Church . . .[26]

After 165 years of independent history, Methodism in New South Wales had 'finished its course' and only time, and the value placed on them by 'the people called Methodists', would tell which of the 'essential features' from its 'accumulated inheritance of faith and devotion' would pass into the 'common treasury'. In the meantime, it remained for former members and adherents to ponder how far they had 'kept the faith' and to what extent they had realised the visions of their prophets.

Notes

Introduction

1 H.A. Snyder, *The Radical Wesley and Patterns for Church Renewal*, Downers' Grove, Illinois, 1980, pp. 19–22.

2 Quoted in A.D. Hunt, *This Side of Heaven*, Adelaide, 1985, p. 2.

3 *The Works of the Rev. John Wesley, AM* (London, 1872), Journal, 1, May 1776, vol. 4, p. 73; R.E. Davies and E.G. Rupp, *A History of the Methodist Church in Great Britain*, vol. 1, London, 1965, p. 30; J.S. Udy and E.G. Clancy (eds), *Dig or Die*, Sydney, 1981, p. 37.

4 W. Daniels, *The History of Methodism*, Sydney and Melbourne, nd, p. 184; Davies and Rupp, *History of the Methodist Church*, vol. 1, p. 79; W.J. Townsend, H.B. Workman and G. Eayrs (eds), *A New History of Methodism*, 2 vols, London, 1909, vol. 1, p. 322.

5 C. Davey, *The Methodist Story*, London, 1955, p. 24–5, gives the date 1795 but F. Baker in Davies and Rupp, *History of the Methodist Church*, vol. 1, p. 226, gives it as 1797; G.T. Brake, *Policy and Politics in British Methodism, 1932–1972*, London, 1984, p. 352.

6 Townsend et al., *New History*, vol. 1, pp. 401–06.

7 Davies and Rupp, *History of the Methodist Church*, vol. 1, p. xxi.

8 Abel Stevens, *The History of Methodism*, London, 1864, vol. 1, p. 16; C. Williams, *John Wesley's Theology To-day*, London, 1960, p. 5.

9 ibid., p. 78; Wesley, *Works*, vol. XI, p. 442; vol. XIII, p. 9 (15 September 1790); W.R. Cannon, *The Theology of John Wesley*, New York, 1946, p. 216.

10 Wesley, *Works*, vol. VIII, pp. 340–3.

11 Stevens, *History of Methodism*, vol. 1, p. 16; Townsend et al., *New History*, vol. 1, pp. 368–9, vol. 2, p. 294.

Chapter 1

1 Bowden to Wesleyan Methodist Missionary Society (WMMS), 20 July 1812; Bowden and Hosking to WMMS, n.d., see J. Colwell, *The Illustrated History of Methodism*, Sydney, 1904, pp. 36–39; G.S. Udy, *Spark of Grace*, Parramatta, 1977, p. 16; Eagar to G. Howe Snr, 20 June 1812, Mitchell Library (ML), Bonwick Transcripts (BT) 49, pp. 308–14.

2 Leigh to WMMS, 2 March 1816, WMMS Correspondence 1812–89, Aust. box 514/1812–16.

3 Leigh to WMMS, 2 March 1816, Bowden to WMMS, 14 March 1816, ibid.; Lawry to WMMS, 24 March 1819, ML, BT 50, pp. 433–37.

4 Committee Minute Book (CMB), 10 January 1817, pp. 20–22, WMMS Papers 1804–69; Minutes of Quarterly Meeting (QMM), 14 September 1815, ML, ms B291, 1815–32, p. 1.

5 Leigh to WMMS, 9 September 1817, ML, BT 50, pp. 280–95; First Report of the Auxiliary Bible Society of NSW, 1817, ibid., pp. 260–65.

6 Walter Lawry's Diary, 8 August, 4 September 1818, ML, ms. A1973.

7 ibid., 22 March 1819; Lawry to parents, 13 March 1821, Lawry Papers 1818–25, ML, ms. A402; W. Hames, 'Walter Lawry and the Wesleyan Mission in the South Seas', Wesley Historical Society (New Zealand), *Proceedings*, 23/4, September 1967, pp. 8–9; Colwell, *Illustrated History*, p. 97.

8 ibid., pp. 57, 67, 99.

9 Leigh to Committee, 22 June 1820 (from Portsmouth), ML, BT 51, pp. 670–77; Mansfield to WMMS, 16 March 1821, ibid., pp. 783–87; CMB 28 June 1820, WMMS Papers 1804–89.

10 Lawry to WMMS, 24 March 1819, ML, BT 50, pp. 433–37; WMMS to Lawry, 9 December 1819, WMMS Correspondence (out) 1812–89; Eager to WMMS, 24 February 1820, ML, BT 51, pp. 599–603.

11 Carvosso to WMMS, 23 January 1822, ML, BT 52, pp. 1074–78; CMB 13 March 1822, WMMS, Papers 1804–89; Colwell, *Illustrated History*, p. 136.

12 Missionaries to WMMS, 30 July 1821, ML, BT 51, pp. 835–40; Leigh to WMMS, 16 November 1821, WMMS Correspondence (in) 1812–89, Aust. box 514/1821; Finance Sub-Committee Minutes, CMB 3 July 1822, pp. 400–01, WMMS Papers 1804–89, Aust. box 514/1821.

13 CMB 11 November 1814, WMMS Papers 1804–89; Lawry to WMMS, 15 July 1819, ML, BT 50, pp. 453–59; Carvosso to WMMS, 2 January 1821, ML, BT 51, pp. 735–38; Lawry Diary, 1 June 1821, ML, ms. A1973.

14 Marsden to Lawry, 21 May 1821, ML, BT 51, pp. 805–07; Lawry to Marsden, 25 May 1821 enclosing Lawry to WMMS, 24 May 1821, ibid., pp. 808–11.

15 Petition of Leaders to WMMS, 22 October 1821, ibid., pp. 950–952.

16 Leigh to WMMS, 23 October 1821, ML, BT 52, pp. 955–58; Mansfield to WMMS, 23 November 1821, ibid., pp. 1029–37.

17 CMB 3 July 1822, WMMS Papers 1804–89.

18 Wesleyan Methodist Church District Minutes, Australia (Aust.), Van Diemen's Land (VDL) and New Zealand (NZ), 2 October 1822, ibid.

19 For a more extensive treatment see Don Wright, 'The First Wesleyan Mission to the Aborigines of New South Wales—A Brief Historical Note', *Church Heritage*, 4/4, September 1986, pp. 245–53.

20 ML, BT 50, pp. 453–59.

21 Lawry to parents, 31 May, 16 November 1821, Lawry Papers, 1815–25, ML, ms. A402; Lawry's diary, 5, 14 January 1825, ibid., A1973.

22 CMB 5 September 1821, WMMS Papers 1804–89.

23 Carvosso to WMMS, 2 January 1821, BT 51, pp. 735–38; ibid., 26 August 1822, BT 52, pp. 1133–34; Wesleyan District Minutes 31 December 1822, pp. 2–4, 6–7, 9, 14, WMMS Papers 1804–89.

24 WMMS Correspondence (in) 1812–89, Aust. box 514/1823.

25 Mansfield to WMMS, 27 October 1825, ibid., Aust. box 514/1825; Erskine to WMMS, 4 April 1826, ibid., box 514/1826; CMB 1 November 1826, WMMS Papers 1804–89; WMMS to Leigh, 25 March 1820, WMMS Correspondence (out) 1812–89; Erskine to WMMS, 9 November 1822, ML, BT 52, pp. 1195–96.

26 Wesleyan District Despatches nos. 54, 58, 61, 19 February, 23 May, 9 October 1827, WMMS Papers 1804–89.

27 Colwell, *Illustrated History*, pp. 150–51.

28 WMMS to Mansfield, 22 September 1830, WMMS Correspondence (out) 1812–89.

29 Wesleyan District Minutes 22 March 1831 and 10 January 1832, Minute Book of NSW District, vol. 3, Dixson Library (DL), ms. Q4.

30 Journal of Joseph Orton, 1832–39, 1 February 1836, ML, ms. A1714.

31 Wesleyan District Minutes, 15 January 1833, p. 17, WMMS Papers, 1812–89; 10 January 1837, ibid. Full members were up almost three times.

32 Schofield to WMMS, 1 May 1835, WMMS Correspondence (in) 1812–89, Aust. Box 515/1835.

33 Wesleyan District Minutes, 10 January 1832, Question XXXIV (Bathurst), DL, ms. Q4, District Minute Book vol. 3, pp. 249–50; WMMS to Orton, 15 September 1832, WMMS Correspondence (out) 1812–89; Orton to WMMS, 24 November 1832, ibid. (in); Eric G. Clancy, 'Twelve Lay Apostles of New South Wales Country Methodism', *Church Heritage*, 2/1, March 1981, pp. 27–8.

34 Orton to WMMS, 29 July 1835, WMMS Correspondence (in) 1812–89; CMB 2 September 1835, WMMS Papers 1804–89; WMMS to McKenny, 6 November 1837, WMMS Correspondence (out) 1812–89; Colwell, *Illustrated History*, p. 217.

35 Draper to WMMS, 25 January 1837, Lewis to WMMS, 18 April 1837, WMMS Correspondence (in) 1812–89; Wilkinson to WMMS, 28 May 1839, ibid., Aust. box 516/1839; Udy, *Spark of Grace*, pp. 126–31.

36 Schofield to WMMS, 14 February 1837, WMMS Correspondence (in) 1812–89.

37 McKenny to WMMS, 20 July 1838, ibid.; District Minutes, 11 January 1838, Misc. Q3, WMMS Papers 1812–89; J. Barrett, *That Better Country*, Melbourne, 1966, ch. 2; Colwell, *Illustrated History*, p. 352.

38 Hurst to WMMS, 31 March 1843, WMMS Correspondence (in) 1812–89.

39 A. Wheen, *A Brief History of Ashfield Methodism 1840–75*, Ashfield, 1975, p. 1; W.C. McClelland, *Centenary of Newtown Methodism 1840–1940* (no details), p. 6; *Wesley Church Chippendale Sabbath School Diamond Jubilee Anniversary 1844 to 1904: Souvenir*, Sydney, 1904, p. 3; Colwell, *Illustrated History*, pp. 228–31.

40 Wesleyan District Minutes, 11 January 1838, 14 January 1841, WMMS Papers 1812–89; Innes to WMMS, 26 May 1840, WMMS Correspondence (in) 1812–89, box 516/1840/F51–2; Newcastle and Hunter District Historical Society *Monthly Journal*, New Series, vol. IX/BIII (May 1955), pp. 114–15; R.P. Whitehouse, *West Maitland Methodist Centenary Record 1837–1937*, Maitland, 1937; V. Bleazard, *A Centenary of Methodism in East Maitland, 1845–1945*, Maitland, 1945, p. 6.

41 Wesleyan District Minutes, 31 July 1845, Appendix 1, WMMS Papers 1812–89; Lewis to WMMS, 12 December 1844, WMMS Correspondence (in) 1812–89.

42 Eric G. Clancy, *A Giant for Jesus* (Waitara, 1972), p. 20; Eric G. Clancy, *Methodism in the Lilac City*, Goulburn, 1958, p. 11; Colwell, *Illustrated History*, pp. 275–83.

43 Schofield to WMMS, 1 April 1841, WMMS Correspondence 1812–89, Box 516/1841/F61; P. Tibbs, 'Illawarra Methodism in the Nineteenth Century: a Comparative Study of Wesleyan and Primitive Methodism in Wollongong, 1838–1902', BA Hons, University of Wollongong, 1981, pp. 2, 35–7; Colwell, *Illustrated History*, pp. 358–9.

44 Schofield to WMMS, 18 October 1838, WMMS Correspondence (in) 1812–89; McKenny to WMMS, 14 February 1839, ibid.

45 Wesleyan District Minutes, 14 January 1841, WMMS Papers 1812–89; Hurst to WMMS, 10 May, 20 July 1844, McKenny to WMMS, 6 September 1844, Boyce to WMMS, 31 January 1846, 20 April, 15 November 1847, WMMS Correspondence (in) 1812–89; WMMS to Boyce, 21 September 1845, ibid., (out).

46 *New South Wales Primitive Methodist Messenger (PM Messenger)*, July 1872, p. 231; *Sydney Morning Herald (SMH)*, 9 February 1875.

47 *Methodist*, 20 May 1899.

48 *Maitland Mercury*, 5 April 1888; Wesleyan District Minutes, 1845, WMMS Papers 1812–89.

49 J. Petty, *History of the Primitive Methodist Connexion from its Origin to the Conference of 1860*, London, 1864, pp. 478–81, 484; *SMH*, 20 February 1846, 23, 25 December 1847.

50 Petty, *Primitive Methodist Connexion*, p. 485.

51 *Maitland Mercury*, 2 February, 1 April 1848; H. Ikin, Autobiography (typescript, c. 1898–99), ML, ms. 3333.

52 E. Cook Pritchard, *Under the Southern Cross*, London, 1914, pp. 25–6; Petty, *Primitive Methodist Connexion*, p. 385.

53 British Primitive Methodist Conference Minutes, 1853, p. 39; see also obituary of E. Tear, ibid., 1895.

54 Sydney Primitive Methodist Preaching Plan, January–April 1860; Pritchard, *Under the Southern Cross*, pp. 25–6, though he confuses Moss and Tear; Petty, *Primitive Methodist Connexion*, p. 417.

55 *Primitive Methodist Magazine (PM Magazine)*, 1857, p. 248; *SMH*, 22 October 1855.

56 *PM Magazine*, 1845, p. 386, 1848, p. 106; British PM Conference Minutes, 1852, pp. 33–35.

57 WMMS to McKenny, 22 October 1844, WMMS Correspondence (out) 1812–89; WMMS to Boyce, 21 September 1845, ibid.

58 Boyce to WMMS, 25 June 1847, 6 January, 1 February 1848, 6 April, 8 August 1850, 1 March 1852, ibid.

59 Boyce to WMMS, 29 December 1846, 10 November 1851, ibid.; N. Turner *Sinews of Sectarian Warfare?*, Canberra, 1972, pp. 62–3.

60 Boyce to WMMS, 22 July, 15 August, 20 November 1851, 4 March 1852, WMMS Correspondence (in) 1812–89; see also exchange between Boyce and E. Deas Thompson, October–December 1851, and subsequent note by Boyce ibid.; Wilkinson to WMMS, 18 May 1852, ibid.; extracts re Methodism from the private diary of the late Rev. J. Oram, ML, Uncat. ms. 197/4, pp. 5–6.

61 CMB 3 December 1851, pp. 23–25, 16 June 1852, pp. 58–59, WMMS Papers 1804–89; WMMS to J.A. Manton, 31 December 1849, WMMS to Boyce, 30 December 1851, WMMS Correspondence (out) 1812–89; Boyce to WMMS, 6 June 1852, ibid. (in); see also, R. Young, *The Southern World*, London, 1855.

62 'Plan for Forming the Wesleyan Missionary Society's Australasian and Polynesian Missions into a Distinct Affiliated Connexion; Adopted by the English Conference held at Birmingham, in 1854', WMMS Correspondence (out) 1812–89.

63 Boyce to WMMS, 1 September, 20 November 1854, ibid., (in).

Chapter 2

1 R.H. Doust, *After One Hundred Years*, Bathurst, 1932, pp. 124–37; E.G. Clancy, *More Precious Than Gold*, Orange, 1960.

2 P.H. Curtis, 'Mudgee Methodism', Australian Methodist Historical Society (AMHS), *Journal and Proceedings*, III/2, January 1935, p. 135.

3 Whitehouse, *West Maitland Centenary Record*, p. 13; J.S. Scott, *Feed My Sheep: The Story of Methodism in the South-West of New South Wales*, Temora, 1976/7; R.W. Hartley and A.M. Grocott, *Around the circuit, Methodism in Northern New England*, Glen Innes, typescript, 1975.

4 McClelland, *Centenary of Newtown Methodism*, p. 16; H.T. Williams, *Hornsby Circuit. A Brief Record In the Settling of Methodism on the North Shore*, 1968, p. 2.

5 Colwell, *Illustrated History*, pp. 405–06, 449–51, 501.

6 K.J. Cable, 'Protestant Problems in New South Wales in the Mid-Nineteenth Century', *Journal of Religious History (JRH)*, 3/2, December 1964, pp. 125–127.

7 *Christian Advocate and Weekly Record (CA&WR)*, 2 May 1871; *Methodist*, 1 July 1905; Doust, *After One Hundred Years*, p. 34.

8 George Hurst to WMMS, 22 May 1863, WMMS Correspondence

(in) 1812–1889, box 519/1863; *Methodist*, 19 March 1904; R. Broome, *Treasure in Earthen Vessels*, St Lucia, 1980, p. 20.

9 Colwell, *Illustrated History*, pp. 499–604; *CA&WR*, 15 February 1866, 9 February 1869; *Methodist*, 19 March 1892, 31 October 1908, 5 March 1910, 28 November 1914; *Daily Telegraph*, 19 April 1915.

10 *CA&WR*, 21 June 1858; *Wesleyan Advocate (WA)*, 21 December 1878, 23 October 1880; *Methodist*, 11 February 1893, 24 October 1903, 11 October 1913.

11 *CA&WR*, 1 October 1873; *WA*, 23 May 1891; *Methodist*, 16 May 1908; Manly QMM 16 July 1913, UCA M2/3/M6, box 1.

12 *CA&WR*, 3 October 1867, 30 June, 14 July 1877; *WA*, 15 February 1879; NSW Wesleyan Conf. Mins, 1894, p. 89, p. 131; *Methodist*, 4 June 1892, 1 August 1896, 11 February 1899, 10 October 1908.

13 Windsor QMM 16 October 1883, ML, MCP552; Walter Phillips, *Defending 'A Christian Country'*, St Lucia, 1981, p. 50 n. 52.

14 *Methodist*, 28 September 1895, 25 January 1896, 27 February 1897, 2 January 1904.

15 J. Colwell, *The Church Sustentation and Extension Society* (ML, typescript, c. 1908), p. 2; *CA&WR*, 22 November 1858, 31 March 1859.

16 First Annual Report of Wesleyan Methodist Church Sustentation and Extension Society of NSW (CSES) 1863, pp. 12–15; 1874, p. 15; 1880, p. 16; 1883, p. 17; 1885, p. 15; 1895–96, pp. 10–11; 1913, pp. 12–3. *CA&WR*, 19 June 1866; J. Colwell, *The Church Sustentation and Extension Society*, pp. 26–7.

17 Broome, *Treasure in Earthen Vessels*, p. 30; *The Jubilee Souvenir, 1859–1909*, UCA, M2/1/12, box 2, Home Missions; *WA*, 15 June 1878, 27 April 1889; *Methodist*, 6 August 1898, 1 October 1910.

18 *SMH*, 4 September 1855, 12, 18 March, 2, 21, 27 May 1857, 15 April 1858; British PM Minutes, 1895 (obituary).

19 *Methodist Union—Federal Council Report*, 1895.

20 *Australian Dictionary of Biography (ADB)*, vol. 4, p. 267; H. Carruthers, *Rehoboth Methodist Church* (Forest Lodge, n.d.), p. 11.

21 *Maitland Mercury*, 7, 10 March 1855, 5 April 1888; *Methodist*, 13 February 1915; *PM Messenger*, January 1874, p. 89, 1880, pp. 42–3; *Australian Christian World (ACW)*, 30 May 1889; *Primitive Methodist*, 5 April 1899.

22 J.C. Docherty, *Newcastle, The Making of an Australian City*, Sydney, 1983, p. 170; E.M. McEwen, 'The Newcastle Coal-Mining District of New South Wales, 1860–1900', PhD, University of Sydney, 1979, pp. 262–63.

23 E. Lingard and N.F. Charge, *Glory Be* (Newcastle, 1945), p. 16.

24 *Primitive Methodist*, 8 March 1899; *Newcastle Morning Herald (NMH)*, 16 August 1900; *Methodist*, 9 January 1904; *Encyclopaedia of New South Wales*, Sydney, 1907, N36.

25 E.G. Clancy, 'The Primitive Methodist Church in New South Wales, 1845–1902', MA, Macquarie University, 1985, pp. 105, 163.

26 *PM Messenger*, July 1869, p. 311; July 1873, p. 34; July 1879, p. 35; 1881, p. 119.

27 Clancy, 'Primitive Methodist Church', pp. 119–32; *Cumberland Argus*, 19 June 1897.

28 Clancy, 'Primitive Methodist Church', pp. 141, 143–44, 237–44

29 ibid., pp. 152, 155–56, 234; British PM Minutes, 1854; *SMH*, 24 January 1894.

30 *Primitive Methodist*, 4 August 1899.

31 Townsend et al., *New History*, vol. 1, p. 486; R.E. Davies, *Methodism*, London, 1963, p. 144; R.E. Davies, A.R. George, E.G. Rupp, *A History of the Methodist Church in Great Britain*, London, 1978, vol. 2, pp. 316–22.

32 Rev. Dr O. Beckerlegge (York) to E.G. Clancy, 4 February 1987.

33 *Quarterly Record of the United Methodist Free Churches (UMFC)*, April 1869, p. 5, July 1873, p. 105, Latrobe Library. See generally Eric G. Clancy, 'The United Methodist Free Churches in NSW', *Church Heritage*, 5/3 (March 1988), pp. 146–170.

34 *NMH*, 12 November 1870, 30 July 1880; Lingard, *Glory Be*, p. 19; J.C. Docherty, 'The Second City–Social and Urban change in Newcastle, NSW, 1900–1929', PhD, ANU, 1977, p. 21; McEwen, 'The Newcastle Coal-mining District', p. 269.

35 NSW Methodist Conf. Mins, 1902, pp. 67, 281, 297; McEwen, 'The Newcastle Coal-mining District', p. 283.

36 J.S. Werner, *The Primitive Methodist Connexion: Its Background and Early History*, Madison, Wisconsin, 1984, p. 19.

37 J. Hughes, 'The Lay Methodist Church', AMHS *Journal and Proceedings*, no. 73, October 1957, pp. 984–5; Werner, *The Primitive Methodist Connexion*, p. 129; McEwen, 'The Newcastle Coal-mining District', p. 278.

38 Hughes, 'The Lay Methodist Church', pp. 984–5; McEwen, 'The Newcastle Coal-mining District', p. 280.

39 *Declaration of Faith and Order of the Adamstown Lay Methodist Church*, Newcastle, 1933, UCA, LMC file.

40 *NMH*, 18 July 1902; Hughes, 'Lay Methodist Church', pp. 985–86; F. Hughes to E.G. Clancy, 14 May 1987.

41 See, generally, annual reports of WMMS for period, UCA, M1/14,

box 2; see, in particular, reports for 1855, 1859, 1891; *Methodist*, 14 September 1906, 10 October 1908; Colwell, *Illustrated History*, pp. 460–66.

42   *Methodist*, 11 June 1892. On this whole question, see Eric G. Clancy, 'The Lay Methodist Church', *Church Heritage*, 5/4, September 1988, pp. 273–97.

43   *CA&WR*, 1 July 1871—the article is signed 'Egmont', Ward's nom-de-plume; *WA*, 24 November 1877, 13 November 1880.

44   *WA* 13 December 1884. See also *Methodist*, 21 April 1900.

45   NSW Wesleyan Conf. Mins, 1885, pp. 67, 77, 1888, p. 88, 1889, pp. 97–8.

46   ibid., 1892, pp. 123–4.

47   *Methodist*, 2 July, 19 November 1892.

48   NSW Wesleyan Conf. Mins, 1893, p. 86–7; *Methodist*, 14 October, 11 November 1893, 17 March 1894.

49   *Methodist*, 6 February, 13 March 1897.

50   *Methodist*, 30 September 1893, 17 March (2), April 1894, 18 March 1899.

51   ibid., 7, 21 October 1893, 7 July 1894, 14 March 1896, 25 March 1899.

52   *SMH*, 21 January 1896; Sydney First PMC QMM 7 September, 13 December 1900, 14 March 1901; letters between W.H. Puddicombe and Rev. J.W. Holden, 28, 30 July, 5 September 1900, ML, MCP 266.

53   *Methodist*, 24 February, 4 August 1900.

54   ibid., 10, 31 March 1900.

55   Colwell, *Illustrated History*, p. 612. Some Primitive Methodists in the Newcastle District associated with the Lay Methodists, elsewhere some joined other denominations.

56   *Methodist*, 7 September 1895.

57   *SMH*, 6 March 1901.

58   K.J. Cable, 'Religious Controversies in New South Wales in the Mid-Nineteenth Century. (ii) The Dissenting Sects and Education', Royal Australian Historical Society *Journal (RAHSJ)*, 49/2, July 1963, pp. 137–38; W.W. Phillips, 'The Social Composition of Religious Denominations in Late Nineteenth Century Australia', *Church Heritage*, 4/2, September 1985; Clancy, 'Primitive Methodist Church', pp. 122–32; R.B. Walker, 'The Growth and Typology of the Wesleyan Methodist Church in NSW, 1812–1901', *JRH*, 6/4, December 1971, pp. 340–41; *CA&WR*, 20 June 1865; *WA*, 19 October 1889.

59   Walker, 'Growth and Typology', p. 333; W.W. Phillips, 'Religious

Profession and Practice in New South Wales, 1850–1901: The Statistical Evidence', *Historical Studies*, 15/59, October 1972, pp. 381–2, 391–3; J.D. Bollen, *Protestantism and Social Reform in New South Wales 1890–1910*, Melbourne 1972, pp. 183, 185; Phillips, *Defending 'A Christian Country'*, p. 22; *WA*, 26 October 1889; *Methodist*, 9 February 1895, 12 October 1901, 5 August 1905, 6 January, 14, 28 September 1912, 25 July 1914; *ACW*, 25 January 1895; *SMH*, 24 January 1894. See also Conference statistics for various years.

Chapter 3

1 *Glad Tidings*, 4 May 1910, 4 September 1911, 2 September 1912.

2 Aust. Wesleyan Conf. Mins, 1855, p. 37.

3 *CA&WR*, 21 July 1858; *Methodist*, 19 September 1942; W.J.M. Campbell, *'Old Tom Brown' of Wesley Vale*, Dalton, p. 11

4 *WA*, 19 May 1888, 6 April 1889; *Methodist*, 17 May 1902; Parramatta PM QMM, 1 June 1887, ML, MP 439; paper in UCA, M2/3/M2, West Maitland, box 5; B. Wibberley, *Marks of Methodism*, Adelaide, 1905, p. 51.

5 *CA&WR*, 1 August, 1 September 1873; *WA*, 17 September, 1, 8, 29 October 1887; *Methodist*, 26 August 1905; Colwell, *Illustrated History*, p. 406; Parramatta PM QMM, 28 February 1883, ML, MP 439.

6 *WA*, 1 October 1887. The CMM band was formed in February 1886.

7 Udy, *Spark of Grace*, p. 156; Colwell, *Illustrated History*, pp. 370–71; *CA&WR*, 3 January 1861.

8 NSW Methodist Conf. Mins, 1902, p. 56; Wesleyan Methodist Laws (1885), nos 11, 46; *CA&WR*, 19 February 1867, 1 July 1875; *WA*, 18 February 1888; *Methodist*, 12 January 1907; Clancy, *Methodism in Lilac City*, p. 69; Goulburn PM QMM, 5 December 1890, ML, MCP 439; R.W. Hartley, 'The Eucharist in New South Wales Methodism from Methodist Union (1902) to the Uniting Church (1977)', *Church Heritage*, 1/4, September 1980, pp. 305, 317.

9 *CA&WR*, 31 March, 1 September 1859; *WA*, 20 January 1883, 20 November 1886, 22 January 1887, 3 November 1888, 1 June 1889; *NSW PM Messenger*, October 1868, p. 219, April 1869, p. 280; Colwell, *Illustrated History*, pp. 226, 339; Clancy, *Methodism in Lilac City*, p. 69; Lingard, *Glory Be*, pp. 11, 18.

10 H. Carter, *The Methodist Heritage*, London, 1951, pp. 96–9, 132–3; Colwell, *Illustrated History*, p. 394; Aust. Wesleyan Conf. Mins,

1856, p. 28; *CA&WR*, 21 July 1859, 1 September, 30 December 1871; *WA*, 25 February 1888.

11 *CA&WR*, 1 September 1859, 16 August 1860, 19 December 1867, 1 August, 1871; Aust. Wesleyan Conf. Mins, 1862, p. 43.

12 *Proceedings of the United Methodist Convention for the Spread of Scriptural Holiness*, 9–11 December 1885; *WA*, 26 December 1885, 30 January, 6 June 1886; Kempsey QMM, 30 September 1889, ML, MCP 380; *Glad Tidings*, 4 July 1911, 4 July 1912.

13 Papers of William Hall Pryor, Journal 1876–86, UCA, quotation dated 23 January 1881; *Methodist*, 16 July 1927.

14 *CA&WR*, 1 March 1873; *WA*, 20 October 1877, 2 March 1889; W. Hall, *The Basis of Membership Question: the Problem Stated and the Remedy Suggested*, Sydney, 1889; NSW Wesleyan Conf. Mins, 1890, p. 101; Wesleyan General Conf. Mins., 1890, pp. 39–41; 1904, pp. 60–61. See NSW Wesleyan and Methodist Conference statistics for various years.

15 Broome, *Treasure in Earthen Vessels*, p. 29; *CA&WR*, 22 November 1858, 2 February 1874; *WA*, 13 September 1879; for Century Fund see *Methodist*, 1898–1901; for Methodist Centenary Fund, ibid., 8 August 1914.

16 Aust. Wesleyan Conf. Mins, 1855, p. 14; *CA&WR*, 26 May, 29 September 1859, 27 October 1866, 2 September 1874; *WA*, 2 August, 20 September 1879. See also Phillips, *Defending 'A Christian Country'*, pp. 4, 207–08, 236–38.

17 Colwell, *Illustrated History*, pp. 558–90; D.S. MacMillan, *Newington College 1863–1963*, Sydney, 1963, especially chapters 1 and 2; Boyce to London Committee, 3 January 1856, WMMS (London) Correspondence (in) 1812–1889, box 878/1855–56/1–122; minutes of Education Committee, January 1861–January 1865, ML, MCP 591; *CA&WR*, 23 June 1864, 14 January 1868.

18 Colwell, *Illustrated History*, pp. 591–98; *MLC Burwood, Jubilee Souvenir*, 1886–1936, pp. 10–28; *WA*, 19 May 1883.

19 Colwell, *Illustrated History*, p. 231; *Wesley Church Chippendale Sabbath School Jubilee Anniversary 1844–1904: Souvenir*, Sydney, 1904, pp. 5–6.

20 C.C. Jones, *An Australian Sunday School at Work. Rockdale, 1855–1915*, Sydney, 1915, p. 9; *CA&WR*, 2 February, 16 August, 1860; *WA*, November 1878–March 1879; Aust. Wesleyan Conf. Mins, 1870, p. 47, NSW 1875, pp. 62–9.

21 ibid., 1877, p. 50, 1904, pp. 66–7; *WA*, 7 June 1879, 6 January 1883, 20 February, 30 October 1886, 26 October 1889; *Methodist*, 11 February 1899, 30 June, 10 August 1906, 22 March 1913; Jones, *An Australian Sunday School at Work*, part 2.

22 *CA&WR*, 19 July, 13 August, 8 September 1864, 5, 30 September 1865, 1 May 1869; *WA*, 23 March 1878.

23 *Methodist*, 24 February, 28 September 1906.

Chapter 4

1 Don Wright, *Mantle of Christ*, St Lucia, 1984, ch. 1.

2 J.R. Green, *Short History of the English People*, London, 1902, pp. 736–37; J.W. Bready, *England Before and After Wesley*, London, 1938, pp. 317–18.

3 *CA&WR*, 21 July 1858; Colwell, *Illustrated History*, p. 36; Aust. Wesleyan Conf. Mins, 1855, pp. 36–9.

4 Colwell, *Illustrated History*, pp. 80, 85; Davies, George and Rupp, *Methodist Church in Great Britain*, vol. 2, p. 384.

5 *ACW*, 25 January 1895.

6 F. Fowler, in F.K. Crowley, *A Documentary History of Australia*, 3 vols, Melbourne, 1980, vol. 2, p. 372; NSW *PM Messenger*, October 1866, p. 288; *Methodist*, 27 October 1894.

7 *CA&WR*, 17 March 1859; Aust. Wesleyan Conf. Mins, 1860, p. 38; 1864, p. 49; *Methodist*, 15 March 1902; J.D. Bollen, 'The Temperance Movement and the Liberal Party in New South Wales Politics, 1900–1904', *JRH*, 1/3, June 1961, p. 160.

8 *Methodist*, 26 November 1892, 13 August 1898; Aust. Wesleyan Conf. Mins, 1862, p. 43; 1889, p. 87; Broome, *Treasure in Earthen Vessels*, pp. 149–54.

9 *Wesleyan Laws and Regulations*, 1890, p. 8; Phillips, *Defending 'A Christian Country'*, p. 177.

10 For a discussion of the activities of the Lord's Day Observance Society, see ibid., pp. 175–93; *CA&WR*, 21 May 1858, 1 June 1871; *WA*, 19 May 1877; NSW Wesleyan Conf. Mins, 1899, p. 85.

11 Newtown Wesleyan Local Preachers' Minutes, 6 October 1859, ML, MCP 194; J.S. Austin, *Missionary Enterprise and Home Mission Service*, Sydney, n.d.), p. 367; Aust. Wesleyan Conf. Mins, 1871, p. 52.

12 J. Gale, *Canberra*, Queanbeyan, 1927, p. 50.

13 W.T. Waters, *The Waters Saga, 1815–1977*, 1979, pp. 1–3.

14 *WA*, 10, 24 April, 1, 8 May 1886; Phillips, *Defending 'A Christian Country'*, pp. 198, 201.

15 *WA*, 18 August 1883, 16 May 1891; *Methodist*, 26 January, 2 March 1895, 6 June 1896, 4, 18 January 1908, 20 September 1913.

16 *CA&WR*, 20 December 1860; *WA*, 6 July 1878; *Methodist*, 29 May, 26 June 1897, 20 January, 29 September 1900.

17 *Methodist*, 19 June 1897, 5, 19 January 1901, 1 February 1902; NSW Wesleyan Conf. Mins, 1900, p. 192.

18 *CA&WR*, 2 May 1871; *WA*, 7 August 1880; NSW Wesleyan Conf. Mins, 1895, pp. 89–90; 1897, p. 81; *Methodist*, 7 October 1899.

19 *Australian Protestant Banner*, 14 November 1868; J. Sharpe, *The Young Minister Counselled*, Sydney, 1871, p. 10; *Empire*, 4 June 1855; *PM Messenger*, 1857, pp. 246–47; Wright, 'The First Wesleyan Mission to Aborigines', *Church Heritage*, 4/4, September 1986, pp. 245–51; Colwell, *Illustrated History*, pp. 168–84.

20 *WA*, 23, 30 November 1878; *Methodist*, 13 June 1896.

21 *WA*, 28 April 1888; *Methodist*, 13 November 1897, 12 October 1901.

22 *Methodist*, 8, 15 October 1898, 29 July, 9 September, 14 October 1899.

23 *WA*, 28 February, 29 May 1880, 16 December 1882.

24 *WA*, 16, 30 August, 1890; *Methodist*, 28 August, 11 September, 23 October 1897.

25 NSW Wesleyan Conf. Mins, 1892, p. 33; *Methodist*, 24 March 1894; Stead to William Lee, 8 March 1892, UCA, M2/1/5, NSW Conference Letterbook 1890–1907.

26 *PM Messenger*, March 1857, p. 15, July 1866, p. 242; *Daily Telegraph*, 24 April 1896; *Methodist*, 2 September 1899; *NMH*, 11 April 1885, 29 March 1886.

27 *Freeman's Journal*, 21 November 1896; *Daily Telegraph*, 4 June 1891; *Methodist*, 16 June 1894.

28 *WA*, 16 August, 29 November 1890; *Methodist*, 15 April 1893, 8, 15, September 1894, 11 September, 23 October 1897, 9 January, 19 March, 29 October 1904.

29 ibid., 13 July 1901, 29 April 1905.

30 ibid., 19 March 1904, 22 December 1906, 2 February, 21 September 1907; *SMH*, 26 January 1907.

31 K.S. Inglis, 'English Non-Conformity and Social Change' *Past and Present*, 13 April 1958, p. 75; *SMH*, 25 January 1894; *Methodist*, 5 October 1907.

32 *WA*, 16 August 1890; *Methodist*, 14 March 1896, 13 August 1898. For a fuller survey, see Clancy, 'The Primitive Methodist Church'.

33 *WA*, 13 June 1891; *Methodist*, 9 December 1893.

34 *WA*, 23 December 1882.

35 *Methodist*, 11 March 1905.

36 A detailed discussion of the Central Mission concept and the history

of the Sydney Central Mission, with full references, may be found in Wright, *Mantle of Christ*.

37 See Sir Alan Walker, 'The Concept of Central Missions in Australia', in Udy and Clancy, *Dig or Die*, pp. 129–39.

38 *WA*, 13 September 1890, 21 March 1891; *Methodist*, 28 November 1903, 27 February 1904, 7 July 1906.

39 ibid., 3 August 1906, 20 April 1907, 20 May 1911, 30 March 1912, 18 July 1914.

40 ibid., 12 June 1897, 11 March, 5 August 1899.

41 *NMH*, 22 November 1902; *Methodist*, 15 November 1902, 6 February 1904; *Northern Light (NL)*, 1 January 1909.

42 Newcastle Central Methodist Mission (NCMM), General Committee Minutes 1905–09, pp. 119–20, 166–67, 173, 175–76, UCA, M2/3/N5, box 2; *Methodist*, 27 November 1909.

43 NCMM, General Committee Minutes 1909–17, pp. 53, 63, 178, 191, 195–96, UCA, M2/3/N5, box 3; *NL*, 1 January 1913.

44 ibid., 3 April, 1 December 1909, 1 October 1912, 1 August, 1 September 1913; NCMM, General Committee minutes 1905–09, pp. 67–68, 78, UCA, M2/3/N5, box 2.

45 Annual Report, CSES, 1859, p. 21; See also Margaret Reeson, *Certain Lives*, Sutherland, NSW, 1989, pp. 113–14.

46 *CA&WR*, 29 September 1859, 2 February, 13 September, 25 October 1860, 17 January 1861.

47 Eric G. Clancy, 'William ("California") Taylor: First Overseas Evangelist to Australia', *Church Heritage*, 6/3, March 1990, pp. 41–62; *CA&WR*, 19 July, 13 August 1864, 8 June 1865; extract from diary, Joseph Oram, ML, uncat. ms. 197/4, p. 32; Orange QMM, 1860–1927, meetings July 1869–January 1875, ML, MCP 430. See also Reeson, *Certain Lives*, pp. 133–34.

48 See generally *WA* for the year stated. For the Maitland case see *WA*, 18 September 1880.

49 Reports are scattered through the *Methodist* for 1892–93. See especially 18 June, 2 July, 20 August 1892, 17 June 1893, 12 August 1899.

50 See *Methodist*, January 1902 to March 1904, also 5 June 1897, 30 November 1901, 8 February 1902, 25 April 1903, 2 July 1904; Tent Mission File in UCA; *The Methodist Quarterly Record* (Lismore), 1 November 1902, UCA, M2/3/L7, box 2. See also Broome, *Treasure in Earthen Vessels*, pp. 59–62.

51 *Methodist*, 8 April 1905, 20 January, 3 February, 19 May 1906.

Chapter 5

1 *CA&WR*, 2 May 1871; *WA*, 26 April 1879, 7 August 1880; NSW Wesleyan Conf. Mins, 1895, pp. 89–90, 1897, p. 81, (Methodist) 1901, p. 216; *Methodist*, 7 October 1899, 6 January 1900, 22 March 1913; *Glad Tidings*, 4 May 1911; F.W. Walker, 'Books, Men and Movements—The Peace Movement', *NL*, 1 September 1911.

2 M. McKernan, *Australian Churches at War*, Sydney and Canberra, 1980, p. 26; NSW Methodist Conf. Mins, 1914, p. 68.

3 ibid., 1915, p. 271; *Methodist*, 22 May 1915, 15 January 1916; *NL*, 1 September, 1 December 1915; Merewether QMM, 7 July 1915, UCA, M2/3/M10, box 1; W. Burston to President, 5 December 1915, UCA, M2/1/6, box 1.

4 B.L. Webb, *The Religious Significance of the War*, Sydney, 1915; *Methodist*, 26 June to 14 August 1915; *Glad Tidings*, 1 July 1915, 1 February 1916; Hay QMM, November 1915 to October 1916, UCA, M2/3/H4, box 1.

5 The correspondence is in UCA, M2/1/6, NSW Methodist Conference Correspondence, 1917 folder.

6 *Glad Tidings*, 1 November 1916; *Methodist*, 9 June 1917.

7 ibid., 18 September, 18 December 1915; Rev. J. Woodhouse to Rev. Henry Howard, 21 July 1915, UCA, M2/1/6, President's Correspondence, box 1, 1913–16; F.E. Donnison (Coonabarabran) to J.G.M. Taylor, 18 August 1915, ibid.

8 *Glad Tidings*, 1 March 1917, 1 March 1920; *Methodist*, 9 November 1918, 5 August 1922.

9 ibid., 11, 18 January, 26 July 1919, 12 February 1921, 25 November 1922, 8 March 1924.

10 For work of Evangelistic Committee, see UCA, M2/1/27, box 1; *Methodist*, 20 July, 5 October 1912, 1 August, 19 September 1914, 3 December 1932; A.E. Walker to President, 9 October 1909, UCA, M2/1/6, box 2, folder 1909–10; NSW Methodist Conf. Mins, 1914, p. 90. On Preston, see W. Kingscote-Greenland, *Raymond Preston: British and Australian Evangelist*, London, 1930.

11 *Methodist*, 30 March, 4 May 1929.

12 Evangelistic Committee Minutes, 25 November 1935, Report of Committee, 25 October 1938, UCA, M2/1/27, box 1; *Methodist*, 14 October 1933, 27 September, 16 October 1937, 28 May, 3 December 1938, 11 February 1939.

13 ibid., 12 November 1938. Donald Hansen, 'The Churches and Society in New South Wales: 1919–1939', PhD, Macquarie University, 1978, pp. 171, 409, argues that circuit ministers were still

heavily involved in evangelism but lacked the doctrinal assurance to succeed. There appears to be little evidence for the first part of his statement, while the second seems to involve a misunderstanding of the nature of Methodist conversion.

14 Orange QMM, 27 January 1917, ML, MCP 430; Parramatta QMM, 10 April 1929, UCA, M2/3/P3, box 1; *Methodist*, 31 October 1936.

15 ibid., 3, 24 July 1920, 6 August 1921, 21 May 1927, 31 July 1943.

16 Methodist Missionary Society of Australasia (MMSA), Report for 1921, pp. 3, 7, 82; 1933, pp. 4, 33; 1938, pp. 62–3; 1945, pp. 34–6, UCA, M1/14, box 2; *Methodist*, 16 March 1929, 21 February 1931, 20 February 1943.

17 ibid., 20 October 1914, 24 June 1944; WAOM Reports are found in UCA, M2/1/13.

18 *Methodist*, 13 September 1930, 22 August 1936, 12 March 1938, 30 January, 2 October 1943, 5 February, 6 May 1944.

19 ibid., January–October 1922, 19 January, 5 April 1924, 1 May 1926.

20 'Australian Horizons', UCA, M2/1/12, Home Missions, box 12; *Methodist*, 18 March 1916, 10 October 1931, 15 October 1932, 14 March 1936.

21 ibid., 10 November 1917, 17 July 1920, 30 January 1937, 11 November 1939, 31 January 1942, 21 August 1943; H.S. Doust, *Early Years of the Far West Mission (1917–24)*; Cobar QMM, 7 January 1926, UCA, M2/F2, box 1.

22 'Australian Horizons', UCA, M1/2/12, box 2; *Methodist*, 2 August 1924, 15, 29 August 1925, 24 October 1931.

23 *NL*, 1 December 1916; *Methodist*, 17 February 1923, 31 May 1924, 16 July 1927, 21 July, 29 September 1928, 1, 8 May, 30 October 1937; Don Wright, 'Manly Methodist Circuit, 1887–1977: Paradigm of a Methodist Middle-class Suburban Circuit', part I: 1887–1954, *Church Heritage*, 5/3, March 1988, pp. 176–79.

24 References to suburban missions are scattered through *Methodist*. For Newtown, see also UCA, M2/3/N7, box 1, Newtown QMM for period from 1927. For Sydney central mission, see Wright, *Mantle of Christ*, ch. 5. For Newcastle Central Mission, see *NL* and NCMM General Committee Minutes 1917–35 and Executive Committee Minutes, 1915–27, UCA, M2/3/N5, boxes 2 and 4.

25 *Methodist*, 12 March 1921, 21 September 1929, 9 September 1933, 24 February 1934.

26 ibid., 6, 13 March 1926, 13 April, 13 July 1929; 16 January 1932, 2 October 1943; Cessnock QMM, 15 January 1921, UCA, M2/3/C10, box 1.

27 *Methodist*, 17 April 1915, 7 May, 15 October 1927, 3 November 1928, 17 May 1930.

28 ibid., 25 June 1927, 8 August 1936, 26 August, 4 November, 2 December 1939; Women's Home Mission League (WHML), Minutes, 19, 25 June 1930, UCA, M2/1/12, WHML, box 1.

29 A comprehensive survey of the union movement may be found in J.S. Udy, 'Church Union in Australia', MA (Hons), Sydney University, 1983, see also articles by Udy in *Church Heritage*, 1/1, September 1978; and 4/2, September 1985; 'Wesley Heritage in the Formation of the Uniting Church in Australia' in Udy and Clancy, *Dig or Die*, pp. 177–201. Cornelius Uidam, *Union and Renewal*, Sydney, 1970; Frank Engel, *Australian Christians in Conflict and Unity*, Melbourne, 1984.

30 *Blue Book of the General Assembly of New South Wales*, 1901, p. 23; *Blue Book of the General Assembly of Australia*, 1901, pp. 42, 93; Methodist General Conf. Mins, 1904, pp. 61–2; Udy, 'Church Union', p. 39.

31 Udy, 'Church Union', p. 45; J.E. Carruthers, *Memories of an Australian Ministry* (London, 1922), pp. 242–45; *SMH*, 11 May 1901; Uidam, *Union and Renewal*, p. 19; General Conf. Mins, 1913, p. 113.

32 *Blue Book of the General Assembly of Australia*, 1916, minute 37, p. 29; Methodist General Conf. Mins, 1917, p. 95; *Methodist*, 29 March 1919; Carruthers, *Memories*, pp. 246–7; Engel, *Australian Christians in Conflict and Unity*, p. 240.

33 *Methodist*, 5 April, 12, 26 July, 2 August, 27 September, 8 November 119, 17 January, 28 February 1920; Casino QMM, October 1919, UCA, M2/3/C8, box 1; *Basis of Union*, 1918.

34 *Methodist*, 9 October, 6 November 1920; D.E. Hansen, 'The Long Road to Union', *Church Heritage*, 1/2, September 1979, pp. 95–6; Uidam, *Union and Renewal*, p. 21.

35 Methodist General Conf. Mins, 1926, pp. 254–55; *Methodist*, 15 May 1920, 20 September 1924.

36 J.S. Udy, *Living Stones*, Sydney, 1974, p. 76; Udy, 'Church Union', pp. 151–180; *Canberra Times*, 23 August 1934.

37 'The Report of the Youth Work Commission of the Young People's Department, New South Wales Conference, of the Methodist Church of Australasia, 1933–36', UCA, M2/1/15, box file 4; see also copy of letter and questionnaire to all ministers, ibid.' *Methodist*, 24 February 1934.

38 ibid., 7 August 1937, 21 January 1939, 27 July 1940.

39 Young People's Department (YPD) Executive Minutes, 10 May 1915, UCA, M2/1/15, box 1; YPD Council Minutes, 10 April

1922, ML, MCP 610; ibid., 11 February 1935, UCA, M2/1/15, box 1; *Methodist*, 20 March 1937.

40 YPD Council Minutes, 12 April 1915, ML, MCP 610; *Methodist*, 15 May, 20 November 1915.

41 'An Authentic History of the Foundation and Early Development of the Methodist Order of Knights. Founded Hurstville 1914', UCA, M2/1/15; F.R. Swynny to L. King, 27 September 1927, ibid.; 'Extracts from Early OK Records and Diary of Alec W. Bray', ibid.; YPD Council Minutes, 21 October 1935, ibid.; *Methodist*, 6 October 1923, 25 June 1932.

42 'Methodist Youth Organisations. No. 4. The Crusader Movement', AMHS, *Journal and Proceedings*, no. 63 (January 1952), pp. 853–55; Hyde, Betty and Dudley (eds), *Lo! Here Is Fellowship*, Sydney, 1979; YPD Council Minutes, November–December 1929, UCA, M2/1/15, box 1; *Methodist*, 21 August 1937.

43 NSW Methodist Conf. Mins, 1921, p. 110; *Methodist*, 7 June 1919, 8 August, 17 October 1925, 21 July 1928, 27 July 1929, 11 January 1930, 22 May 1937; J.W. Hill, 'The history and administration of the Methodist system of secondary education in New South Wales, with particular reference to the period 1919–1960', University of Sydney, MEd, 1975, especially pp. 74–7; 'Ravenswood in Retrospect', UCA, M2/1/18, Methodist Colleges; J.C. Potts (ed.) *Wolaroi College Orange. A Pictorial History*, Orange, 1977; Colleges Advisory Board Minutes, 1940–62, UCA, M2/1/18.

44 YPD Executive Committee Minutes, December 1918 to January 1919, September 1921 to February 1922, December 1923 to January 1924; YPD Council Minutes, 10 August 1925, UCA, M2/1/15, box 1; *Methodist*, 11 March 1922, 21 February 1931.

45 ibid., 14 April 1945.

46 See UCA, M2/1/12, Methodist Women's Federation, box 1; *Methodist*, 8 January, 11, 25 June 1921; Newtown QMM, 13 October 1931, UCA, M2/3/N7, box 1.

47 NCMM General Committee Minutes, 6 July 1915, UCA, M2/3/N5, box 2; NSW Methodist Conf. Mins, 1918, p. 197; *Methodist*, 28 May 1927, 4, 18 August 1928; *NL*, 1 May 1931.

48 *Methodist*, 26 March, 7 May 1921, 6 April 1929, 22 February, 29 March 1930, 4 March 1933, 5 March 1938, 15 (14) February 1948.

49 *Glad Tidings*, 1 May 1920; *Methodist*, August–September 1921, 19 May, 1 September 1923, 14 February 1925, 19 January 1935, 14 June 1941, February–March 1945. For material re Angus, see Hansen, 'Churches and Society', pp. 66–7, 82 and S. Emilsen, *A Whiff of Heresy: Samuel Angus and the Presbyterian Church in New South Wales*, Sydney, 1990.

50 *Methodist*, 1 July 1930.

51 ibid., 10 February 1923, 10 March 1928, 12 March 1938; NSW Methodist Conf. Mins, 1926, pp. 122–24.

52 Hansen, 'Churches and Society', pp. 338–56; *Glad Tidings*, 1 April 1917; *Methodist*, 5 June 1920, 3 April–17 June 1922; W.C. Francis to all Methodist Ministers, 19 February 1935, UCA, M2/1/6, box 5, 1935 folder.

53 Manly QMM, 15 January 1917, 6 January, 14 April 1919, UCA, M2/3/M6, box 6; Weston QMM, 4 July 1931, 8 July 1933, UCA, M2/3/W11, box 1; *Methodist*, 2 January 1932, 6 August 1938; UCA, Restricted papers, 'Bathurst Football Case'.

54 Orange QMM, 14 July 1924, ML, MCP 430; *Methodist*, 8 September 128; Social Questions Committee (SQC) Minutes, 14 August 1933, UCA, M2/1/16, box 1; Tighes Hill QMM, 27 April 1936, UCA, M2/3/T9, box 1.

55 *Methodist*, 14 August, 27 November 1920, 27 August 1921, 27 December 1930, 8 June 1935.

56 For a detailed discussion of Men's Own Movement, see Don Wright, 'The Methodist Men's Own Movement', *Church Heritage*, 4/1, March 1985, pp. 1–24.

57 *The Sentinel*, 1 February 1919, UCA, M2/3/M9, box 5; *Methodist*, 8, 15 February, 1 March 1919, 9 January 1932, 3 June 1933, 6 May 1944; Weston QMM, 8 October 1935, UCA, M2/3/W11, box 1; *NL*, 1 December 1942.

58 *NL*, 1 May 1931; *Methodist*, 23 May 1931; Wright, *Mantle of Christ*, pp. 113–14.

59 Wright, 'Manly Methodist Circuit', part I, p. 179; Lambton QMM, 14 October 1930, UCA, M2/3/L2, box 2; *Methodist*, 23 November 1929, 14 February, 4 July, 19 September 1931, 2 August 1947; SQC Minutes, 2 June 1930, UCA, M2/1/16, box 1.

60 *Methodist*, 9 August 1930, 4 April, 29 August 1931, 14 August 1937; Newtown QMM, 16 January 1933, UCA, M2/3/N7, box 1; NCMM, Men's Hostel Log Book, 1938–41, p. 3, UCA, M2/3/N5, box 7.

61 *Methodist*, 27 October 1928, 2 August 1930, 27 February to 23 July 1932; Hill, 'History and Administration of the Methodist System of Education', p. 54; NSW Methodist Conf. Mins, 1932, p. 155.

62 *Methodist*, 9 March, 24, 31 August 1935, 27 February 1937; circular issued by United Christian Peace Movement, 27 March 1937, UCA, M2/1/6, box 5, 1937–38 folder.

63 *Methodist*, 18 November, 2 December 1939, 16 March 1940 (Statement Issued by Conference and paper by P.L. Black), 1, 22 March 1941, 1 September 1942.

64 ibid., 29 June 1940 (Women's War Work), 9 September 1944; HMD, 82nd Annual Report, 1941–42, pp. 9–10.
65 Statement by A.G. Manefield, HMD, 82nd Annual Report, 1941–42, p. 5; *NL*, 1 March 1943 (Alan Walker); *Methodist*, 21 November 1942, 11 December 1943; PQC Minutes, 6 December 1943, UCA, M2/1/16, box 1.
66 Rev. R.H. Campbell, HMD, 75th Annual Report, 1933–34, p. 4; *Methodist*, 21 June, 20 September 1941, 2 August 1947. Statistics are calculated from NSW Methodist Conf. Mins for the relevant years.

Chapter 6

1 *Methodist*, 29 May 1948.
2 ibid., 11 May, 17 August, 9 November 1946, 30 July, 13 August, 10, 17, 24 September 1949, 5 October 1963; *The Challenge*, April 1960, UCA, M2/3/L2, box 9.
3 *The Spire*, September 1944, UCA, M2/3/W7, box 1; *Methodist*, 12 March 1949, 8 April, 2 September 1950, 6 August 1960, 4 August 1962, 23 February 1963, 27 February 1965.
4 ibid., 7 August, 20 November 1965, 9, 23 April, 7, 21 May, 18 June, 19 November 1966, 13 May, 28 October, 25 November 1967; Press release by D.A. Trathen, 16 June 1970, M2/1/18, Newington College, box 1 (which also contains a mass of other interesting material on this issue).
5 *Methodist*, 2 March 1946, 19 June 1948, 21 August 1954, 16 June 1956, 15 March, 24 May, 12 July, 27 September, 11 October 1958, 9 April 1960, 26 August 1961, 2 March 1963, 18 December 1965, 20 May 1967, 4 July 1970, 23 June 1971, 18 July 1983.
6 ibid., 19 December 1953, 18 May 1957, 26 April 1958.
7 ibid., 13, 20, 27 November 1954, 21 July 1956, 10 May 1958, 17 January 1970; Watson Report presented at meeting of Methodist Social Services Department, 20 October 1958, UCA, M2/1/16, Minute Book no. 1; Narromine correspondence, July–August 1962, President's Correspondence 1961–62, Restricted Papers, UCA; Goulburn QMM, 17 July 1956, UCA, M2/3/G10, box 1.
8 *Methodist*, 24 August, 14 September 1946, September–November 1947, 12 June 1954.
9 Wright, *Mantle of Christ*, pp. 152–58, 194–96; List of Aged Persons' Homes of the Methodist Church, October 1975, UCA, M2/1/16, Department of Christian Citizenship, box 2; *The Leichhardt Story* (Leichhardt, 1963).

10 *Methodist*, 24 December 1949, 19 March 1960; Newtown QMM, 4 February 1952, 12 April 1954, 21 September 1954 UCA, M2/3/N7, box 1.

11 Wright, *Mantle of Christ*, pp. 192–94. A more detailed treatment of this work will be given in a book to be published by the same author in 1993.

12 Wright, *Mantle of Christ*, pp. 206, 212–16; Wright, 'Manly Methodist Circuit', pt II, *Church Heritage*, 5/4 (September 1988), pp. 240–41; see also NCMM LMM and QMM 1964–66; *Methodist*, 30 April 1966; *NL*, June 1966; Wollongong QMM, 12 July 1967, UCA, M2/3/W16, box 1; West Maitland QMM, 4 October 1967, UCA, M2/3/M2, box 1; Udy, *Spark of Grace*, pp. 200–01.

13 G.W. Walker, *The Crossroads Story* (Kotara Heights, 1986); Wright, *Mantle of Christ*, pp. 200–01; *Methodist*, 5 May 1962, 27 July 1968, 1 February 1969; DCC council minutes, April 1964 to June 1965, 17 December 1974, UCA, M2/1/16, box 2; 'Westwood' (typed pamphlet), ibid.

14 Wright, *Mantle of Christ*, pp. 197–200; Udy, *Spark of Grace*, p. 203.

15 DCC Council minutes, 11 November 1955, 21 January 1959, UCA, M2/1/16; Report of Committee for Community Welfare, 28 March 1974, ibid; *Methodist*, 17 November 1956, 6 February 1965; *Methodist and Congregationalist*, 10 April 1976.

16 DCC Council Minutes, 7 June, 5 July 1955, 29 April 1963, 7 December 1964, 19 February 1969, 23 June 1971, UCA, M2/1/16; *Methodist*, 5 November 1960.

17 Hamilton QMM, 27 October 1965, QMM 18 July 1969 (Report), UCA, M2/3/H2, box 3; *Methodist*, 19 February, 9 July 1966, 18 February, 30 September 1967, 30 March 1968.

18 ibid., 23 August 1919, 8 July 1944, 13 January, 10, 24 February, 28 April 1945, 1 June, 27 July, 26 October 1946, 17 May, 13 December 1947, 24 January, 21, 28 February 1948, 29 July 1950, 25 February 1961, 5 May 1962; *The Spire*, June 1944; *NL*, November 1949, June 1961; Wright, *Mantle of Christ*, pp. 184–87, 206–08.

19 Ted Noffs, *The Wayside Chapel. A Radical Christian Experiment in Today's World*, London, 1969; *Methodist*, 30 May, 24 October, 28 November 1964, 20 March, 25 December 1965, 22 April, 9 September, 21 October 1967.

20 HMD, 88th Annual Report, p. 5; *Methodist*, 3 May 1947, 9, 16 September 1950, 6 September 1952, 1 August 1953.

21 Manly QMM, 22 June 1955, UCA, M2/3/M6, box 1; Charlestown QMM, 18 October 1955, UCA, M2/3/C11, box 1; Report of Commission Appointed to Enquire into Working, Development . . .', 4 September 1947, UCA, M2/3/W16, box 1 (attached to p.

84); *Methodist*, 19 February 1955, 14 September 1957; 'Special Commission . . . to deal with New Australian Outreach . . .', 30 September 1965, 25 August 1966, UCA, M2/3/W16, box 1.

22 'Australian Horizons', UCA, M2/1/12, box 1; *Methodist*, 27 April, 31 August 1946, 29 January 1949, 12 June, 31 July 1965, 9 May 1970, 15 January 1972.

23 ibid., 9, 23 September, 7 October 1967, 10 April 1971; Udy, *Spark of Grace*, ch. 12.

24 Goulburn QMM, 9 October 1951, UCA, M2/3/G10, box 1; Manly QMM, 4 April 1960, UCA, M2/3/M6, box 1; *Methodist*, 6 July 1957, 7 February 1970.

25 ibid., 2 August 1947, 21 October 1950; 'Crusade for Christ MANUAL', UCA, M1/11, Crusade for Christ/Mission to the Nation (CC/MN), 1949–54.

26 Manly QMM, 11 January 1949, UCA, M2/3/M6, box 1; *Methodist*, 5 March, 7 May, 27 August 1949, 20 January, 14 July 1951, 17 May 1952; 'The Crusade for Christ . . .', by Norman G. Pardey, UCA, M1/11, CC/MN, 1949–54; State Director's Report to Synods 1951, ibid.

27 *Methodist*, 19 July 1952, 3 October 1953; 'The Plan and Purpose of a Nation-Wide Mission', N.G. Pardey, UCA, M1/11, CC/MN, 1949–54; minutes of planning meeting, 30 April 1952; *Argus*, 9 April 1953; *SMH*, 21 September 1953; *NMH*, 25 May 1953. See also Rex Mathias, *Mission to the Nation* (Melbourne, 1986).

28 *Methodist*, 16 May, 14 November 1953, 8 May, 14 August 1954.

29 ibid., 20 June, 26 September, 3 October 1953; Goulburn QMM, 18 March 1953, UCA, M2/3/G10, box 1; *SMH*, 21 September 1953.

30 *Methodist*, 1 May, 1954; Federal Report 1954, Alan Walker and Rex Mathias, NSW Report 1954, UCA, M1/11, CC/MN, 1949–54.

31 Mathias, *Mission to the Nation*, pp. 71–3; *SMH*, 15, 17, 24 January 1955.

32 *Methodist*, 8 January, 20 August, 29 October 1955; *SMH*, 28, 30 May 1955; Manly QMM, 22 June 1955, UCA, M2/3/M6, box 1; Mathias, *Mission to the Nation*, p. 65.

33 *Methodist*, 19 December 1953, 10, 17 September 1955; Mathias, *Mission to the Nation*, pp. 91–6. Percentages calculated from statistics for relevant years in NSW Methodist Conf. Mins.

34 Minutes of Special Meeting of Committee of Management of Home Missions & Evangelism Dept, 18 February 1970, UCA, MN2/1/12, box 3; minutes inaugural meeting Com. for Mission to NSW, 6 May 1970, ibid.; *Methodist*, 16 May, 19 September, 21

November 1970; *SMH*, 22 October, 2 November 1970; *Parramatta and Hills News*, 22 October 1970.
35 *Gosford Star*, 6, 13 January 1971; *Methodist*, 9, 23 January, 27 February 1971.
36 *SMH*, 26 April 1971; *Methodist*, 1, 8, 15 May 1971.
37 ibid., 29 May 1971; *SMH*, 21 June 1971.
38 *Methodist*, 27 November 1971; 'Newness News', October 1971, UCA, M2/1/12, box 3.

Chapter 7

1 *Methodist*, 6 August 1966. Figures are based on a quinquennial sampling of official NSW Methodist Conference statistics found in the Minutes.
2 *Methodist*, 13 May 1946, 11 August 1951, 1 February, 7 March 1964, 18 September, 23 October 1965.
3 ibid., 15 February 1947, 1 November 1958, 8 October 1960; YPD, Executive Council Minutes, 9 June 1948, UCA, M2/1/15, box 1.
4 Wright, 'Manly Methodist Circuit', pt II, pp. 239–40; Wright, *Mantle of Christ*, pp. 145–49, 188–89; *Methodist*, 26 October 1968, 8 March 1969.
5 ibid., 30 July 1949, 18 May 1957, 9 January 1960, 4 February, 5 August 1961.
6 ibid., 25 January 1947, 23 January 1954, 15 August 1959, 11 November 1961; *Methodist Messenger* (Manly), August–November 1966, May–August 1972, February–May 1973; Balgowlah LMM, 4 May 1973, Seaforth LMM, 9 May 1973, UCA, M2/3/M6, boxes 15, 16; *Methodist and Congregationalist*, 12 February 1977.
7 *Methodist*, 6 July 1968, 13 November 1971; 'The work of the Holy Spirit'. The Report of the Charismatic Committee of the NSW Methodist Conference. Presented to Conference October 1973, UCA, M2/1/12, box 3.
8 *NL*, June 1953; *Methodist*, 20 April 1963, 8 November 1969; Wright, *Mantle of Christ*, p. 190; *SMH*, 3 April 1991.
9 NSW Methodist Conference Agenda, 1964, p. 111.
10 *Methodist*, 5 March 1955, 29 October 1960; Wright, 'Manly Methodist Circuit', part I, p. 182; see NSW MWF Annual Reports in UCA, M2/1/12, boxes 1–2.
11 Membership and attendance figures are taken from the NSW Methodist Conf. Mins.
12 *Methodist*, 21 February 1948, 2 February 1952, 27 June 1953, 20

October 1962, 18 May 1968, 1 July 1972, 16 February 1974. Statistics are from NSW Methodist Conf. Mins.

13 Raymond Terrace QMM, 6 April 1948, UCA, M2/3/R3, box 1; Goulburn QMM, 31 January 1949, UCA, M2/3/G10, box 1; Wollongong QMM, 17 January 1951, UCA, M2/3/W16, box 1; Weston QMM, 12 October 1953, UCA, M2/3/W11, box 1.

14 'Commission on Stewardship–Report to Conference, 1968', UCA, M2/1/12, box 3; *Methodist*, 14 July, 10 November 1956, 13 July, 31 August 1957; *Methodist Messenger*, November 1957 to January 1958, UCA, M2/3/M6; Mayfield QMM, 19 July 1956, 10 April 1962, 30 April 1963, UCA, M2/3/M9, boxes 5, 10.

15 Report of the Convenors of the Victorian State Sections of the Church Unity Committee of the Presbyterian, Methodist and Congregational Churches, 21 December 1943, Methodist General Conf. Mins, 1945, supplement, pp. 249–52, 1948, pp. 197–205; *The Presbyterian Register*, April 1946; *Methodist*, 12 June 1954; J.S. Udy, 'Australian Negotiations Towards Union', *Church Heritage*, 1/1 (September 1978), p. 19.

16 Methodist General Conf. Mins, 1966, pp. 152–58.

17 ibid., p. 152; *Methodist*, 8, 15, 29 August, 5 September 1964.

18 NSW Methodist Conf. Agenda, 1962, pp. 165–67; *Methodist*, 29 August 1964; Joint Advisory Council Report to NSW Conference, 1977.

19 Methodist General Conf. Mins, 1975, pp. 276–81; NSW Methodist Conf. Mins, 1972, p. 117; *Methodist*, 8 May 1972; Udy, 'Church Union', pp. 356–8.

20 ibid., pp. 362.

21 *Methodist*, 12 August 1972.

22 A.H. Wood, *Our Heritage in the Uniting Church*, Melbourne, 1977, p. 1.

23 For details see Special General Conf. Mins, June 1977, pp. 48–80.

24 Udy, 'Church Union', pp. 415–17.

25 Proposed Basis of Union, 1964, *The Church, its Nature, Function and Ordering*, Melbourne, 1964, p. 77.

26 Methodist General Conf. Mins, 1948, p. 51.

Bibliographical notes

It is not intended to provide a full and complete list of all the materials read to prepare this volume as that would virtually require a second volume. The endnotes will provide a complete indication of those materials, both primary and secondary, which have directly shaped the printed page. What follows simply offers some further assistance for non-specialist readers who are unwilling to risk becoming lost in the endnotes.

Primary sources

In general terms, the classes of primary materials used have included the following:

Circuit records from a wide range of circuits in each of the different regions of the state, found in either the Uniting Church Archives (North Parramatta), the Mitchell Library or, very rarely, the Dixson Library.

Personal papers, more likely to be in the Mitchell Library but occasionally in the Uniting Church Archives.

Papers relating to youth work, schools and colleges, the Church Sustentation and Extension Society, Home and Overseas Mission work, (the 'Departments' of the church), Conference correspondence, adult fellowships and the like were usually in the Uniting Church Archives.

Conference Minutes may be found in either repository.

Methodist papers: *The Weekly Advocate, The Christian Advocate and Weekly Record, The Methodist* and *The Methodist and Congrega-*

tionalist are all available in both the Mitchell Library and the Uniting Church Archives in both hard copy and microfilm. The microfilm version is also available in the Auchmuty Library, University of Newcastle. *Glad Tidings* is in the Mitchell Library.

Other church papers referred to are generally from the Mitchell Library, though there are a few copies of the *New South Wales Primitive Methodist Messenger* and the *Primitive Methodist Magazine* in the Uniting Church Archives.

The Uniting Church Archives holds full sets of the Australian Methodist Historical Society *Journal and Proceedings* and of its Uniting Church successor, *Church Heritage*. It also holds a large collection of local church histories.

Select bibliography of major secondary sources

Bollen, J.D., *Protestantism and social reform in New South Wales 1890-1910*, Melbourne University Press, Melbourne, 1972

Brake, G.T., *Policy and politics in British Methodism 1932-1972*, Edsall, London, 1984

Broome, R., *Treasure in earthen vessels*, University of Queensland Press, St Lucia, 1980

Cannon, W.R., *The theology of John Wesley*, Abingdon-Cokesbury, New York, 1946

Carter, H., *The Methodist heritage*, Epworth, London, 1951

Clancy, E.G., *A giant for Jesus*, Clancy, Waitara, 1972

—— 'The Primitive Methodist Church in New South Wales, 1845-1902', MA, Macquarie University, 1985

Colwell, J., *The illustrated history of Methodism*, William Brooks, Sydney, 1904

Daniels, W., *The history of Methodism*, James & Coffey, Sydney and Melbourne

Davey, C., *The Methodist story*, Epworth, London, 1955

Davies, R.E., and Rupp, E.G., *History of the Methodist church in Great Britain*, vol. 1, Epworth, London, 1965

Davies, R.E., George, A.R. and Rupp, E.G., *A history of the Methodist church in Great Britain*, vol.2, Epworth, London, 1978

Docherty, J.C., *Newcastle, The making of an Australian city*, Hale & Iremonger, Sydney, 1983

Emilsen, S., *A whiff of heresy: Samuel Angus and the Presbyterian church in New South Wales*, UNSW Press, Kensington, 1990

Engel, F., *Australian Christians in conflict and unity*, Joint Board of Christian Education, Melbourne, 1984

Hansen, D., 'The Churches and Society in New South Wales: 1919–39', PhD, Macquarie University, 1978

Hill, J.W., 'The history and administration of the Methodist system of secondary education in New South Wales . . .', MEd, University of Sydney, 1975

Hunt, A.D., *This side of heaven*, Lutheran Publishing House, Adelaide, 1985

Hyde, B. and D.(eds), *Lo! here is fellowship*, Methodist YPD, Sydney, 1979

Jones, C.C., *An Australian Sunday school at work. Rockdale, 1855–1915*, Epworth, Sydney, 1915

McEwen, E.M., 'The Newcastle Coal-Mining District of New South Wales, 1860–1900', PhD, University of Sydney, 1979

McKernan, M., *Australian churches at war*, Catholic Theological Faculty and Australian War Memorial, Sydney and Canberra, 1980

Mathias, R., *Mission to the nation*, Joint Board of Christian Education, Melbourne, 1986

Noffs, Ted, *The Wayside Chapel. A radical Christian experiment in today's world*, Fontana, London, 1969

Petty, J., *History of the Primitive Methodist connexion from its origin to the Conference of 1860*, R. Davies, London, 1860

Phillips, W.W., *Defending 'A Christian Country'*, University of Queensland Press, St Lucia, 1981

Pritchard, E.C., *Under the southern cross*, W.A. Hammond, London, 1914

Reeson, M., *Certain lives*, Albatross, Sutherland, NSW, 1989

Sharpe, J., *The young minister counselled*, E.E. Pritchard, Sydney, 1871

Snyder, H.A., *The radical Wesley and patterns for church renewal*, Downer's Grove, Illinois, 1980

Stevens, A., *The History of Methodism*, William Tegg, London, 1864

Tibbs, P., 'Illawarra Methodism in the Nineteenth Century: a Comparative Study of Primitive and Wesleyan Methodism in Wollongong, 1838–1902', BA, University of Wollongong, 1981

Townsend, W.J., Workman, H.B. and Earys, G. (eds), *A new history of Methodism*, 2 vols, Hodder and Stoughton, London, 1909

Turner, N., *Sinews of sectarian warfare*, ANU, Canberra, 1972

Udy, G.S., *Spark of Grace*, Epworth, Parramatta, 1977

Udy, J.S., 'Church Union in Australia', MA, University of Sydney, 1983

Udy, J.S., and Clancy, E.G. (eds), *Dig or Die*, World Methodist Historical Society, Sydney, 1981

Uidam, C., *Union and Renewal*, Sydney, 1970

Webb, B.L., *The religious significance of the war*, Sydney, 1915

Werner, J.S., *The Primitive Methodist connexion: its background and early history*, University of Wisconsin Press, Madison, 1984

Wesley, J., *The works of the Rev. John Wesley, AM*, Epworth, London, 1872

Wibberley, B., *Marks of Methodism*, Whillas & Ormiston, Adelaide, 1905

Williams, C., *John Wesley's Theology Today*, Epworth, London, 1960

Wood, A.H., *Our heritage in the Uniting Church*, Aldersgate Press, Melbourne, 1977

Wright, D., *Mantle of Christ*, University of Queensland Press, St Lucia, 1984

Young, R., *The southern world*, Hamilton, Adams & Co, London, 1855

Local histories

Bleazard, V., *A Centenary of Methodism in East Maitland, 1845–1945*, East Maitland Methodist Circuit, Maitland, 1945

Carruthers, H., *Rehoboth Methodist Church*, Forest Lodge Primitive Methodist Circuit, Forest Lodge

Clancy, E.G., *Methodism in the Lilac City*, Goulburn Methodist Circuit, Goulburn, 1958

—— *More Precious Than Gold*, Orange Methodist Circuit, Orange, 1960

Doust, H.S., *Early Years of the Far West Mission (1917–24)*

Doust, R.H., *After One Hundred Years*, Bathurst Methodist Circuit, Bathurst, 1932

Hartley, R.W., and Grocott, A.M., *Around the Circuit: Methodism in Northern New England*, typescript, Glen Innes, 1975

Lingard, E., and Charge, N.F., *Glory Be*, CMM, Newcastle, 1945

McClelland, W.C., *Centenary of Newtown Methodism*

Scott, J.S., *Feed My Sheep: The Story of Methodism in the South-West of New South Wales*, Temora, 1976

The Leichhardt Story, Leichhardt Methodist Mission, Leichhardt, 1963

Udy, J.S., *Living Stones*, Sacha Books, Sydney, 1974

Wheen, A., *A Brief History of Ashfield Methodism*, Ashfield Methodist Circuit, Ashfield, 1975

Whitehouse, R.P., *West Maitland Methodist Centenary Record 1837–1937*, West Maitland Methodist Circuit, Maitland, 1937

Williams, H.T., *Hornsby Circuit. A Brief Record in the Settling of Methodism on the North Shore*, 1968

Articles

Cable, K.J., 'Protestant Problems in New South Wales in the Mid-Nineteenth Century', *JRH*, vol. 3, no. 2, December 1964

—— 'Religious Controversies in New South Wales in the Mid-Nineteenth Century: (ii) The Dissenting Sects and Education', *RAHSJ*, vol. 49, no. 2, July 1963

Clancy, E.G., 'Twelve Lay Apostles of New South Wales Country Methodism', *Church Heritage*, vol. 2, no. 1, March 1981

—— 'The Lay Methodist Church', *Church Heritage*, vol. 5, no. 4, September 1988

—— 'William (California) Taylor: First Overseas Evangelist to Australia', *Church Heritage*, vol. 6, no. 3, March 1990

Curtis, P.H., 'Mudgee Methodism', AMHS, *Journal and Proceedings*, vol. III, no. 2, January 1935

Hames, W., 'Walter Lawry and the Wesleyan Mission in the South Seas', Wesley Historical Society (New Zealand), *Proceedings*, vol. 23, no. 4, September 1967

Hansen, D., 'The Long Road to Union', *Church Heritage*, vol. 1, no. 2, September 1979

Hartley, R.W., 'The Eucharist in New South Wales Methodism from Methodist Union (1902) to the Uniting Church (1977), *Church Heritage*, vol. 1, no. 4, September 1980

Hughes, J., 'The Lay Methodist Church', AMHS, *Journal and Proceedings*, no. 73, October 1957

Phillips, W.W., 'The Social Composition of Religious Denominations in Late Nineteenth Century Australia, *Church Heritage*, vol. 4, no. 2, September 1985

Walker, R.B., 'The Growth and Typology of the Wesleyan Methodist Church in NSW 1812–1901, *JRH*, vol. 6, no. 4, December 1971

Wright, D.,'Paradigm of a Methodist Middle-Class Suburban Circuit', *Church Heritage*, vol. 5, no. 3, March 1988; no. 4, September 1988

—— 'The First Wesleyan Mission to the Aborigines of New South Wales–a Brief Historical Note', *Church Heritage*, vol. 4, no. 4, September 1986

—— 'The Methodist Men's Own Movement', *Church Heritage*, vol. 4, no. 1, March 1985

Index